KU-152-018

South Dublin Libraries

Trials of A
Legal Secretary

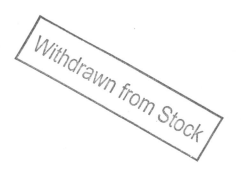
Withdrawn from Stock

Mary Mannion

chipmunkapublishing
the mental health publisher

All rights reserved, no part of this publication may be reproduced by any means, electronic, mechanical photocopying, documentary, film or in any other format without prior written permission of the publisher.

Published by
Chipmunkapublishing
United Kingdom

http://www.chipmunkapublishing.com

Copyright © 2014 Mary Mannion

ISBN   978-1-78382-103-7

Chipmunkapublishing gratefully acknowledge the support of Arts Council England.

Marjorie was sitting in state behind her desk when I got in. I noticed she'd dyed her hair a deep shade of purple. Combined with the orange fake tan she always wore she looked a proper sight. She wasn't exactly skin and bone and wore deep plunging necklines to show off her large bosom. She was living with her boyfriend, a Chartered Surveyor, but they were bored to distraction with each other.

'Are you better?' she asked me with mock-interest.

'I'm fine. Jeepers your hair looks great!' I always tried to butter her up to keep the atmosphere halfway bearable between us. Anything for a peaceful life.

'Thanks. I must say I love it myself.' She glowed when you gave her a compliment. Wouldn't give you one yourself unless lighted matches were put under her fingernails. Why did I suffer these people? Maybe that's what they paid me for, not the work.

I was just slithering into my chair when I was nabbed by Leonard. Checking his watch as ever. I knew I was in trouble. I mumbled something about the Dart being late. He didn't even condescend to answer, just glared at me like an angry bull and walked away.

At least he hadn't actually said anything. Heart giving a few strange jumps though. Gave a quick feel of my pulse. So so. Calm down. Deep breaths.

I barely had turned on the computer when Fiona came marching over.

'In at last,' she sniffed.

'Sorry but it wasn't my fault. The Dart was late again.'

'Isn't it always? Are you over your bug? We wouldn't want you spreading germs', she said sarcastically.

'Grand again, thanks.'

'OK, we've a busy day ahead of us. Chop, chop. I need a contract out this morning. After that you might tackle the filing. Don't forget you still haven't finished that Deed you were working on. I'd appreciate it if you'd get started immediately. I have to leave early today. Nadine has a dental appointment and I need to pick her up after school.'

Pressure. Just what I needed. Bloody little Nadine, if it wasn't her arse it was her elbow. Piano lessons on Monday, ballet on Tuesday, horse-riding on Thursdays. Spoilt rotten by her doting architect dad and solicitor mummy.

Fiona was 37 six years younger than me. Before her I'd worked for Mr Purcell, the senior partner, for ten years until he retired. He'd been a real dote. None of his children had any interest in doing law and that's how Fiona managed to become a Senior Partner. I remembered her as an apprentice. She'd never been a sad-eyed Rita but she'd been friendly, thanking you profusely if you typed a letter for her. It sounded like it was too good to be true - and it was.

Things changed once she qualified. From then on we were the lowest form of animal life. She had her coffee brought to her desk and insisted it came in a china cup. Two spoons of honey well stirred in for her ladyship. Also insisted I put an envelope between cup and saucer in case a drop spilled. Sometimes she'd phone me to make a cup for her even though I was only sitting three feet away. Phoned, mind you. To call out would have been beneath her. Posh Spice her middle name.

When I worked for Mr Purcell all my work was Probate. It was done at a leisurely pace. The dead never came knocking at the door for requisitions on title. Wills were done on electric typewriters in those days and if one went against me he'd cover for me. If the client was waiting he'd say an urgent matter had come up and to come back later. Then we'd both have a cup of tea and a biscuit and I'd be ready to tackle the Will again. When he retired I was miserable. To add to my woes I was then given the, ahem, 'privilege' of becoming Fiona's secretary. It was a shock to my system. Her clients actually had pulses. They were capable of doing things like walking and talking. They also had voices, which they used for the horrible practice of complaining about me. They weren't safely six feet under - though sometimes I felt like putting them there.

In fairness to her, Fiona could be reasonable at times. She was very generous at Christmas and always gave me expensive perfume. But if something went wrong she became a total harridan. We sometimes called her Atilla the Hen. She looked a bit like a hen too with those mincing little legs. She also seemed to shake her feathers when she was in a rage. She mostly favoured pin-striped trouser suits and very high heels to give herself a bit of stature. Her hairstyle was Married Woman Perm. Sensible and clipped. The tight blond curls nestled in behind her pink ears. Just when it would start to fluff out a bit and look half feminine, she's have it permed again. Her perfume was Chanel No. 5, Marilyn Monroe's favourite. But she was certainly no Marilyn.

I was ploughing through her work when two symbols disappeared from the toolbar for no apparent reason. The B for bold type and the I for italics. Damn and blast, just what I needed. I searched frantically for them but it was as if they'd been gobbled up in a black hole. My immediate impulse was to try the old-fashioned cure and give the machine a good kick. When in doubt, give it a clout. Why did technology have no respect for these treasured solutions of yore?

'Are you through with the contract yet?' Fiona asked from behind my shoulder. The hen was clucking again.

'Almost there.'

There was nothing for it but to call on Sandra.

'Sandra, could you come over for a second. My machine is acting up.'

She gave me a hard stare. That was Sandra for you. Definitely not a Mother Teresa.

'I'll see what I can do but you'll have to wait. I'm out the door with work myself.'

I felt like a child waiting for her to give me her Quality Time It would take her two minutes to sort me out, but I was totally dependent on her and had to sit waiting.

After twiddling my thumbs for ten minutes I finally saw Her Highness hove towards me. In about twenty seconds, by pressing various combinations of keys, all was back to normal.

'I hope that's okay,' she said as she walked away, speaking at the top of her voice so Fiona would overhear, 'If you have any more problems you know where I am.' Little bitch.

Fiona cocked her head round the corner.

'You know I've to leave early, don't you?'

'I do. You told me. But the machine is acting up.'

'Hmm. I heard Sandra helping you again. Maybe you could do with a refresher course on the computers. We could pay for it for you. What do you think?'

I could see Sandra smirking to herself as she pounded her keys.

'Honestly, I'm fine. It'll be ready in two minutes.'

I finished the contract at last. While I was doing the photocopying I got all the sheets mixed up and it took me half an hour to get them sorted. It was almost lunchtime before I had the completed job on her hallowed desk. She grabbed it and marched out for her lunch.

I worked right through lunch hour on the Deed from last week. The sweat was pouring out of me by now. Left arm numb. Pinchy pains in right side. Dryness of the mouth. Churning in the stomach, Slight dizzy sensation when I turned my head. But I kept on typing. Deed finally completed and now to my favourite job: binding.

It never went right for me, I was back again to the frightened nine year old trying to turn the heel of a stocking in third class. Needles and wool going in all directions and other good girls producing dainty perfect little woolly socks. I punched the little square holes as best I could but made a pig's ear of it. All the other secretaries were brilliant at this job, but for me the holes were just not coming through. And pages of the Deed were in bits. .

Back up to the machine to run off another copy. Four o'clock now and Fiona would be leaving in ten minutes. I called Joanie. She usually helped without making too much of a big deal out of it.

Joanie was married to an alcoholic who hadn't worked for years. They had five children but he never lifted a finger to help her. Her life was a constant dash. Shopping at lunch-time, racing out in a panic at 5.20, lashing down to the Dart like a mad thing, breaking her neck each morning to get in early so she could chop a few minutes off the end of the day to avoid the crowds on the rush-hour train. No wonder the poor woman was skin and bone.

'I'm up to my eyes with my own stuff,' she groaned. 'Here, give it to me. I don't know why you can't do it. A four-year-old could do this.'

Off she whizzed. Holes punched to perfection. Little curly spiral things pressed into place. Down comes the lever and she hands me her masterpiece.

'Thanks, Joanie. You're a life-saver. Fiona is like a demon today.'

'Not to worry. You should be able to do it, though. It's simple.' Sure, and so was the square on the hippopotamus.

'Maybe for you but it's a nightmare for me. Why was I born so clumsy?'

'It's all in the mind,' she said with a laugh, 'all you need is a bit of confidence.'

Five-thirty came round at last. I gathered up my things and was about to go home when Sandra stopped by my desk.

'We're going next door for a few bevvies,' she said, 'Like to come along?' I wasn't usually asked. The oldies in the firm put dampers on things, didn't they? But she was in a good mood after our little encounter.

'I'm sorry, I have something on.' It was a lie. It was going to be another boring night in but I knew what her 'few' consisted of: slugging back shorts until closing-time and then on to one of those places off Grafton Street until the small hours. Then roll home footless, hardly able to remember your name. I liked my drink as much as the next woman but I knew my limits. The younger ones in the office seemed to have kidneys like camels.

'That's a pity. Maybe next time'. She knew I was lying but I didn't care. Only wanted me to make up the numbers.

I decided to walk home. I needed the air. Couldn't face the stuffy old Dart. All those sweaty bodies pressed up on top of each other. No choice in the mornings but now I could dilly-dally. A walk always relaxed me.

It took me the usual length of time, an hour and seventeen minutes. When I got to the house I found it dark and empty.

Surprise surprise - Nigel was working late again.

CHAPTER 2

The next morning I didn't even hear the alarm clock. Woke at 11 a.m. to hear the phone ringing and the answering machine clicking into place.

'This is Marjorie. Please get in touch. Fiona asked me to ring you.'

Oh God. What now? I leapt out of bed. No shower again this morning. I'd have to stink for the day. The hair would also have to do. I rang for a taxi and was in the office by half eleven, dripping with sweat and full of jitters.

Fiona had a face like thunder. Not a word of appreciation for all the work I'd done the day before. She didn't address me once, just kept dictating tapes all morning. Again I worked through my lunch break.

By the way,' said Fiona as I was getting ready to leave, 'You did get my gardening magazine, didn't you?"

'Oh Lord, I never thought of it. I can run across the road and get it now.'

'Forget it.'

Wednesday. How could I have forgotten? It showed the way my head was. Anyhow, pity about her. It wouldn't kill her to pick up her own stupid magazine.

I got a phone call from Nigel in the evening.

'Hi. Just finished up in Drogheda. A real.stinker of a job. Anyway, it's wiped out. I'll see you later on. Gotta rush.' Just as effusive as ever.

Went out for some chips from the take-away and treated myself to some large battered onion rings.

He was there when I got back to the house and gave me a light peck on the cheek. Not exactly hot passion but we were together for a long time now so what did I expect? .Mr Rochester pressing me to his bosom and whispering in my ear that we were attached to each other by a cord coming from our ribs? We'd never been love's young dream, even in our early dating days.

He was meticulous in every way. In some ways that was what had attracted me to him. He always wore the right clothes and was groomed like a prize pony. He was tall, wore glasses and had the finest set of teeth I'd ever seen in a human being. His hair was going a bit thin on top which bothered him greatly. He spent hours in front of the mirror combing it round and round his head in order to hide the bald spot. This worked out fine until he was out in a storm and the whole concoction would stand up in the air, exposing his bald pate.

We'd dated for a while and moved in together after six months. We did have one thing in common but in many ways were like chalk and cheese. We both were fond of expensive clothes. The difference was that he took care of his stuff. He had his suits dry-cleaned regularly. They were always right up to fashion. At present he favoured linen suits. His colouring was tending towards the beige and I felt his pale linen suits made his whole appearance look sort of anaemic. His ties were colour-coordinated with various rig-outs. If I didn't iron his shirts to perfection he'd take the iron from me and do a far better job himself.

As for me, I'd hold up hems with safety pins. I'd often destroy a beautiful blouse by spilling my dinner all over it. More often than not my clothes were an unholy mass of wrinkles.

I decided to tell him about all my symptoms, hoping for sympathy. Lots of pinchy pains occurring intermittently. Cold foot every now and again. And tingly sensations down my spine, dry mouth, palpitations and vague sensation of depression. . He sat there like a statue as I spoke, mumbling as he foostered around the room looking for something.

'Did you get the paper today?' he asked finally, and now it was my turn to be in a daze. 'Hello?' he said waving his hands in front of my face, 'The paper? Lots of print on it? Comes out every day?' What a sarcastic bastard.

'Have you heard a word I've said?'

'Every bit of it, but I can't help you until you start helping yourself. Listen, I think I'll bed down in the spare room tonight if you don't mind. Got a hard day tomorrow.'

With that he was gone. Didn't even rise to the occasion of saying goodnight.

I stayed awake with racing thoughts. Crawled downstairs at 4 a.m. and got myself tea and biscuits. The doctor told me not to eat at night but I didn't have the willpower. By the time the alarm went off the next morning I could just about have slept.

CHAPTER 3

Next morning the journey into work went by in a daze. Reminded me of my young days when I'd walk in at dawn after an all-night party. No party now though, just troubled thoughts and nervous feelings.

Fiona was a bit more civil than usual. It wasn't long before I realised why.

'Nadine won first prize for her English essay yesterday,' she informed me with a big beam.

'That's great. She must be very bright.'

'Bright? She's a proper little genius. Been top of her class for as long as I can remember.'

I tried to sound enthusiastic but I always despised those studious types. I remembered them from my own schooldays, waving their arms to attract attention. 'Please, Sister this' and 'Please, Sister that'. Writing furiously at exams as if they were getting electric shocks. Meanwhile I sat poring over empty pages, dying a death from shame.

'I heard a good joke last night,' she went on, 'we were out to dinner with friends of ours and Tom told us this one. I thought it was hilarious. I was in convulsions all night. What's under the water and shivers?'

'I don't know. I'm useless at these sort of things.'

'A nervous wreck. A nervous wreck! Good one, isn't it? Do you get it? Wreck. You know. Under the water. Shivers.'

I did my best to produce a few chortles. Anything to keep her in good spirits.

Later in the morning I phoned Alice and arranged to meet for lunch. She was cool-headed and I knew she'd take me out of myself. I could trust her. We'd been friends for over fifteen years.

She was a lovely woman but could have done more with her appearance. A bit of colour in her hair and maybe change her sensible neat clothes for something more youthful. But she was her own person and I admired her for this. Certainly no botox or face-fillers for Alice.

We met in a pub just three doors from the office. She looked well, maybe a little overweight. We queued for ten minutes and at last found a corner for ourselves.

'How are you?' she asked, 'I expected to hear from you last week. Were you out sick again?'

'Yes, all last week. Had pains all over and felt very anxious and depressed. Alice, that place is becoming a nightmare. I can't cope anymore. Just when I think I've mastered the computer I muck up again. And as for the binder, it's a total nightmare. You're so lucky taking early retirement.'

Alice had worked in the Civil Service for thirty five years and was now retired for four.

To be honest it was the best move I ever made. I can mooch round town and go over to my niece any afternoon I feel like it. The baby is gorgeous now. Ciara, they called her. Lovely name, don't you think? Already has two teeth, would you believe. My nephew, Conor, is getting married next week. Not to the mother of the child but another girl. She seems nice. I hope they'll be happy. I'm giving them 500 euro. So much expense with weddings these days.'

She was so generous to all her family but they all took her for granted. Sometimes it made me really angry.

We were chatting away and I was quite relaxed when all of a sudden I got a severe pain in my left shoulder blade.

'I'm in a bad state at the moment,' I found myself saying, 'I haven't slept for almost a week. My nerves are in bits and I have a desperate darting pain in my shoulder.'

'Darts don't mean anything. Its continuous pain you have to worry about. How's the numbness in the leg?'

'Did I have that the last time? No, it's more than that. It's my mind, Alice. I really feel I'm losing it.'

'Don't be silly, will you. We're all a bit daft in this life as far as I can see. Learning to live with it is the problem. Give in gracefully is my advice. Memory is my trouble, especially since I gave up work. Half the time I don't know what day of the week it is.'

We finished our lunch. Alice was going down town, no doubt to buy another present for one of her brother's children. When I stood up to leave I got the panic attack sensation. Out of the blue I felt I was going to conk out. I hadn't had that for six months.

I told Alice and she ordered me to sit down, after which I got the 'It's only your nerves' speech.

The whole room was swirling round and my mouth dry as a board. I was afraid to stand up in case I collapsed.

'I'm going to fall, Alice. How will I get back to work?'

'I'll get you a cup of tea. You have fifteen minutes yet. That coffee is only making you worse. You really do drink too much of it. I know it sets my heart crazy.'

I had the tea. The feeling subsided a little. I was able to ask her about the new baby. We chattered on for I don't know how long. She escorted me back to the office. If you were looking down from Mars you'd probably be in convulsions at the pair of us. Alice so small and me nearly 5'9" leaning on her, stark terror written on my face.

Back at my desk I took one of my tranquillisers and just about functioned for the afternoon. 5.30 couldn't have come quick enough.

I got the Dart home, too stressed to walk. Jabbing pain in shoulder again. Of course it had to be the left one, probably my heart. Mouth dry as a board. Tingles in feet Into the bargain.

I stared at a fixed point and tried to turn my mind off, tried to envisage one of those beaches in the Caribbean I heard you were supposed to think of at times like this, with a Mills & Boon style man feeding me grapes. Bruce, or maybe Craig. I was slim as a reed dressed in a stunning bikini to show off my gorgeous tan. This exercise calmed me down for a little while.

The Dart slowed down and came to a halt between Connolly Station and Clontarf. This was all I needed. Back again came all the symptoms. My heart was pounding and giving strange lurches. I tried to focus on the thin long nose of a red-haired schoolboy but still my agony persisted. Finally we were moving again and I stumbled like a drunken woman onto the platform and walked to the house.

Nigel was home before me. Thank God for that. I didn't want to be alone.

I didn't mention my suffering, knowing the way he'd react. Didn't want the same treatment he'd given me last night.

He did the hoovering while I sat and watched him. He was much better at it than me. He got into all the nooks and crannies, as he called them. Was there ever a nook without a cranny? I usually went at it like a mad woman and ended up knocking over the lamp or something. He said I was a lethal weapon with that implement in my hand. Bulls in china shops were more graceful. I nearly took his eye out once or twice with my elbow in mid-action.

Afterwards we sat on the sofa staring vacantly at Sky News with the sound turned down. He talked about his job and I listened politely, or pretended to. The word pressure came up about a hundred times and every so often I gave a sympathetic cluck.

'You poor thing,' I said, 'it's so stressful for you.'

When he was finished he went into the kitchen and took out a beer for himself. Not a mention of asking his lady love to have a drink. He was whistling away, happy as Larry now that he'd pontificated. All he needed was an ear, not dialogue.

I took up the crossword but couldn't get one of the clues to save my life. I could hardly remember my name at this stage.

He turned on Sky Sports to watch an all-important Man United game. The volume was up to the highest pitch, the sounds drumming into my addled brain No hope of concentrating on the crossword with that din.

Sometimes he and his two pals flew to Manchester to watch a game. He was never as happy or excited as he was when he was planning one of these trips. Certainly the few times we'd gone on holiday together he looked more in pain than even mildly contented.

'This is a huge match', he said, 'it's a six- pointer.'

'Right', I said. I didn't have a clue what six-pointer meant but I certainly wasn't going to ask him to explain.

Towards the end of the first half I went to take a few mugs from the coffee table. The roars of him would have shattered the sound barrier.

'Jesus, will you move your big bum. He's about to score.'

'Someone has to wash up,' I snapped back. 'Do you expect the fairies to do them?'

'You sure know how to pick your time, that's all I'll say. You're as a lazy as sin most of the time. This place would be like a pig-sty if it wasn't for me.'

'Give me a break. I've been listening to you moaning about your job since I got in from work. Anyway he didn't even score so you missed nothing.' .

'That's not the point. He could have scored. Now for God's sake let me watch the match in peace.'

In the kitchen I had another shot at the crossword but my nerves were jangling so I threw it aside.

Crosswords and interesting hobbies were supposed to keep you young. Gardening too. I hadn't the remotest interest in gardening but maybe a hobby would take my mind of myself.

I used to enjoy line-dancing but that was years ago. I did love it though, leaping round to *Cotton-Eyed Joe*, or Dolly Parton belting out *Islands in the Stream*. Out of fashion now, though maybe sometime I could look it up on the internet to see if there was a place I could go to in the Dublin area.'

There was another wild roar from the living room. Man U had scored and the match was over.

I brought him in a cup of tea and he held my hand for a moment. Obviously the win had cheered him up.

'I think I'll have an early night,' I said, 'I'm out for the count for some reason.'

'If that had an air I could sing it', he muttered. 'You spend far too much time lying in bed. I hope you don't take this personally but you've put on some weight. You should join a gym or at least take up walking. Why not do a 30 minute walk before you go up. Swing your arms as you go, great aerobic exercise.' He was right there. I was getting a bit large round the hips. Probably middle age spread. I should really cut back on the bad food too.

'The weather forecast says heavy showers,' I said to get out of the walk, 'and besides, I'm exhausted.'

'If you ever need to leave that place you could get a great job in the Met Office. Every time I suggest a walk you say a monsoon is on the way. Do you know what your favourite expression is?'

'You've told me hundreds of times. No need to rub my nose in it.'

'It's "I Don't Like the Look of that Sky." OK, go to bed. Some partner you are. Other girlfriends watch matches with their partners, indeed go to matches just to cheer on his favourite team, but that's too much like hard work for you.'

'I don't need this stress now. My nerves are in bits. I barely made it home this evening. I've dizzy feelings, pins and needles, sharp pains, numbness.'

'Oh, for God's sake go to bed. I can't take any more of this moaning.' I went out to the kitchen and put on the kettle for my hot water bottle. Out of nowhere I started to sob.

Tears ran down my cheeks and I sat at the table trying to dry my eyes with the dishcloth but the tears kept coming. He couldn't bear to see me crying so he came over and put his arms round me. 'Look, I'm sorry, he muttered. 'Tough day myself, didn't mean to upset you.'

The tears just kept coming like a deluge. All my suffering and fears came pouring out of me. He stroked my hair and I nestled up close to him. I felt warm and protected like when I was a small girl sitting on daddy's knee.

He made some toast and tea and gradually we started to chat normally. 'By the way', he said, out of the blue, 'as I was telling you earlier I'm swamped in the office. My secretary is still on maternity leave and her replacement is useless. Could you ever type up a report for me. It's not too long but I'd need it ASAP.' Tea, toast, sympathy. Price report ASAP. Always a catch with him. 'Bring it home and I'll have a go.' 'Thanks you're a lifesaver. Actually I have it in my brief case. Just wanted to check with you to be sure,' and he planted a wet kiss on my lips.

He knew how much I hated doing his reports. He was such a fusspot and the work was mostly figures, which were a million times harder than words. 'I'll start it after work tomorrow so.' On a whim I suggested we go for a drink. 'Oh God, no. Not at this time of night. If you have that much energy, though, maybe you could start on the work now. A few hours and Bob's your uncle.'

CHAPTER 4

The next few days at work passed off without note. No more panicky feelings. I walked the whole way in two mornings in a row which made me feel good about myself. On Monday I did my detox and that helped too. I managed to consume eight glasses of water which had me up to the toilet all night. Still no gain without pain. I rewarded myself at lunchtime by putting a deposit on an absolutely beautiful stone-coloured coat. It was real simple, slightly waisted but it definitely looked the money. The fur collar gave it a sort of Russian look. I told myself I deserved it. God knows if you can't be nice to yourself nobody else will. You could tell immediately from the feel of it that it was pure wool but yet it wasn't like some knobbly tweed effort. Subtle really and it suited my colouring. I need cheering up anyway.

Nigel was busy and worked late most evenings. You wouldn't want to be depending on that fellow to give yourself a little lift. God knows life was tough enough. One afternoon towards the end of the week I got off work early and dropped in to see him with the typed up report. It certainly wasn't a small job. There were pages and pages of figures.

I knew he wouldn't be pleased to see me. The few times I'd been in his office he was embarrassed and rushed me out. He was terrified I'd run into his boss, the notorious Brannigan, and let him down. I wasn't really Chartered Accountant Wife material with my country accent . And of course I wasn't a professional. Had I qualified in law and been another Fiona, Brannigan would probably have been inviting me round to his snazzy Dublin 4 residence every day of the week.

Brannigan was a tiny little runt of a man with a ratty face and beady brown eyes that could see right through you. There was something cunning about him. Not my kind of person putting it mildly.

He was in the reception area when I walked in. He looked at me with an 'Oh you' expression that suggested the bold Nigel had been telling tales out of school about me. I towered over him, which I hated. I found myself buckling my knees to be more on his level.

'Not working today, are we?' he said with an expression on his face that suggested he got a bad smell. I hated that royal plural. It reminded me of doctors. (At least he didn't give me the usual one, 'How's the weather up there?')

'I'm my own boss now,' I said to shut him up. 'Is Nigel around?'

He grunted, telling me to sit in Reception while he went to fetch him. I found myself reading one of those 'How To Lose A Stone In Two Weeks' articles from a magazine. Trish, the receptionist looked very prim in a tight-fitting polo neck with her hair screwed back. She eyed me up and down suspiciously. Had Nigel told her about my nerves too? Or maybe I was just being paranoid. Still, as the saying went, that didn't mean they weren't out to get you.

He came out looking cowed, buried under a sheaf of papers and with his glasses down on his nose. That always made him look slightly demented.

'Is something wrong?' he said, frowning.

'Of course not. Are you not glad to see me?' ('Hello' would have been nice.)

'I'm afraid it's not a great time.' He looked around at Trish nervously and she pretended to be busy with her little computer screen. But I could sense her ears were flapping goodo. Gossip: the food of the bored.

'I know, but I thought you might like that report. I've finished it.'

'What report?' He'd forgotten already.

'Remember the one you asked me to type out for you when the United match was on? You did say it was urgent.'

The penny dropped very, very slowly. He hated references to anything to do with the job when others were listening.

'Oh yes, oh yes. Jesus, that can do anytime. I'm in the middle of an important meeting at the minute. If you have it there I'll take it but I won't be able to look at it for hours'. (This was for Brannigan's benefit, I presumed).

I was tempted to fling it at him, or maybe tear it up into little pieces in front of Trish, just to make her day, but instead I dug it out of my handbag and handed it to him civilly. Once a mouse always a mouse.

He rummaged through the pages but I could see he wasn't concentrating on them.

'You're very good,' he said, thawing out a bit but still looking awkward. Brannigan was hovering in the background. For some strange reason I felt a fit of the giggles coming on and nearly had to pinch myself to stop myself laughing out loud. Nigel was so cocky when we were together and yet here, in his area of excellence as it were, he was like a frightened rabbit. Maybe we were all in the same boat. Office angel, home devil.

We stood there in the silence as I waited for some commendation or acknowledgement but it didn't come. All you could hear was the air conditioning humming loudly. I was baked with the heat coming from it.

'Well,' I said finally when I realised all three of them were willing me to go with their X-ray eyes, 'I suppose I'll be off then.'

'Okay,' he whispered, 'see you tonight.'

I put my head towards him for a kiss but he swung away as if a piece of string was pulling him. He gave a watery smile as he disappeared into the bowels of his office to return to his meeting.

The way Brannigan looked at me you'd imagine I was a piece of dirt.

I shuffled towards the door, bumping against a coffee table on the way as only I could. Trish tried to restrain her laughter. My knee was in agony but I didn't let on. Then at the door there was one of those buzzy things I never know what to do with. I stood there like an idiot till Trish pressed a button. It let out a big noise and I was flushed out onto the street. Relief for all of us.

I tried to be angry with him all the way home but I couldn't. Maybe we were all victims of the labour force no matter how high up the tree we went. I could understand his bluff and swagger in the evenings if it helped him get off some steam. In a way he was ten times worse off than me in my own job. I had my stresses to be sure but I didn't bring my work home with me, either physically or in my head. As soon as the gong sounded I was out of there, baby, and on to other things. Not exactly earth-shattering things, admittedly, but at least they didn't own my soul. Not yet anyway.

That nearly changed on Friday, which was mental. Marjorie was out with flu so we all had to do a stint at the switch. Joanie was dying with her period and Sandra was hungover. She'd been out with a 'goy' the night before who was loaded, so they went to Lillie's to get, like, smashed on Southern Comfort. But, hey, never again. She liked living too much.

Leonard Darcy spent most of the day in the board room in deep conversation with Mr Skelly. It was like the freemasons when that pair got together. Sometimes I felt they were badmouthing me. There you go - my paranoia coming out again. (Nigel used to say I wouldn't go to rugby games without thinking they were having a moan about me in the scrums. Ha ha.) A more likely scenario was they were comparing notes about how to poach clients from Fiona, or even set up on their own. They always seemed to have their minds somewhere else but I could hardly blame them. It wasn't exactly Shangri-La in there.

Fiona was like a bull all morning trying to get a courier to take a Brief down to the Four Courts. She kept getting an engaged tone every time she rang the company. 'We're paying them a bloody fortune,' she said, 'and I'd be quicker walking down.' She was getting ready to send up smoke signals from her pink little ears.

One arrived eventually, barging in the door. He also had his helmet on. It always drove her bananas when they did that. He looked like the missing link.

'T-a-k-e y-o-u-r h-e-l-m-e-t o-f-f,' she growled in the kind of voice that made people listen - even missing links. He was dumbfounded, rooted to the spot.

'Who burst your bubble,?' he said when he recovered his senses, 'Keep your knickers on. I'm not goin' to rob the place.' She was purple with rage. Nobody spoke to Fiona like that and expected to live. We all started to chortle.

'What are you laughing at?' she screamed in her schoolmarmy voice, 'I don't see anything remotely amusing.' She fixed her attention on the courier. 'I'm not going to say anything to you for the moment but that letter is more important to me than your job so I suggest you get down to the Four Courts five minutes ago. I'll be talking to your boss.' She marched out of the room muttering something about muddy footprints on the carpet as we clutched our sides.

I was worthless for the rest of the morning. Couldn't type a word without thinking of the courier's unbelieving face as she lashed into him. She needed to get a life. Herself and Leonard were models for the early coronary. But I knew what she'd say if I told her that - that I was the other extreme.

We all had a good bitching session about her at lunch, even treating ourselves to Irish coffees for dessert. Afterwards I went on one of my trawls round BTs. I'd been trying on a beautiful leather jacket there for ages. It was expensive but in the end I put a deposit on it. Why not, I told myself, enjoy life while you can. It was worth the money, I felt. Lovely soft leather, well cut, and simple lines.

When I got to my desk I was disgusted to see Mummy's little helper plonked in front of my computer. The divine Nadine. She was a miniature version of Fiona. Fiona *beag* I used to call her. She had the same short little legs and she didn't need a perm as her fair hair was a little ball of tight fuzz. She was dressed in her private school uniform, a grey skirt and white blouse. She was eleven years old - eleven going on twenty. I knew Fiona was going to be fuming about my lateness so I made a big fuss of her little darling.

'Hi Nadine,' I said, 'aren't you a great girl. I suppose you know more about computers than I do myself.'

She didn't answer, just continued to move the mouse as if she was the senior partner's secretary and I was the little young one.

Fiona eventually came out of her office and muttered to me to get on with my work. After a struggle she got darling daughter away from the machine, all the time telling her what a wonderful girl she was and how clever Nady would be a solicitor like Mummy when she grew up. The one good thing was that Fiona told me she'd be gone for the rest of the day as she was bringing Nady to her ballet class. The idea of those fat little legs pirouetting round in a tutu made me snigger to myself.

As Fiona was gone for the evening, I took myself out for a break to the Henry Grattan. Occasionally I got the chance to do this and would order tea and biscuits and sit there as if I were a free woman, perfectly entitled to do as I pleased. I knew I had only two letters to run off so went back just before five, planning to dodge off early at 5.15.

I typed up my two letters, put in the headed paper and clicked Print Command. The printer made some odd noises but eventually it vomited out my first letter. Grand, I thought, getting ready to print off the second one, but just then another copy of the first letter proceeded to issue forth. And another. And another. I frantically phoned for Sandra but she'd left the office. Then I tried Joanie but no luck there either. Everybody had availed of Fiona's early departure. The place was deserted.

Copy after copy poured forth. I turned the machine off and then on again. Immediately more copies of the same letter emerged. I went through a whole ream of paper and still couldn't stop the machine. I couldn't understand what had happened as I was convinced I'd given the printer just a One Copy command. Suddenly I remembered Nadine's stint on the machine earlier on. Obviously the little horror had given it a request that was causing all this havoc.

I went into Print Command for the fifth time to try and cancel it. By now the sweat was pouring out of me. I looked at my watch. Seven o'clock. Some early evening I was getting. I clicked the mouse and a set of instructions came up in German.

And still the letter kept on printing. Then a command came up saying 'Reverse Order'. Joy unconfined! I said yes to this, thinking Nadine's command would be obliterated. Dream on. Now the machine started printing the second letter. Again more and more copies kept coming out.

In desperation I thought I'd try Sandra at home. I raced to the reception desk and picked her number from a notebook kept in a drawer. Her answering machine came on. Brilliant. Then I tried to get Joanie, but no reply there either. In desperation I took one of my diazepam tablets and washed it down with a cup of tea. Deep breaths. Let there be no panic.

Back up to the machine to find it had run out of paper and was making a wheezing sort of noise. Nothing for it but to feed the bastard more paper. Another ream almost gobbled up. My waste basket was overflowing, pages piling up on all sides. All the reams of paper in the cupboard were used up. I rushed upstairs to the Probate Section. Yanked out two reams and then the bulging files caught my eye.

Estate after estate danced in front of me. Ghosts peeped out from behind every filing cabinet. John Atkinson deceased. Huge case. Inland Revenue Affidavit form umpteen pages long. I'd got mixed up with figures and the whole thing had to be retyped. Mrs Celia Butler deceased. Her Will had gone missing and it took three weeks to locate it, misfiled as it was by yours truly in the Strong

Room. Cornelius Brady deceased. A legacy to a beneficiary who never existed. Still fresh in my mind after all the years.

'To my friend and companion Terence Dockrell I Give Devise and Bequeathe the Sum of Ten Thousand Pounds (£10,000) for his own use and benefit absolutely.' The distribution of the funds was delayed for months and finally my typing error was discovered. 'To my friend and companion Terence Cockrell.'

Even Mr Purcell had lost his temper over that little effort. I felt I was pretty close to being fired as a result of it. Then I remembered the wretched machine. I nearly broke my leg racing back down the stairs to feed it more paper. Eventually it went quiet. I frantically gathered up a black bag from the broom cupboard and lashed it all into it. Couldn't let Fiona see my Collected Works. She'd have gone ballistic. Herself and her horror daughter. What wouldn't I give to wrap little Nady's tutu round her pampered neck.

I locked up the office and made my way outside, lugging the bag behind me. A part of me felt as if I'd robbed a bank. Baggot Street was like a graveyard, all the sensible office people at home in safe suburbia. Even the sweet shop across the road was closed up for the night. I began to get nervy. I pictured ghosts of long departed Probates filing their way towards me in alphabetical order. Eat the face of me, some of them would.

I walked towards Pearse Street, the weight of the bag killing me. I dumped it in a lane on top of a skip, thankful for small mercies. Running towards the Dart I heard a drunken man scream at me. My teeth chattered and I shook all over. This was no life for an ageing secretary with arthritis in her knees and a numb feeling down her right side.

The Darts were delayed by half an hour due to a signal failure at Tara Street so it was after ten when I finally got home, bloodied and bowed. I was too old for this. Just wanted to fall into a chair and snooze.

The house was empty. Where was Nigel when I needed him? I wanted him to sit me down, make me a cup of tea and listen to my tale of woe. I tried phoning him but only got 'The person you are calling may be out of range. Please try again later.' Out of range. That was apt, all right. In more ways than one.

When he came in he was as sour as ever. In a stink about some problem with a Cost Control clerk from Newtownmountkennedy. Not exactly in the mood to listen to me. So what else was new? I listened to him telling me about the shoddy standards of the young brigade, knowing pretty well that if I dared interrupt I'd get the nose bitten off me. When he took a breath I saw my chance and went for it.

'If you think your day was bad,' I said, 'listen to this.'

I was about two sentences in before he started to lose interest.

'That's good all right,' he said as I told him about my Niagara Falls of paper threading itself through the printer. He thought it was a funny story!

'Nigel,' I screamed, 'you don't know what I've been through. The way I'm feeling I should be signed into St. Pat's mental institution.'

'Join the club,' he yawned.

Numbness on right side, burning sensation in throat, cramps in stomach, panic in office. He put them all into the same actuary folder. Filed under CCL for Couldn't Care Less.

'I had a nightmare at work today and there wasn't a sinner to help me'. He looked at me as if I was giving another of my martyr speeches.

'I don't know why you don't get out of that kip. Tell them to shove their job where the monkey put the nuts.'

I gave up. Pointless to argue when he was in that mood. In his book every problem had a readymade solution if you accessed the right button. Press Function key for Exit from Purcell Fennelly & Co. Unplug Fiona. Disconnect Leonard Darcy. Lower Skelly by a few megabytes. Windows is now shutting down. Press 'Log off' and you'll be grand out.

He often said I should move to a more upmarket firm where I'd get double the money for half the work. If I was interested he could make some calls for me. I didn't like the sound of it. Maybe go from the frying pan into the fire. Too old anyway. They'd take one look at my date of birth and I wouldn't even make it to the interview. Even the confident Marjories of the world were probably past it in these places, overtaken by youngsters straight out school trained in computers since the age of four.

'I know you want me to be a flashy secretary for some yuppie but I just couldn't live with that.'

'Why not? You have all the skills.'

'I don't know. Maybe the little girl in me likes being old-fashioned.'

'That's all very well if you're getting a fair crack of the whip but they seem to be nasty to you in there.'

Talk about the pot calling the kettle black.

'I know I give that impression but it's bearable most of the time.'

'Really? You could have fooled me.'

I didn't blame him for saying that. I was giving him mixed signals. I was a Moaning Minnie most evenings but I never did anything about it.

'Maybe I'm afraid of change. I don't want to end up in one of those trendy places with state-of-the-art furniture where you call your boss by his first name and he brings you out playing golf at the weekend. I'm set in my ways. I need the safety of routine. It's as simple as that.'

'Shit or get off the pot,' he said. Whether he knew it or not, he was part of the same routine. In the morning I buzzed the same bell in the same door each day and climbed the same stairs to the same desk and then in the evening I sat down in the same sofa to watch the same TV with the same man, He was another Fiona in a way, but I preferred to suffer him rather than throwing myself into the minefield of going in search of a new mate.

It had always been my way. I stayed in bad situations because I was afraid of the devil I didn't know.

'Oh I don't care what you do. If you want to stay, stay. But it bugs me when you allow yourself to be a doormat.'

CHAPTER 5

Whether as a result of his words or not, the following morning I decided to go straight in to Fiona to tell her what happened with the delightful Nadine.

'I don't know what you're on about,' she snorted, 'Nady is an expert on computers. She even has her own website.'

'I don't know about that but I had to work till ten to get it all sorted out.'

'That's what you're paid for - sorting things out.' She picked up her phone and started jabbering into it about some missing file from a conveyancing case. Sorry for breathing, Fiona.

One day shortly after that incident I told her I had a dental appointment and would be out for the afternoon. It was a downright lie (I was always good at these since the days of 'forgetting' my copies at school) but I felt I had to get back at her for the torture little Nady put me through. I breezed into a couple of shops and tried on some expensive dresses. There was one pale lilac one that looked really well on me. Payday wasn't for another week so I had to leave it. Also if I didn't pick up the Zhivago coat soon I'd lose the deposit. On the way home, as a kind of consolation prize, I treated myself to a takeaway from the chip shop. One large single, two helpings of onion rings and a greasy cheeseburger.

I put on a CD and lit the fire. Closed the curtains and turned off the light. Ages since I'd listened to Beethoven's Symphony No. 8. The joy I used to get from that music. Years and years ago in the sitting-room in Artane. I'd leave the rest of them at the telly and turn off the light and close the curtains. It could lift me up into the sky and throw me down again. My stomach would go all over the place with the strength of it. I felt the notes were like crashing waves and I was a bit of driftwood tossing and turning under their power. Other times I'd think they were raindrops beating against my whole body and drenching me to the skin. Then again it would be soft and for a little while I'd feel it was lulling me like a mother singing to its baby. Just when I was peaceful it'd lash out again, roaring in my ears until I was almost deaf. I always played my music to the highest pitch.

Why had I stopped listening to it? I could still get that feeling back. It was gratifying to me to know that Beethoven himself loved that one. I read on the sleeve of the tape when I first bought it that the audience hadn't admired it as much as others but Ludwig himself did. What else counted? Always trust the composer, not the critics.

I let the music blare out and began to get back those feelings. I played it four times. Then I put on a Sharon Shannon CD and danced some reels round the sitting-room. I finished with the Sun Collection by Elvis, whirling around like a dervish. After it all I collapsed on the couch feeling rejuvenated. (Except for my knees). That was it: I should have more music in my life. The secret of happiness in your CD set. Who needed doctors?

Nigel and myself went for a walk at the weekend up the hill of Howth. The weather was mild. There was a driving mist at the summit but it was refreshing. I imagined I could smell turf in the air. I had memories of walks in Achill with Daire one summer long ago.

When we finished our climb we stopped at a hotel for tea. Nigel was in good form and didn't speak about work once. We talked about summer, where to this year. Maybe Spain or France. I needed to think of getting away. Life didn't seem too bad suddenly. Only a slight bit of the diarrhoea this morning and the numb leg barely there. Good to be alive. Nice partner. Nice house. Nice world.

Monday at work was when I came back to the planet earth with a bang. I lost a whole document on the machine and the mouse wouldn't operate. Great. I had to call on Sandra again. All sweetness and light, she sorted it in two minutes flat. Later when I was going out to the tea-room I heard her sniggering with Marjorie. I presumed I was the butt of it. Sometimes I thought I gave them great happiness by being so thick. They were able to make themselves feel important by contrast.

I walked down by Stephen's Green at lunchtime and turned into Clarendon Street Church. Lit a candle and thought of my childhood prayer. Please God, mind everybody. Mind Daddy, Mammy, Brian, Angie and me, Cork granny and grandaddy, Glenamaddy granny and grandaddy, uncles and aunts, everybody. All those people dead now. Just me and Angie left.

When I stood up to leave my head felt light. Next of all the whole panic thing hit me like a bolt. Dry mouth, cold foot, feeling of imminent collapse. Have been here before, I thought. Deep breaths. Relax.

I made my way back to the office. Shivering, I sat in the loo for about twenty minutes. How I managed to do my work for the rest of the day I'll never know.

'You're very quiet,' Nigel remarked after we finished our tea, 'Anything bothering you?' How could he have got that idea? Remember you're talking about Ms Ice Cube here.

'Not really. Well I wasn't going to say anything but I got the panic attack back again. Twice in the last few days in fact. Nigel, I'm in a bad way.' There, I chanced it. Brace yourself for Good Samaritan response.

'Oh cry me a river. Not that crap again. Listen, get a grip. There's nothing wrong with you. Get an interest. Start evening classes. Take up bungi-jumping. Scuba dive off the Great Barrier Reef. Join a music appreciation class. You like that classical stuff, don't you?

It's not a cakewalk for any of us. Work at the moment is like World War 3 but do I bring my problems home with me?'

No, I thought, you're too much of a heroic martyr for that. Complaining about something so mundane might jar with your sunny disposition.

'Sorry,' I said, 'You did ask me, though. Believe me, I don't want to be this way. It just hits me out of the blue.'

'Well get yourself sorted. If you need the doctor, go. Get more of those drugs you swallow. I thought they had you sorted out. Become a junkie if you like. It can't be worse than the way you are now.'

'How dare you. They're not drugs, they're prescribed medication.'

'Yeah, Elvis used to say that too and look what happened to him.'

'I don't want to be this way. It's outside my control.'

'Well bring it inside because I'll tell you one thing: I don't need this aggravation. I have enough on my plate with Brannigan on my case all day at work. Maybe if you gave a bit more to the relationship and concentrated on my life you wouldn't have time for these insane attacks.'

'You do enough of that yourself. Why should the two of us be fascinated by you?'

'Not funny.'

'You were saying there I should try music appreciation classes. Well my opinion of these things is that they're a load of rubbish.'

'No they're not. One of the girls from work is going and she's a mensa student.'

If you have to be taught how to appreciate music you have a problem. Who wants to know the difference between a crochet and a semi-quaver, or what andagio is, or if you can identify the third movement? You feel music, Nigel. Feel it.'

'Lay off. It was just a suggestion. I don't personally care what you do with your time.'

'Another thing I can't stomach is wine-tasting classes,' I said, warming to my theme. '*Learning* to taste.

'Come on. Give me a break.'

Nigel looked a bit funny as I went on: 'That has a good nose and a woody flavour to it. Right. It must be good so. It tastes horrible to my mouth but my palette is educated. They have ways of making you enjoy your wine.'

'That's obviously a dig at the course I did last year. Why don't you come straight out with it?'

'Sorry. I didn't remember you did that course. I didn't mean to be sarcastic.'

'Yeah, right.' After that he gave me the silent treatment again. We spent the rest of the night avoiding each other before bed..

Another night of tossing and turning. How could I face work in the morning? What a louse. When he had his sinus trouble I listened to him snorting every night and gave him buckets of sympathy.

I turned up for work the next day feeling miserable. Sneaked a minute between letters to cry on Alice's shoulder over the phone. Afterwards she invited me over to her place for tea. She asked me to stay the night and I said I would. I didn't even bother telling Nigel. A night with her would mean much more to me than jumping off the Barrier Reef.

Sisters were doing it for themselves.

CHAPTER 6

Alice lived in a quiet street in Donaghmede. Her house was small, but neat and tidy like herself. She had a blazing fire on and told me to sit in front of it with a glass of wine while she got the dinner. I knew she preferred to get the food ready without me breathing down her back so I sat still.

What a day. How did I manage to get there? I walked the whole way because I couldn't face the bus. Sitting on her sofa I felt calm but if I stood up I knew I'd get the dizzies again.

'Dinner's up,' she said, ' How about another glass of wine to go with it?'

I didn't talk about myself all through the meal. Major achievement. Helped myself to two more glasses of wine and slumped into the sofa while she tidied up.

'Now,' she said when I was nice and squiffy, 'how are you at all at all? I know there's something up. Is it the leg again?'

'Alice, you don't know what I'm going through. I've always been hyper but in the last few months I've gone into another league. It's like something out of a horror film. Half the time I don't know who I am anymore. Nigel is treating me like dirt and the job is crap and then I have all these pains.'

'Did you tell him about them?'

'Unfortunately.'

'That was a mistake. Cop onto yourself, girl. Us women are in a club of our own when it comes to things like that. Talk to me anytime but men don't understand how sensitive women can be It comes across as nagging. If I were you I'd keep quiet with Nigel about your ailments if you want to hold on to him'.

'I couldn't really care if he puts his head in the oven at this stage.'

'According to yourself you're the more likely one to do that.'

'You don't seem to realise how horrible he is!'

'Come on. You're happy together. You must be nearly ten years with him. You've a gorgeous house.'

She went on, 'My God, look at your new kitchen. It's like something out of a magazine.'

That had been Nigel's idea but I went along with it. We'd spent almost three months having it designed to the snazziest proportions with an integrated fridge and magic presses and whatnot, all state-of-the-art. Now she was using it as a stick to beat me. She was almost as bad as him. I felt like I was in one of those films where everyone is trying to make the main character mad. I threw my heart across the table and she was on about kitchens as if they were the new holy grails. What was mental health compared to a magic press? Don't worry about your head not holding together - just integrate the fridge.

We went on talking but I couldn't get through to her so went to bed early. I slept all night in Alice's little room. I woke about seven and it took me a minute to realise where I was. Maybe I should go to Dr Walsh, I thought. He'd sort me out. He always did.

I just about managed to function at work, spent all day in a kind of dream. Nigel phoned in the afternoon. Friendlyish. He apologised for getting annoyed. He was working late and would see me about ten. He hadn't even noticed that I'd stayed with Alice.

I called into the doctor on my way home. Was nervy waiting to go in. (Nervy – me? Now there was turn-up for the books). At last it was my turn. Legs like jelly as I went into his room.

'How are you? Sit down and take off your coat.'

It all splattered out of me.

'Doctor, I think I'm going crazy. First of all my heart is pounding all the time. Then I feel dizzy. I'm getting those panic attacks back. I had four bouts in the last week. I'm really up the walls. I get a sort of tight pain low down my stomach as well. Could that be anything?'

'Those attacks mean nothing. I've told you that before. It's fear that's making you so nervous. You have nothing to worry about. As for the tummy pain, it's probably a touch of irritable bowel.'

He examined my heart and said it was fine. Well he would say that, wouldn't he? If he looked crooked at me I'd probably have got a major coronary on the spot anyway.

He pressed my stomach and said that was A1 as well. By now I should have been thinking of running the Marathon.

'Are you still taking the anti-depressants?'

'I did feel quite good on these, but doctor but they seem to have stopped working.'

'Yes?'

'Well let me put it this way.'

'Go on.'

'Well I think I'm going round the twist.'

'Now listen here to me, I've known you for twenty years and if you're going mad I'll be the first to let you know. I can guarantee you of that. There's an old saying: 'If you think you're mad you're not. Okay? So let that one go. Tell me now how is the job going? And the relationship?'

'Both horrible.' I thought of the words of granny: 'Better a bad relationship than none.' Granny didn't know too much.

He went to a cupboard and took out some pills. 'What I'm going to do is this. I'll prescribe an extra one of those tablets and two others to help you sleep. Also I'm going to put you on HRT. I know you're still having periods but I see definite signs of the menopause.'

Thoughts came to me of Miss Shaughnessy in my early career in the Department of Posts & Telegraphs. The sniggers and smart comments from us ignoramuses of typists when her poor neck got all flushed. Not so funny now that I was approaching that stage myself. The change of life. How can you change if you've never had a life?

'Why am I like this, doctor?'

'I think it's a combination of things. Women experience a lot of unusual symptoms at this time of life. I'm hopeful that after ten days on this medication you'll feel better. Your private life is your own business but maybe you should look at that, and also the job. In the meantime the medication will help a lot. Nigel tells me you're doing a bit of scribbling.'

Scribbling. That's how people who didn't do it always talked about writing. He meant my - don't laugh – Novel-in-Progress. I'd been at it for about five years now and was going fast nowhere. Ten characters in search of an author. Some author.

'I'm afraid scribbling is the word for it.' You had to play them at their own game.

'Don't be always running yourself down. That's half your problem, low-self-esteem. Ring the bell on your bike.' He gave a grin. 'Like Nigel does.'

I was tempted to say that Nigel rings his bell even though he doesn't have a bike. Instead I said, 'Thanks a lot, doctor.' and shuffled out into the dreary street.

I made it to the late-night chemist and got my prescription. Fat lot of good I expected from it. Placebos.

How did doctors get plates over their doors? Fifty euro for that balderdash. Should diagnose myself from now on. But couldn't refuse to take them on the one in a thousand chance that the man was right. If he put me on any more stuff I'd rattle when I walked.

Nigel arrived in at ten. I told him I'd visited Dr Walsh and that he'd prescribed extra medication. He didn't seem too interested one way or the other, just muttered something about me wearing a path to his door.

'How was your day?' I asked, wanting to let him see I wasn't totally self-absorbed.

'Don't even go there. The sinus has flared up again. I think I'll stay in bed tomorrow. Don't wake me when you're leaving in the morning.'

I sat for a while playing my Beethoven's 8th. Soon I was transported to a happier place. Feck Dr Walsh and his happy pills. Give me good old Ludwig instead.

I felt much calmer for the next week or so. The medication was, as Nigel would put it, starting to kick in. He continued to suffer with his sinus problem. He was clogged up all the time, clearing his throat and making horrible noses like a pig snorting. He complained non-stop. Then one morning it cleared up. He was all smiles at breakfast and when the post came he positively glowed.

'Look - an invitation to a wedding. Brannigan's Lisa is getting married to that Tom fellow. We'll definitely go. Three weeks away. Pick up something trendy for them, will you? And don't stint.'

I looked at the card: 'Nigel and Partner are cordially invited to the wedding of Lisa and Tom blah blah.'

Partner. I was nine years with him. If I was his wife that would be a different day's work. I would have been named, not just called Partner. It was just typical that the Partner had to spend lunch hours trying to get something for the bride and groom. He was too important in himself to even consider looking in a shop.

All that consumed me over the next few days was what I'd look like on the Big Day. At least I had something to wear. The green suit would be just perfect. On the other hand it would probably be a very swanky affair. Maybe I'd treat myself to something more feminine. Suits were fine for office wear. This called for something more dressy. Perhaps a floaty type of dress and maybe a bolero effect thingy to go over it. I'd spotted a lovely one in Pamela Scotts last week. Just as well I forfeited the deposit on the coat. I mean when you think of it, that would have cost me €750 and I had saved €700 by being prudent. Anyway the coat was a bit matronly. Why not get the dress now that I had a reason for getting it? I was sick of being sensible.

I always got worked up if I had to buy something like a birthday or wedding present in a short space of time. It became an obsession. For two weeks of lunch hours I went from shop to shop. One day it was a Waterford glass bowl, the next a lamp, the next set of silver cutlery. I lay awake at night perusing it in my mind. Nigel never lifted a finger to help.

In the end I settled on a wooden salad bowl in Kilkenny Design. It cost over €500 but looked the money. I showed it to Nigel but he just grunted. My nerves were much better for those few weeks. I was sleeping better and only got the panics once. The numb leg was hardly there at all. This was almost too good to be true. Bring on the nuptials.

CHAPTER 7

The wedding day dawned bright and sunny. Pretty warm for March. What we used to call a pet day when I was a child. The dress and matching little jacket gave me confidence. It was a sort of cornflower shade of blue and came down to the mid-calf. It was quite low at the neck but as my old pal Minnie used to say 'if you have it, girl, flaunt it.' Best of all it made my hips look tiny. Even if I say it myself, I really was the business. And, joy of joys, I had a good hair day. Nigel also looked the works in a snazzy grey suit with a sparkling white shirt (which I'd spent an hour trying to iron).

The bride was radiant. I couldn't really see the groom but he seemed older. A woman sang Ave Maria - or should I say murdered it. I was never what you would call much of a singer but I certainly would have made a better job of it myself.

We didn't delay for the photographs. Made our way to the hotel instead. Very fancily laid out, as if for royalty. A sherry reception in the foyer and then the happy couple arrived. She was wearing a beautiful dress. Cream lace just off the shoulder. It was at this point I got my first real look at the groom. He was indeed older. A small butty man with a red face and a very obvious toupee. She towered over him.

When we are at the meal I whispered to Nigel, 'Look at the cut of him. What's she doing with an old geezer like that?'

'He's not that old. Anyway he has a brilliant mind. He's from Cork originally but he's been out of the country for years. They met in Brussels. Appearances don't count for anything. Seemingly it was love at first sight. Brannigan is delighted. I know that for sure. Apparently pots of dough there.'

'Well love must be blind. I'd say she wasn't too blind to the money though.'

'Ever the cynic,' said Nigel. He then proceeded to engage a pretty little blonde in a meaningful discussion about the stock market. I knew the stock market I'd have liked to give the pair of them. A sharp hard kick into both of their stuck-up rear ends.

The meal was your typical wedding fare. Little crabby things for starters, which I hated. The roast beef was all stringy and almost stuck in my gullet. The trifle swam in a sea of sherry. Nigel and his blonde friend appropriated the nearest bottle of wine. There was no water nearby which always freaked me. If I was eating anything at all I had to have a glass of it beside me to make a wild grab at in case of a crisis. It was probably nerves. Hard to believe, I know, in such a sensible woman as myself, but my throat would close up unless I had a drink to clear it. For some reason I always kicked my shoes off when this happened. It was another one of my funny little habits. I didn't want to die with my boots on.

I spotted Trish hovering round looking like a lost soul. Out of the kindness of my heart I asked her if she'd like to join us after the meal. She'd made an effort, in fairness to her, but she was a bit long in the tooth for the baby pink sparkly jacket and her knees were far too agricultural-looking to be uncovered. In the make-up department she'd obviously decided whatever you do, do it in style. The bright orange lipstick clashed with her jacket. As for the blue eye shadow, that went out with the Indians.

'I'd love to join you,' she replied to my invitation, 'I know it's probably a bit awkward for you being here, not working with us and all that.'

I felt like telling her what to do with herself. Instead I just gave her a smarmy grin and said with as much sarcasm as I could muster up, 'Well now that you're here, I just know I'll be fine.'

She was too dense to get the dig and just smiled as if to say 'God love you, if it weren't for me nobody would bid you the time of day.' No mention of the fact that I had an escort while Miss Moneypenny was on her lonesome.

Next came the speeches. They dragged on and on. Blue jokes from the best man caused the elderly priest to go rather pink round the gills. Brannigan rattled on about every day being Christmas with Lisa for a daughter. A drunk uncle from Boris-in-Ossory disgraced himself by toppling into the cake. (Didn't every wedding have one? (A drunk uncle from Boris-in-Ossory, I mean, not a cake). .

The cards were read out and I wanted to hide under the table at Nigel's attempt at wit. 'May more than railings run round your front lawn.' He was getting quite merry and insisted on telling everyone at the table that I was the love of his life.

Then the dancing started. Nigel continued to lash into the red wine and it went straight to his head.

We got up to dance. He pulled me close and started nibbling at my ear. He looked quite sexy with drink. It was like when we first started dating. What with the romantic music and the atmosphere of the wedding I let myself sink into the warmth of his body.

'You know what,' he cooed, snuggling up to me, 'These wedding affairs aren't half bad. Maybe you and I should be doing something about it. What do you think?'

'Married? I don't know. I thought both of us were content enough to live together.'

'The time is right, my dear. Also, it doesn't help my career to be, as they say, living in sin.' Impress Brannigan. To hell with my needs.

No sooner were we seated than Trish descended on us like a leech. 'Nigel,' she said in her little baby voice, 'am I going to get that dance you promised me? It's the tango. I'll show you what I've learnt at those classes I've been telling you about.'

If you lean back in that skirt with those thunder thighs, sweetie , I thought to myself, there'll be a general stampede. Women and children first.

'I'd love to dance,' cooed Nigel, 'if that's okay with you.'

'Be my guest,' I said and went off to the powder-room. Lisa and her new husband were in the hallway chatting. As I passed by them I suddenly felt faint. All the old symptoms came back: dizziness, sharp jabs of pain in left shoulder, numb foot. Definitely a bad idea to combine drink and the medication,

I sat on the staircase for half an hour or so, trying frantically to keep my head together. I tried my old trick of focussing on a beautiful scene but it didn't work. How could you think of a beach in the Caribbean when your brain felt like cotton wool and people were scurrying around you like mad things?

Another trick I had was making up sentences with the same letter. Sometimes it got me off to sleep when I was stressed. A bit like counting sheep. Auntie Ann ate an apple. Bertie Browne beat a baby. Carrie Connolly cut a crust. And so on. (Theoretically to Z). I think I got to G before I dozed off.

'What are you doing? Is this where you've been? I was getting worried.'

Nigel's face was black with rage. He shook me awake. For a minute I didn't know where I was.

'Wake up! Jesus. You'll have me disgraced.' No good-humoured Romeo now. Wanted to marry me one minute, devil incarnate the next.

'I'm feeling terrible,' I muttered groggily. 'I want to go home. I'm half asleep. I can't stay here. Anyway, you were dancing with Trish.'

'Pull yourself together for God's sake. What's your problem? Everyone is staring at you.'

'I couldn't give a fiddler's about them. Do you not care about how I'm feeling?'

'We'll talk about that later. Can you get up? Here, hold on to me.' He lifted me up but I felt like a limp rag doll. The lights might have been on but there was nobody home.

'Call me a taxi, Nigel. Honestly, this is serious. If I don't get out of here quick I'll pass out.'

'There's no way you're going to pass out. Cop on to yourself. It's your imagination. You're conning yourself into thinking you're getting a panic attack. Maybe the drink went down the wrong way.'

'Bullshit.'

'Listen to me. I can't stay here with you. If you want to go, go, but I have to stay. Do you understand?'

And then ,'Brannigan would be vicious if I walked out now.' Brannigan. The man he really loved. I was only a fifth wheel. It was all so insane I nearly had to laugh.

'At least phone for a taxi.'

'Phone yourself. You're the one with the problem.' He walked away.

As he was heading into the function room I saw Trish making a bee-line towards him. There was a time when I would have chased after him and clawed her eyes out but I was just too miserable to care.

I went to the reception desk and somehow managed to ring for a taxi. Can't remember how long it took for him to get to me or how we got home. Minor miracle I even remembered the address.

In bed by seven p.m and snoozed like a sad spinster. So much for one wedding being the making of another. Did anyone miss me? It didn't look like it.

The next day I spent in bed as well. Too upset and frightened to move. Nigel never came near me all day. I heard the door bang with an almighty wallop at about four. I dragged myself down and had a cup of instant soup, shaking all over.

Then back to bed again. Got a hot water bottle and two tranquillisers and fell into a lovely sleep. Woke once in the night and heard Nigel going to the loo. He was in the spare room again. He was obviously furious about my performance at the wedding. Image was more important to him than breathing.

I didn't turn up for work again the next day and didn't ring in either. The longer you stayed out the harder it got to go back. Like in school. There was a short message on the answering machine from Nigel. 'Away for a few days. Be in touch'. Charming. Ever the concerned caring partner.

I thought of phoning Alice, or my old friend Minnie from Galway. Alice was too kind, I decided, it would have been unfair to be using her. As for Minnie, we hadn't been in touch for months but she was always there at the end of the phone. Blood sisters since childhood. We'd sat beside each other in first class and from day one we'd taken to each other. 'Bonded' as they call it now. Why did they always have to put those American-sounding words on things?

She had dark curly hair and huge brown eyes. She was petite and had a lovely little figure, nicely rounded. Her colouring was almost Spanish. In the summer she'd go as dark as a dusky little Indian child.

I was the complete opposite - tall and gawky from childhood. They always put me in the back row at school because of my height. My colouring was delicate. My mother told me she used to pinch my cheeks as a little girl so I'd have a nice pink glow.

The school put on *The Three Children of Fatima* one year and Minnie was chosen to play the part of Lucia. They tested me out for Jacinta's part but I was disastrous. They gave me a part in a crowd scene instead. I only had one line. When the sun fell from the sky I had to shout out, 'I believe, oh my God, I believe.' On the first night of the play, Mammy, Daddy, Angie and Brian were all in the front row waiting for my debut. When it came to the time to deliver the words my mouth went dry and I froze. No words came out. I upset the whole scene because the other children were waiting for their cues. After that night they took the line from me and passed it on to Teresa Duggan. It was my first experience of rejection. (How did The Abbey survive without me?)

Minnie shone in the part of Lucia. I always felt she should have taken up acting. She was a natural. Instead she got married at twenty and dropped all those kinds of thoughts.

Maybe I'd give her a call in a few days. It was a pity Angie was in the States. She'd understand too.

Four days went by with me going from bed to kitchen, nowhere else. Half woman, half mattress. I lived on tea and toast until the bread ran out and then tackled the digestive biscuits, lorrying them back like peanuts. In the mirror I thought I looked a hundred. Couldn't remember when I'd last washed my hair. Unheard of for me, forever with a bottle of shampoo in my hand. My father used to say he was convinced I was drinking the stuff. You couldn't move without falling over it in the bathroom.

Daddy. I drove him mad with my disorderly ways. He was the opposite. He had these little notebooks with all his appointments in them and all our birthdays. A totally dependable man. Steady as a rock. Even after he retired he kept his routines.

He was always after me to tidy my room. I'd put on a glazed look and tell him I'd do it tomorrow. It was always tomorrow with me. Like Scarlett O'Hara.

I once thought he had all the answers but I realised as I got older that he was nervous too. He didn't show it much because he grew up in an age when you weren't allowed to. Big boys didn't cry. I made up for him, of.course. Had to be taken out of two schools because of my whinging. Sometimes I thought he fought his nerves too hard. Maybe bottling things up had caused his heart problems. I always thought he liked my scattiness. Nigel used to too - once. Like Daddy he was ordered. Opposites attracted, at least for a while.

I wasn't very attractive to Nigel now. He thought he was getting a social butterfly, a coper, not this couch potato on medication. How could he sympathise with me when he had no nerves himself? It wasn't like a broken leg where you had plaster of Paris over you, or a black eye or a cut on your finger. He kept saying 'Pull yourself together'. The old joke: 'Doctor, doctor, I think I'm a pair of curtains'. 'Well pull yourself together then.'

CHAPTER 8

On Day 5 of my isolation I remembered Dr Walsh's advice about getting back to my writing. I rummaged through old papers in the attic and eventually dug up my masterpiece. I'd started it probably ten years ago but there were long gaps where I would forget it existed. I had lots of ideas in my head but what was actually on paper was pretty pathetic. I surveyed my opening chapter anew: My heroine was a lost sort of woman. She was in her mid-fifties and wasn't a success on the romantic field nor in her career either. She struggled with new technology and was a grey sad lady. This was how I wrote about her:

Bridget Small lived in a small house in Rialto. She was nothing to write home about in appearance. Your typical secretarial type: mousy and conscientious. But what nobody realised was that inside herself Bridget was a seething cauldron of emotion.

One time years ago she'd sent off an application form to go to Canada. Reams and reams of stuff she'd filled in: Do you enjoy sport? Are you a leader? What were your grades at school? Do you debate? No, no, no, and a big fat no, she replied. She was lousy on the playing fields, definitely no leader, grade e-minus at school and as for debating, goodnight Irene.

'Any distinguishing feature?' asked the application form. 'None,' she answered, 'but am willing to be tattooed.' Afterwards she got a snotty letter back from the Canadian Embassy denying her request to go to that country. Just as well, she thought to herself, they must be as dull as ditchwater over there. (She'd heard someone once said that it was such a boring country, even the female impersonators were women).

Even though Bridget was a mousy secretary, she did have an outside life. She invented a character called John that she'd been married to since she was about seven. Oh how her parents had fretted when she'd ramble on to this make believe husband. Even now, John came to her rescue when the job was getting her down.

She worked in an office with mouses and seals. The seals were her workmates and the mouses the little thingies sitting snugly beside her computer. She was always making mistakes at her computer and it always said the same thing: 'Are you sure?' Every time Bridget made a mistake that question would come up. Except it wasn't really a question because when the computer said that you knew you had rightly mucked up. It was sarcastic. So you see, thought Bridget, even computers can be cruel and try to make you feel small. Which was really hard for Bridget because she was so small anyway - in name, in body and in her mind as well.

Every day of her working life Bridget was the loyal secretary, trundling down to the Dart in her best bib and tucker and then seating herself at her desk, plugging in her earphones and typing away until elevenses, or whatever. She'd never master the computer, she knew, but she remembered with some pride the first day she'd managed to type the sentence The Quick Brown Fox Jumped Over The Lazy Dog. That was the one that had all the letters of the alphabet in it. It was part of her training course. Weren't they clever to think up a sentence like that?

After work Bridget usually went home and played classical music to relax herself and forget about the tensions of the day. She made up some more situations with John which she then acted out to her heart's content in the privacy of her room. She also told herself jokes from her past. There was one about Michael Delaney's dog which used to cheer her up. 'How is the dog?' asked his friend Tom one day when the dog was sick. 'I'll put it this way, Tom,' said Michael, 'she's civil but dishtant.' It became a family quote. Sometimes Bridget would ask her sister Niamh how she was and Niamh would reply, 'I'm civil but dishtant.'

Thinking about things like that took Bridget's mind off mouses and seals and bad memories of school when she couldn't do her geometry or graphs and Bright Young Things with bobbed hair like the two Flannery sisters from Taylor's Hill who shot their hands up and asked intelligent questions about algebra and theorems, their eyes hopping out of their sockets with excitement. Meanwhile she broke out into a sweat thinking she might be asked a question next about Euclid or Pythagoras' theorum or those funny sguiggly graphs she drew but didn't have a clue about. To her they were just hills of things you might draw in an art class to dress up a page.

One day when Bridget was eight years old hers mother called the doctor because she was worried about this imaginary John character she kept talking about. (She even had a song about him but she couldn't remember the air of it). The doctor said it was just a bit of fantasy and to leave her at it, that she'd grow out of it. But she didn't.

Bridget also missed her Confirmation question and worried that the bishop might tell her to leave the church. Then there was a play where she only had one line which she managed to mess up, her voice drying up totally just as she got her cue.

In later years the bright young things from the classroom got replaced with the performing seals in the office who knew everything about computers and were never asked 'Are you sure?', but Bridget was just the same Bridget, a frightened little girl that would never be up to scratch, living in permanent dread that one day they'd find out she knew nothing and turf her out onto the roadside without a penny to her name..."

So that was it. Chapter 1 of my delightful novel. Maybe one fine day I'd take Bridget a step further and make her go crazy in her office - as I felt like doing in mine. As for now, there were days to be got through in my supposedly real life.

On the Friday Alice phoned.

'I tried to get you at work. What's wrong?'

'I'm sick, Alice, just sick.'

'Is it the flu? It's going round. I wish I could do your shopping for you or something.'

I told her I was fine, that Nigel was taking care of everything. (And pigs might fly).

She knew I was antsy so she got off the phone quick. On an impulse I decided to phone Nigel but his mobile was turned off. Between the jigs and the reels I'd forgotten his marriage proposal. A crazy part of me thought: Why not go for it? We knew each other long enough.

It would be a quiet wedding, a small select affair. I wouldn't wear white. Maybe a cream silk would look well with my slim figure, which was getting slimmer with my nerves. I thought I'd fit into a size twelve now. Minnie could be the bridesmaid, or maybe Alice. Charlie, Nigel's brother, could be a groomsman, and maybe Brannigan. Angie might fly over from the States for it, with Louise and Jennifer in tow. They could be the flower girls.

'The bride is beautiful,' they'd all remark as I tripped down the aisle in a haze of silk, 'she doesn't look a day over thirty-five.'

CHAPTER 9

I walked into work the next day. Nigel had arrived back the night before. He was quite civil and dropped me to the Bull Wall and I put on my sensible shoes and walked from there. No bunion aches but the heavens opened when I got to the Five Lamps. Knew it was down for the day. Murphy's Law. Soaked to the skin when I got to the office.

Waiting for me at the door was Fiona, the unofficial sentry.

'We can't have this sort of thing,' was her opening comment, 'You have to ring in or send a doctor's cert.'

She went on about expecting more from me, giving good example to the juniors and so on. I tried to look suitably crestfallen. How long did she spend every night rehearsing these little diatribes?

I soaked up the punishment but my mind was a million miles away. They only owned my body, not my mind. As soon as elevenses came I was released from captivity for those ten minutes of relative peace with my brown scone.

At the tea-break I started telling them about my early days in the Civil Service and they seemed to enjoy it. Even Rita and Mairead got a kick out of me. I told them about a little cloakroom we had and whenever a girl got her Auntie Jane, she vamoosed in there with a hot water bottle and a grey warm blanket. You could lie there for two or three hours and nobody would bother you.

'Imagine that happening here,' Sandra said, clearly flummoxed. She told me I was a panic. Not such a bad young one really, I concluded. I'd be friendly with anyone who laughed at my anecdotes. I didn't really care if they cut hell out of me behind my back.

Marjorie asked me was I free for lunch, which stopped me in my tracks. I always got the impression she'd only pick me if I was the last woman on the planet.

We went to a local place and as soon as we sat down she started telling me all about her relationship, which was going through a very bad patch. Nothing new there. She obviously needed somebody to moan to and muggins was the only game in town. I didn't mind what her reasons were, I was still complimented she took me into her confidence. To be honest, there seemed to be a pair of them in it. Her boyfriend was no great shakes but in a way I felt they deserved each other.

She was worried that he hadn't given her a commitment. It was mooted a few times but kicked into touch by her knight in shining armour. Not that these things mattered to her, love, but you had to know if there was a future in something, didn't you?

To shut her up I came out with my usual quip: 'There's more married than can churn milk.'

'You're a riot,' she said, 'I must remember that one. More married than can churn milk.' It seemed to quell her fears, at least for the moment.

Back at work my mind was on what we talked about instead of my work so I made the usual number of typing mistakes and got the usual dirty looks from the top dogs. Who cared? I kept looking at the clock until Release Time.

The rain was still bucketing down when I left. I ducked into Kilkenny Design on the way home. Spotted this Michael Mortell waxed coat. The medium size fitted me perfectly. It was a bit 'Going to the Races' sort of coat, and I don't mean Best Dressed Woman gear. More horsey English type with hip flasks in the roomy pockets type of get-up. It had a sort of cape effect too but the thing I really liked was the leather trim on the collar and cuffs. It was expensive but as the shop assistant said, 'Ideal for our lovely Irish weather'. And it would last for years.

Delighted with my purchase, I sailed home on the Dart. En route I got into a chat with a woman who was working in the Dental Hospital. Apparently the pressure was terrible there too. The stories we told each other were like mirror-images of each other. We clicked so much I ended up giving her my phone number. Eva was her name. Not married either and about my own age. I gave her a peep at the coat and she said it definitely looked the money. Nigel was there when I got home. He had his nose in the paper as per usual and didn't even say hello. I decided to act totally normal. I didn't even ask him where he'd been.

'Hi,' I said, 'busy day?'

He grunted.

I was all set to model the coat for him but didn't bother when I saw the puss on him. Probably something upset him at work. Hopefully he'd come out of it in his own time. I read an article once in a book about the difference between the sexes. It said men prefer to retire into their caves after an argument whereas women want to come and talk it all out. Was that why men were so screwed up and women so balanced? Probably.

He surprised me by coming in to me during the night. Strange for me to be with him in this way again.

That's how things were between us. .Love's young dream every now and then. Total strangers at most other times. But snug in his arms now I felt safe. Would we go the distance? Who knew.

I was feeling in top form the next day at work.

'What's up with you?' one of the younger secretaries said, 'You look like you're hiding some guilty secret.' I wanted to reply, 'I'm in love. Nigel and me are together again. And he proposed a week ago. Mind you he hasn't mentioned it since and he just sort of said it would be a good idea, but it was a proposal. Definitely a proposal.'

I could just see the wedding day scenario:' Here comes the bride, fifty inches wide.' Maybe if I got the hair cut now it would take people's attention off my weight, which was going up again.

I thought of phoning Alice. Maybe I'd meet her this evening and tell her how I was feeling. Then I thought, no. Instead I'd go home. Get a bottle of wine and rustle up something special for Nigel.

I did that. The steak and onions were delicious, potatoes and peas perfecto. An apple tart I cooked with my own fair hands also turned out just right. When Galway were playing in All-Irelands, Mammy used to spell out 'Up Galway' on her apple tarts with sticks of pastry. I should have put 'Nigel, the love of my heart' on this one.

We had an early night and again slept wrapped in each other's arms. He had his new after-shave on and it was intoxicating. I could hardly breathe from the scent but it was a nice way not to be able to breathe.

I trotted off to work a new woman the next day. No pains, no aches, no numbness or feeling I was going to pass out or freak or disgrace myself. I didn't even have to do the 'Focus on a still point' thing, or the ABC game. A barrel of laughs again at coffee break. 'You're a pantomime,' they said, 'where do you come up with them?' They thought I should be on the telly.

My good humour was short-lived. When I went back to my desk, Nady was sprawled over my machine. If she starts to muck things up again, I thought, I'll swing for her.

'Oh God, Nadine,' I said, 'could I get in at my desk? I'm very busy today.'

No response.

'Nadine,' I repeated, 'your mummy needs her work done. Wouldn't it be nice if you let me in there?'

Still nothing. She was actually playing Patience. I desperately needed some.

I started to fantasise about pulling at her tight curls when a happy accident happened. Dame Margot Fontaine caught her toe under the leg of the desk and let out an almighty roar. She uttered screams that would waken the dead. A minute later, Fiona put her head round the corner. 'What's going on here?' she bellowed.

'Nadine hurt her toe.'

She put her arms round Nadine's shoulders as if she'd just had open heart surgery. I tried to look soulful as I sniggered to myself inside. Score: one-all. Going home on the Dart that evening my symptoms erupted again with a huge gush. Pinchy pains, numb fingers, weight on chest, dry mouth and dragging sensation in the pit of my stomach. When I reached the safety of the house I flung myself on the sofa. My heart was palpitating and I couldn't get my breath.

It was late when Nigel arrived in from work, laden down with the inevitable sheaf of papers. I ran into his arms and burst into tears telling him I felt terrible.

'Cool it,' he said, 'you're the picture of health.'

'No I'm not, actually. Dr Walsh said I had irritable bowel problems.'

'It's not the only irritable thing about you,' he said, "I'll ring the doctor tomorrow and he'll sort you out. As for now, I'll make the tea. Watch the telly for yourself. *Coronation Street* is on.'

I sat staring into space. Didn't hear one word of Corrie. Unusual for me. Even if there was an earthquake in Dublin I had to see it. Like a second religion. I let my mind wander. Pictures of this irritable bowel thing inside me drifted before my eyes. I imagined a squelchy thing with a sour face on it, and a sourer disposition. The cares of the world on it, cross as a bag of cats. That 'Nobody knows all I've suffered' sort of mentality. Probably pushing other organs all over the place. 'Get out of my way there, kidneys. Would you ever shove off, bladder, I'm sick of looking at you.' I thought of the other intestines and gallstones shunning it and saying to each other, 'Here comes cheery bowel again, a laugh a minute.' Somehow these thoughts calmed me down.

When Nigel presented me with a toasted cheese I swallowed it without a word. He didn't have a clue how to make it. No onion, and the toast all burned. 'Are you still taking those concoctions the doctor has you on?' he asked as I nibbled at it, 'I think you should visit him in the morning.'

I didn't want to tell him I'd eased off on the medication. He'd say that's what it was all about.

For the rest of the evening I tried to get him to listen to me but he kept putting his hand over my mouth, or in his own ears. Subtle Nigel. Then he told me it was bedtime, as if I was his daughter instead of his lover.

He brought his computer to bed with him and clicked the mouse for what seemed like hours on some report he was doing. I had a rival in the love stakes. Other men went with lapdancers but my one was falling for a lapTOP. Which was worse?

I tossed and turned all night as he accessed websites. Clickety-click like a tap dripping hour after hour. I didn't dare interrupt him for fear of getting the old line: 'This is what's paying the mortgage, my dear.'

CHAPTER 10

He was up at dawn and brought me breakfast in bed, wonder of wonders.

'I've rung the office,' he said, almost throwing the tea at me, 'and also the doctor. He'll be here at ten. I'm staying off work until he sees you.' There was always a catch.

I lay in a stupor until Dr Walsh arrived. It was the first time he'd ever called to the house. Everywhere was in rag order. Usually this would have upset me. I would have tidied it up a bit. I didn't look in great nick myself either but then who wants to look well when the doctor is calling? Better resemble the wreck of the Hesperus to get your fix of tabbies.

'I feel terrible,' I told him, holding my nose and diving straight to the heart of it.

'Is that so? Let me listen to those lungs. I think you're a bit chesty. Now, how many of these anti-ds have I you on - two, isn't it?'

'I cut them down. I felt great for a while and felt better to ease off.'

'What?'

'I'm sorry. I thought...'

'You shouldn't think. That's what you pay me for. I'm a doctor, remember? It's no wonder you're in a state. It's withdrawal. That can create havoc. You must never, I repeat never, come off medication without my telling you. You have to be weaned off these little babies. You must realise that.'

'Minnie always says they cause more problems than they cure. It's much better to fight it yourself. I was just as bad on them anyway.'

'And who may I ask is this Minnie - your new doctor?'

'She works in a chemist shop in Galway. She had some bad experiences with tablets.'

'A chemist shop. She'd know how to prescribe, to be sure. Now listen to me. I'm going to put you on a different tablet. Maybe the last ones didn't suit you. You're to take three of those tranquillisers. I'll give you a cert for work for two weeks. You need total rest. Get out in the afternoon, take a little walk. Fresh air is good. You have a good man downstairs. He's very worried about you. Be thankful for what you have. I'll leave the prescription with Nigel and in the meantime don't leave that bed.'

He asked me about my diet and my general routines but every answer I gave seemed to be wrong. I didn't get enough exercise, I worried too much, and pigged out on junk food. In other words I was an accident waiting to happen. A healthy body meant a healthy mind and vice versa.

He told me to take more fruit and vegetables and also more fish. 'It's good for the brain,' he said, giving me a funny look. I was about to say 'Is that why they travel in schools?' but thought better of it. This was deadly serious stuff as far as he was concerned. He talked about the food pyramid, about saturated fats, about cholesterol and blood pressure and all those other things sensible people worry about, instead of dizzy heads and cold numb feet.

I listened to it all in a half-daze. I was funny like that. I was the most nervous person on the planet when I had a symptom but when I didn't I was nonchalance personified. It was like when I was at school: nervous half the time and bone lazy the other half. Always terrified I'd get caught for not having my lessons done but never willing to clean up my act. Everyone knew I was a ditherer - Daddy, Big Knickers (the most horrible nun on planet Earth) and now this man of medicine. That's probably why he spent extra time with me. Probably knew I hadn't the foggiest what he was on about and cared less.

After he left the room I heard himself and Nigel in conspiratorial chat downstairs. No doubt he was telling him I'd come off the medication. He'd be bucking mad with me. Neither of them understood this was nothing to do with medication. Could it be something like the woman I read about who had multiple personalities? Maybe. My thoughts kept racing round in circles.

When Nigel finally came upstairs he put on his Snotty Parent mask, telling me I'd been a naughty little girl but now everything was going to be all AOK because he was going out to get my new medication. I almost expected him to lock me in till he came back.

I buried myself under the duvet for the next few days, my favourite hiding-place when things got too bad. Nigel came home every lunchtime to cook something for me. He was like a mad thing on his mobile, bawling instructions to the other people in the office. It was reassuring to me that I wasn't the only one he acted the anti-christ with.

I developed a passion for Bovril, which he made for me as well. He administered my medication to me as if he was a male nurse caring for a private patient. I slept for hours and hours. I must have been totally zonked on tablets but I wasn't afraid anymore, just not really there. He stayed out late most evenings, either to make up for the lunchtimes or because I was such lousy company.

When I felt I was cracking up from boredom I ventured downstairs but hadn't the energy of a duck. I sat in the living-room like a total vegetable watching television. Dr Phil, Jeremy Kyle, Oprah. If you worked it out properly, I concluded, you could have back-to-back talk shows from dawn till dusk. To avoid the nervous breakdown caused by missing one it was always necessary to have your remote on hand to record it.

The shows had one positive aspect. They made me realise most other people's lives were almost as mad as my own. Fat American mothers wheeled out equally fat American children and bellyached about the fact that their excuses for boyfriends were cheating on them with majorettes from Idaho. Anorexic teenagers went into graphic detail about their last suicide attempt. Weedy teenagers paraded themselves about the studio as if to the manner born and I didn't know whether to laugh or cry.

Nigel told me the end of civilisation must be near if he caught a few minutes of these shows but as far as I was concerned they were quite jolly. A bit like Mills & Boon on the small screen. I sat button-hopping for hours. It was like having all these guests in your house without having to go to the trouble of cooking or tidying up.

Every evening when he came in it was the same routine.

'How are we today - any better?' He'd even adopted the royal plural beloved of Dr Walsh.

'On the mend,' I'd tell him because I knew it was what he wanted to hear. In actual fact I didn't know if I was or not - or if I'd even been sick.

Then he'd put on the Bovril and carefully count out my tablets in his accountant's fingers. Woe betide me if I forgot one. He was the provider now and me the liability. But it was a role I slotted myself into with some relish.

When the time came to go back to work I totally lost my nerve. Old solution to all my problems so decided to pay the good old doc another visit. Would ask for another two week's leave. I felt a further fortnight of the good life would sort me out nicely. I also bought a few books for myself. More Mills & Boons. To hell with good literature. These sort of books always made me feel happy. Dark cruel men called Bruce being horrible to little delicate girls named Fern and in the end, no matter how horrible he was or how he seemed to love the total hard bitch, Fern got her man and they lived happily ever after. My kind of story.

The doctor wasn't over the moon about my proposal but I toughed it out with him and he eventually wrote the cert out.

'But remember now,' he warned as he gave it to me, 'you must get out and about. You've had your rest and don't need to stay in bed anymore. Take some long walks. Get your hair done. Do what women do to cheer themselves up. Above all, take care of that lovely man of yours. He's very concerned about you, you know.'

I knew that. Almost, in fact, as concerned as he was about himself.

When I got back to the house I was in seventh heaven. I lashed on my Beethoven No.8 and danced round the sitting-room for myself as I played it over and over again. One time I was the conductor, waving my hands at the orchestra, another time I was a leaf dancing about in the air, up and down, hither and thither. I jumped up on the table at one wild part of the music and leapt off.

The pain in my arthritic knee was terrible, but Dancing Delia wasn't to be denied.

The next few days were like a dream. Nigel worked late a lot but the evenings were getting brighter and I didn't mind being alone. Every morning I was up at dawn, getting energy from somewhere just when I didn't need it. My system was funny. I could bounce around the place at weekends but was always sluggish on work days. My subconscious was probably trying to tell me something.

I continued to feed myself on the dumbed-down telly shows where sad fat people tore the living daylights out of each other and then hugged and kissed for the benefit of the resident psychiatrist. I also added a new scene to the Bridget Small business, the one where she goes barmy in the office:

One day in June 1995 it all came to a head. She was sitting at her screen typing away to beat the band, moving the mouse about and feeling reasonably comfortable with herself. Suddenly she couldn't remember a single thing she'd learnt. It brought back all the bad old days at school when she didn't know her geometry and graphs and all the bright-as-button girls were shooting their hands up to Sister Benignus, also known as Sister Big Knickers.

She looked across at all the efficient young secretaries and the room started to spin and the mouse grew ears and a long curly tail just like her brother had for a pantomime in the Columban Hall. Dressed in a lovely suit her mother made for him.

The screen spun in front of her and the mouse looked up at her with an ugly grin. 'Look at yourself,' he said, 'you're past your sell-by date. You're useless, feckin' useless.' Her face got hot and she left her seat and went into the Ladies. She sat on the floor bawling her eyes out. 'God help me,' she said, 'I'm truly bunched.' She could hear the mouse laughing outside. After a while one of the Bright Young Things knocked on the door. 'Are you all right?' she asked, 'you look a bit on the peaky side.'

She went back into the typing pool where all the clever young performing seals sat. She opened her drawer and pulled out a load of old photos from long ago. Pictures from the Ark,, a letter from a penfriend, a few sticks of lipstick, and many crumpled cigarette packets.

'Excuse me, Bridget,' said the supervisor, 'Are you all right? What are you doing?'

'I'm going,' she snapped back, 'I'm off. You can keep your old mouses. Send me out my P45 if you wouldn't mind.'

'Sit down, sit down,' said the supervisor lady, 'you're not well. This is so unlike you, you've always been a lady. Can we phone home for you to be collected?' She heard a few of the young seals giggling and one whispering about changes of life.

'Yes,' she said, 'yes, it's the change but I don't care anymore. You know what? I just don't care.'

Next of all Mr O'Brien from the Taxation Department arrived in. 'Take it easy, Bridget,' he said, 'you're fine, I'll drive you home. You need a break. It happens to the best of us.'

She tried to push him aside but he grabbed her and led her out to his car. She could see the goggling seals gaping from their windows into the car park and imagine the chat of them. But she let Mr O'Brien drive her home. What did it matter now?

A few days later a deputation of the seals arrived out to the house. They brought flowers and cards and all other sorts of junk. 'Isn't it well for some?' Mr O'Brien said. She told him it was indeed but she had it coming to her after all those years slaving in the Dublin 2 Torture Chamber. He didn't get the joke. 'Don't come back till you're good and ready,' he said, putting on his sweetest smile. 'That'll be when I'm about 85,' she informed him.

The following Saturday morning she got up bright and early and went to the Dart station and off into town with her. She got off at the usual stop and with her personal key let herself into the office.

Everything was as still as a graveyard there. Empty seats sat facing empty silent screens and scores of mice huddled up on desks waiting for the seals to return on Monday.

She pulled the mice from their sockets and flung them in a mass of tangles into the centre of the floor. Then she threw big chunks of cheese at them and also large dollops of mouse poison.

'Eat up,' she said, 'enjoy yourselves my boyos.'

She turned on screens and watched them flashing and demanding passwords. Then she keyed in gibberish words. 'Are you sure?' asked the screens. 'Yes,' she replied, 'I was never more sure of anything in my life.' Then she went to the filing cabinet behind which Ms Lady Supervisor sat and pulled out every file she could see and ripped them all to shreds. 'Eat up,' she said to the mice, 'eat up, you bastards.'

CHAPTER 11

The weather was like summer during those endless March days. In Fairview Park the trees were just coming into bloom, all pink and rosy and perfectly suiting my mood. Getting ready for Easter in their new rig-outs. Soon in Galway it would have been time for white ankle socks, black patent shoes and the knee socks and bootees thrown into a cupboard to lie in the dark for months and months. Jack 'O'Leary would have his homemade ice cream for sale. It was lovely biting into the bottom part of the cone and scooping the delicious cream with your tongue. Heaven, Summer on the way, at least when summer was summer, and wandering down the winding lane that led to the sea.

This break was good for me. I needed to be out of the pressure cooker atmosphere of the office. Maybe it was time I thought about early retirement. Everybody I knew seemed to be going for it now. Look at Alice. Never happier. Maybe I'd discuss it with Nigel.

I cooked him a lot of dinners at this time, atoning for past sins of almost starving the poor man when I was a dying duck of a patient. Lasagne, spaghetti bolognese, chicken *a la* king. After one of my particularly imaginative creations, while he sipped his wine, I broached the subject. My four week's holidays were coming to an end and I knew I'd have to face back to the queer place. If I could give in my notice immediately I'd be free by the end of April.

His reaction was predictable, to say the least.

'You're far too young to retire. Anyway, my salary wouldn't pay the mortgage. What would we live on - fresh air?'

'I know, but what if I got a job temping? Maybe I could have the summer off and then look for something totally different.'

'I can't see it working. Do you think I like turning in every morning myself? You don't know the meaning of pressure in your soft little number. It's dog-eat-dog where I am. Survival of the fittest. You're only as good as your last audit. If it's a break you want we'll have a holiday in August, maybe go to the sun. Anyway you need the routine.'

'But I feel so good these days. All those horrible experiences I've been having. They stopped when I took the time off.'

'We all need discipline in our lives. You have too much time to think. Get back into harness. Everybody needs to work. Wake up and smell the coffee.'

'I don't want to smell the coffee. I just want to drink it.'

'What's that supposed to mean? Look, work is good for you. You need to meet those friends of yours for lunch. Get back into real life. Dr Walsh said you're ready.' And so on. The two of us were like broken records.

The following drizzly Monday morning I was again a respectable member of the working community, off the Live Register and battling my way onto the Dart like all the other world-weary wage slaves. Once more into the breach.

We didn't have swords, we had umbrellas. My Michael Mortell coat gave me a small lift as it was just the weather for it but my heart was elsewhere than with the toffs in Pinstripe Suit Land.

It was more with Jack, my homeless friend. I spotted him huddled up on his usual bench. He was still bedraggled and still half frozen-looking. I threw him a few euro as I passed and he looked up at me as if I was Lady Bountiful.

'I missed you,' he called after me in gratitude.

'And me you,' I returned. It was true too. More than Fiona Fennelly anyway.

Connolly, Tara Street, all the familiar stops popped up as I busied myself looking at people's mangy little gardens in the inner city and wondered if I still remembered what a Deed of Conveyance looked like, or if I was liable to mistake it for an Affidavit of Attesting Witness..

I felt like staying on and going all the way to Bray. Why did I have to get off at Pearse Street? Why couldn't I stay on the same train all day, going back and forth admiring the scenery? Fiona wasn't exactly creating a masterpiece or re-inventing the wheel. What made the people in the office superior to the ones outside?

Everyone was friendly to me at work but in a self-conscious way. Four people made special trips to my desk to welcome me back. Fiona even told me to take it easy and go at four for the first few days. All this niceness made me even more of a butterfingers than ever. For some reason I felt she was killing me with kindness. When a bitch stopped being a bitch it was time to get worried. The joke in the office was that if she put her arm around you it was only so she'd get closer to your throat.

I phoned Alice and she agreed to meet me for lunch. She was pleased to see me back and talked away about her nephew's marriage. For a change she got a chance to speak and for a change I actually listened.

'Do you know,' she said as she was saying goodbye, 'I've never heard you sound so well. Not once did you mention your nerves. Whatever you're on, keep taking it.'

For two weeks everything was normal. Nigel made a special effort to be home early and we went to Howth or Dollymount for long walks. He was so nice to me I had to pinch myself to believe it. As long as I was active the demons seemed to keep at bay. That was my weapon. It was hard to hit a moving target.

One evening I was sitting in the kitchen reading when Nigel came in carrying a big bunch of flowers. I had to brace myself when he got down on one knee and asked me to marry him.

'There's no point in going on like this,' he said, 'let's name the day'. As I looked at him kneeling there with a big grin I thought he'd freaked. Maybe some way we got our medication mixed up and he was taking mine by mistake.

'Are you sure about this?'

'I was never surer of anything in my life. You're the girl for me. Always have been. And now that you've put that spot of bother behind you.'

I hoped that wasn't a factor in his decision but I still said yes. I always told myself I'd never marry for the sake of it but in the back of my mind I kept hoping this day would come. Now that it had, it was like everything in my life was clicking into place.

We met in town for lunch later that week and bought my engagement ring together. It was a solitaire, huge on my finger. I didn't tell anyone at work. The next morning, however, Fiona copped it. Of all people. Soon I was the centre of attention. Cards from the staff, a cake at coffee break, everybody asking me when Nigel was going to make an honest woman of me.

When I was in company I was the perfect fulfilled fiancé but when I was alone thoughts of my first love came back to me. I had almost gone up the aisle before with Daire all those years ago. My mind drifted back to the first time I saw him. Not in real life but in a photograph. . Angie, my sister, had a picture of some friends of hers and he was in the background. It was at a Halloween party in Shantalla. He was stretched out on a sofa, the picture of contentment. 'Who's yer man?' I asked Angie, 'Rip Van Winkle?' She said she didn't know much about him except that his name was Daire and he came from outside Spiddal. I liked something about his eyes - they reminded me of the sea - and said I'd like to meet him. I was that impulsive then. She said she was seeing some people she knew in a few weeks and if I wanted to join them he might be there. It was to be in the Crane Bar.

For the next few weeks he kept running through my mind. I didn't know why I fell for him in the first place because he had fair hair and I didn't usually like fair-haired men. I started picturing how he'd talk and walk, just like when I was a child. I used to have this imaginary boyfriend called John and made up stories about him. I'd conduct conversations with him as if he was there, answering my own questions. My parents thought I had a bit missing. They were probably right.

I recognised him the minute he came into the bar. His fair hair was streaked from the sun and his eyes weren't so much looking at me as through me. He said nothing and neither did I. We just listened to an old man in a cloth cap playing 'An Staicin Eorna' on an accordion.

Angie introduced me to him but I felt I knew him already. The music got wilder and he took me out onto the floor. He put his arms round me and they were so strong I felt he must have been a fisherman or a farmer. In fact he was the son of a man who died at sea. He said he refused to learn to swim as a result of that. That's the only thing he told me about himself as we sat over a drink. I nursed mine but he knocked his back in a shot as if it was water. At the end of the night he walked me home to the B & B I was staying in. I wanted him to ask me out and eventually he did. I tried to act casual but I wasn't a very good actress.

We met outside Lydons café for our first date. He was twenty and me just eighteen. We had cappucinos and sat at a table looking out at the people passing by. Then we walked towards the Corrib and wandered towards the Spanish Arch. I was tense with anticipation. I felt I was going down a road I was half-afraid of, a road that might have meant more to me than him. I didn't know anything about him but maybe that added to the excitement.

I had to get back to Dublin the next day but we exchanged addresses. All that winter long we wrote to each other and then in the summer he went to study engineering in the university in Dublin. He told me he would have gone to UCG but he wanted to be near me. We met three times a week outside Demesne Products on Eden Quay. I stood opposite the same magazine rack waiting to see his green anorak coming round the corner at O'Connell Street Bridge.

We always went into the same pub in Abbey Street. I remember I was trying to get off cigarettes and was smoking burnt out matches instead. That amused him. My clumsiness also made him laugh. One night I spilt a pint of Smithwicks over his trousers.

When we got to know each other better he brought me out to UCD. I now felt as if I was a brainy student type with my duffle coat and black tights, not just a boring typist, grade 3, who ran out of school after the Inter Cert. He was fascinated by Thomas Hardy and talked a lot about him. I knew nothing about Hardy. One birthday he gave me a copy of *The Mayor of Casterbridge* as a present and I read it over and over till the pages fell out.

We were going out for ages before we had our first kiss. It was down a lane off Baggot Street one freezing night in January outside a disco called Bumbles. I felt like I was going to swoon like some Victorian lady laced into her corset.

He often picked me up after work. I'd see his motorbike coming from way down the street. He'd clip his spare blue helmet onto me and we'd snuggle up on the bike. We used to drive out to his flat in Sandymount and listen to Leonard Cohen tapes. 'Famous Blue

Raincoat' was our song. I knew if off by heart. I'd never forget the images in it. A rose in her teeth. A flake of your life. The music on Clinton Street all through the evening.

We liked the same films too. *La Strada* was being shown in a film club, our film for always. I had a video of it but hadn't looked at it for ages. Poor little Gelsomena and Anthony Quinn and the lovely haunting music. Every time I saw it I cried at the end.

We sat in the State cinema in Phibsboro watching that and other foreign films shot in grainy soft focus. I loved the foreign accents, the beautiful sad love stories, couples mating and separating in cars on rainy beaches as windshield wipers slapped back and forth. He tried to explain Method acting to me but I was only interested in watching him talk. He was reading books by Jean-Paul Sartre too and trying to get to grips with what existentialism meant. I was more into Simone de Beauvoir, Sartre's lover.

We used to go Tramore on the bike at weekends. We nearly froze to death in the cheap and cheerful B & B joints. I thought of The Everly Brothers playing on a radio programme, golden hits from the past, the rain lashing down against the window pane as they belted out 'Wake Up Little Susie'. Strange to think that was banned once. So innocent compared to what they were playing now.

He proposed to me on a train. We were reaching Dublin and I saw a woman hanging out clothes on a line, just like the end scene in *La Strada* when Anthony Quinn finally realised he loved Gelsomina but she was dead. I saw myself in a suburban house, eternally hanging out clothes. That's why I told him no. 'Not yet,' I said, 'I love you but I'm too young to be tied down'.

He never asked me again and we drifted apart. He went to America and me to Cork with Jeanie Dalton. I got a job in an accountant's office in The Mall. We wrote for a while. After three months I decided to come back to Dublin. Someone told me he'd been seen in Chicago working on a building site. I never heard from him after that. I used to phone the digs in Cork every now and then asking if there were any letters but eventually I stopped doing that.

It was probably for the best, I told myself - but I didn't really believe it.

CHAPTER 12

Nigel visited various hotels over the next few weeks comparing prices and menus. As for myself, I started looking at outfits that might hide my bulging shape. Things got worse for me at work. I still couldn't concentrate and found myself making even more stupid mistakes than usual. Fiona turned a blind eye to a few of them but then she'd lose her patience and bring me into her office for a roasting. That always made me worse. I felt like ten years old again with Sister Big Knickers standing over me trying to explain the finer points of Long Division.

Marjorie and Sandra were like the two wicked sisters in *Cinderella*. They more or less sent me to Coventry. At elevenses I was ostracised from conversations. When I walked into a room they suddenly stopped talking. I couldn't understand that. It wasn't as if they were paying my wages.

One morning I was coming out of the toilet when I heard the pair of them deep in chat about me.

'God love her,' Marjorie enthused, 'she finally got the rock on her finger. Good old Nigel, he turned up trumps in the end. I'm relieved for her.'

'Especially after that attack of depression,' echoed Sandra, 'That can come back any time, you know. She's zonked up to the eyes on tablets. And did you ever see anything like the way she poured on the weight? Goes with it, I think, side effect of all those drugs she's taking.'

'She looks half asleep to me most of the time. Fiona lets her away with murder. It's not fair that the rest of us have to fill in for her. I know Joanie covers for her too. Clueless really.'

I walked in on them, singing dumb about what I'd heard.

'Speak of the devil!' Sandra piped up, 'We were just saying how great you're looking. Give us a goo at that gorgeous diamond again.' Neither of them were getting married. What did that say? I told myself they were jealous but I couldn't stop it affecting me. Was Fiona really handing my work over to Joanie? I'd have to check that out. I never saw myself as Secretary of the Year but this pair took things onto a different level. Was I really that pathetic?

The overheard bitching session was small potatoes in comparison to what happened next. One Sunday Nigel and myself were out driving. We still hadn't set the actual date for the wedding and I knew he was getting bogged down with hotels and bookings. He stopped the car just outside Portmarnock.

'I have something to say to you,' he rasped, screeching to a halt. It sounded serious. Had he changed his mind? 'Don't take this the wrong way.' When someone talks to you like that, you know you're in for a right kick in the teeth.

'Don't take what the wrong way?'

'Did you notice your weight? You must have put on a stone in the last few weeks.'

'So?'

'Well do you not think.....'

He paused.

'Is that a problem for you?'

'To be honest, it is.'

'A bad one?'

'Let's put it this way. For our wedding I'd be a lot happier if – '

'Our wedding? You're bringing my weight into a discussion of our wedding?' Jesus, was this guy for real?

He got uncomfortable. 'I don't know how to put this. The fact is, you've always had a great figure. It's one of the reasons I was so attracted to you. I can't stand women who let themselves go. Take your friend Minnie for instance, look at the state of her. She was a good-looking bird when I met her a few years ago but now she's a disaster zone. The hips on her, and her stomach. She looks nine months gone.'

'Get to the point, Nigel. You're asking me to go on a diet, right?'

'I know you think I'm being a little insensitive, but – '

'If it means that much to you I'll think about it.'

'There's a good girl.'

'And if I don't become a stick insect in three weeks the wedding is off, is that the deal?'

'There's no need for that. I just think we should take a raincheck until you get sorted, for your own sake too.' I felt like one of his clients after finding out someone in the company had cooked the books. Those digestive biscuits must have had more calories than I thought.

That night in bed I felt as if I'd been kicked in the stomach by a horse. What did I represent for him - a model or a woman? If he was this obsessed with my shape before we even walked down the aisle what would he be like after a few years when I started breaking out in cellulite and other mysterious bumps? I knew if he was weighty it wouldn't have made any odds to me. So different to Daire. He never gave a damn about my appearance. Neither did I then, of course. Funny what time does. Or tragic.

I decided to join a slimming group not so much for Nigel as myself. My pride wouldn't let me be an embarrassment to him. I also started to walk into work every morning. If he offered me a biscuit after tea I almost felt guilty.

The hall we had our classes in was like a war zone. All human life was there. Compared to some of the ladies I was almost anorexic. I looked at one woman and thought: If I spent six months gorging myself on Bounty bars and nothing else I couldn't approximate to your girth, missus. Every time I felt low in spirit I looked at this lady and she revived me. I had a bit to go yet before I became like her.

I was determined I'd fit into a size ten for the wedding day. To this end I exercised like a mad thing. Every week you were weighed in and if you lost a pound or two the other people all applauded. I lost two pounds the first week. Full steam ahead.

On the second week I got no applause. Wendy, our leader, said it worked that way sometimes: you lost a few pounds at the beginning and then it stopped. She asked me if I was sticking to my healthy eating plan and I told her yes. It was a barefaced lie. The truth of it was I was becoming addicted to chocolate éclairs instead of her low-fat biscuits. To hell with being sensible, I thought. I was entitled to a bit of pleasure and I loved my little treats.

One woman lost seven pounds in a week and was over the moon with herself. I pictured all that excess fat sliding to the floor as we did our physical jerks. Where would it go? Perhaps it would be made into a fat pile like the butter mountain and sent out to poor countries and grafted onto thin little starved women. The flesh was Irish flesh, fat pink little thighs, but the black women could roast in the sun for a few weeks and who'd know the difference. Those poor dames wouldn't want to be in need of few pounds of my pink thighs because I was gaining weight instead of losing.

I decided to give up the classes but not tell Nigel because I knew he'd go crazy. To keep him happy I used to go for walks on the Tuesday evenings till the class time had elapsed. He was so wrapped up in his own life he didn't suspect anything but once or twice I thought I saw him looking at my stomach in a way you could hardly call admiring. (Pity he wouldn't do anything about his own nicely developing little beer belly, I thought.)

In June they came around at work with the holiday list. Nigel hadn't mentioned holidays so that evening I asked him when he'd be free and where we might go.

'I don't know,' he said nervously, 'I have two audits down the country in the next two months. Let's leave it till later in the year. There'll be better bargains then as well.' Even our time away together was computed on debits and credits. I sometimes wondered if I was part of his expenses list as he kept receipts for everything from car hire costs to B&Bs.

'But I really need a break. Couldn't we even have a long weekend away?'

'That's out of the question. Work is manic at the minute. I haven't time to blow my nose, never mind swan around in the sunshine. Why don't you go off with one of your pals?'

'It's not the same. We both need the break.'

'Look, if we're planning getting married later this year we'll have a honeymoon. I think you're being a bit greedy.'

Greedy? He wrote the book on greedy. Why did I always have to be the bad guy? I was fuming to myself. I went to bed thinking I'd call his bluff and head off somewhere. But who would I go with? Alice was the most likely choice.

I phoned her on an impulse the next day.

Any chance you'd be free to get away for a short break, Alice?'

She knew me well enough not to delve. That was the great thing about Alice, she was up for anything on a moment's notice. She said she was available anytime so we decided on a trip to Killarney in the first week in July. Just like that. I'd show him I had a life, I'd give him a taste of his own medicine.

I kept on with taking the tablets. I had a bit more energy now. Every Tuesday I continued my pretence and detoured from the Slim Trim premises, stuffing myself in the chipper when Nigel thought I was breaking out into a sweat on bench presses and treadmills. I knew I was piling on the pounds but thought it better to be fat and happy than thin and a walking nerve case. (Nigel would hardly have agreed, needless to say).

One evening after work I thought I'd go to Clarendon Street and get evening Mass. Sometimes they had benediction afterwards. I loved the Latin hymns: 'Tantum Ergo Sacramentum in particular. There was a part of it that sounded like 'Jenny told me Jenny told you, lies about you she did so.' I always sang it that way when I was a child, only discovering the real Latin words years later. In the Hail Mary we said 'Blessed is the fruit of thy wound Jesus.' We rhymed them off like so many poems. The meaning didn't matter, all we were consciousof was the rhythm

There were just a few elderly people at the benediction but we all sang our hearts out. We finished with 'Hail Queen of Heaven'. I felt really peaceful and lit two candles, one for Nigel and one for me.

I walked the whole way home again. Nigel was sitting at the table surrounded with paperwork.

'You're late,' he said, 'Did you have a good day?'

'Not too bad.'

'I'll be with you in a few minutes. You wouldn't be an angel and rustle me up a fry there, would you?'

I put on rashers and eggs for him and he gobbled them up, hardly noticing me. Then he did some work stuff for a while. We didn't talk much - amazingly.

In bed he was in a romantic mood. Well, as close as Nigel could ever come to romantic. He gave me a lecherous eye and I knew that meant down to business. Nothing like a bit of rumpy-bumpy to wind down from those debits. From balance sheets to silk ones, paper figures to fleshy ones, emphasis on the fleshy ones in my case . He wanted more responses from me but I wasn't up for it. I thought of the old joke: 'Moan,' he said. 'The ceiling needs re-painting,' she replied.

The next day I rang in sick. Nigel hated when I did that so I had to pretend I had a tummy bug. It was easier to fool the office than him. I had to refuse breakfast and then sneak a few éclairs from the fridge while he wasn't looking. It was like all those years ago when I lay under the covers trying to work up a blush for Mammy when I wanted to get off school.

I stayed in bed most of the day and in the evening watched TV. My appetite was back so I wolfed down two bars of chocolate, a frozen curry and a toasted cheese sandwich. I spent the evening checking myself in the mirror and pacing the room.

I went back to Stalag 17 the following day. I knew I'd have to go out in the evening or he'd be cribbing about the slimming class. So off with me to my beloved chip shop. I brought my trusty Mills & Boon with me but couldn't concentrate, not even on that bilge. The same sentence kept swimming before my eyes.

I arrived home a bit later than usual. I'd braved it out in the chipper till closing-time. This bingeing was serious business. You really had to work at it but like most dedicated foodaholics I persevered.

'Where were you?' he quizzed, as stony-faced as ever.

'Where do you think? I'm exhausted. It was very strenuous tonight.' Actually it was. I had a pain in my face from stuffing it.

'I hope you got a clap. How many pounds did you lose this week - Five? Ten?' What was this all about, I wondered.

'What did I lose? Let me see. Four pounds I think.' I didn't want to bump it up too much because I probably looked like Roseanne Barr.

'Four pounds. Well done. You deserve a really big clap for that. I'll tell you what else you deserve a medal for. Lying through your teeth.' Surely he couldn't know.

'What are you talking about?'

'I decided out of the goodness of my heart to collect you this evening. I watched all the women coming out of the building but there was no sign of my lovely fiancée. Eventually I went into the hall and met Wendy. You know Wendy, don't you? Wendy the Group Leader stroke Facilitator?' Oops.

'Hold on a minute, Nigel. Okay, you're right. I admit it, I didn't go tonight I had a pounding headache and went for a walk instead. I didn't like to tell you.'

'That was thoughtful of you. Afraid Doodles would get upset, were we?'

'Well I know how much it means to you that I trim down a bit. Don't worry, I'll get back into the swing of it next week. Everyone bottoms out now and again.' (Speaking of bottoms, I was wondering how far my own one was sticking out. Probably as far as the neighbour's house).

'So you'll get back into it next week. That's funny because Wendy told me you'd only been to four classes. Guess what — when she realized I didn't know, she thought you were having it off with someone. She was so embarrassed she didn't know where to look.'

'I'm sorry, Nigel.'

'I can't stand lies, you know that? I can forgive anything but them. Are you having an affair? If not, where in God's name do you spend these Tuesday evenings?'

'An affair? Me? That's a laugh. I'm afraid it's nothing that spicy. The truth of it is, I haven't been too well with the nerves lately.'

'Oh change the record, will you? I can't take any more of that self-pitying stuff.'

'No, this is different. Do you remember me telling you I was having visions?'

'Just leave it out, will you? We'll talk again. I have to be up at cock crow. Goodnight.'

He banged the door and I sat there in the dark, too miserable even to cry. I wondered if I was losing him, or how I might get him back. How about a present tomorrow? No, that wouldn't work. He'd just fling it in the bin. The only thing that'd please him would be if I could transform myself into Gwyneth Paltrow.

Where was Mandrake the magician when you really wanted him?

I sat up for ages, my head whizzing with ideas that inevitably came to nothing. When I got to the bedroom I wasn't too surprised to see that he'd moved his stuff out of it. Again.

By now the spare room was turning into the new marital bed.

CHAPTER 13

It was a beautiful summer. Everybody looked brown, not just the people who'd been abroad. My nerves calmed down and Alice and myself travelled to Killarney on the train. Nigel was still in a sulk over the slimming business and hardly exchanged a word with me unless he had to. He was in the spare room more often than not and when he wasn't I almost wished he was. We arranged our schedules round each other like work colleagues.

The farther I grew away from Nigel, the more I started to think of my past. Before I left for Killarney I resurrected an old picture of my Glenamaddy grandfather. It was his wedding photograph. He was seated in it like most of the men in photos from that time and granny stood with her hand on his shoulder. He had a top hat and a moustache. My memory of him was a white-haired man with a beard and eyes like Paul Newman. At night when I was lying awake I imagined myself dressing up in clothes like his and making my way down Grafton Street. I had the height and if I tucked my hair under the top hat I could probably pass for him.

Funny the thoughts that come to you at night. He was a gentleman and quite a dandy. Mammy used to tell us stories of him taking her and her sisters back to boarding school, the Dominican Convent in Cabra. I pictured it like Lowood in *Jane Eyre*. Mammy used to say how her Dad would keep them out of school for an extra few nights and bring them to the Gaiety to see a show. He had such charm he could wind the nuns round his little finger. They'd giggle and fuss over him, serving him sherry and cakes in the convent dining-room.

The first time I got my 'Auntie Jane' I was in Glenamaddy. I was slow getting it, just like everything else I did in life. My periods were less frequent now but when they came they very heavy. I was up to ninety before they arrived and afterwards totally drained. I supposed they'd soon be a thing of the past. Maybe that's why I kept remembering my first one. It was the summer after my fifteenth birthday after we'd just moved to Dublin. I'd gone to Glenamaddy for the month of July and was alone in the house with granddaddy. He was upstairs playing 'Go Home and Wash Your Father's Shirt' on the piano. I felt a trickle down my legs. I rushed out to the toilet and there it was, a little red river running down my thighs. Years before, Tessie Tyrrell had tried to prepare me for the cataclysmic moment. I was hardly more than nine at the time.

'It happens every month,' she said to me, 'there's blood when you do a wee-wee.'

'I don't believe you,' I said back to her.

'It's true. I heard it from my big sister Mary and she doesn't lie.'

'But Santy was a lie, wasn't he?'

'Yeah, but this is different.'

I couldn't tell granddaddy a word about the blood because he was a man. I had to wait for hours until Auntie Eileen came home. She fixed me up with pads and told me I was a woman now. The pads were bulky and felt huge in my panties. So many months and years to follow of being a woman. Oh for the freedom of white ankle socks and my hair in pigtails.

I didn't tell Alice any of this, determined to 'stay in the moment' as the psychology books said. In Killarney I was quite chirpy. The first day there I treated myself to two pairs of cords in summery colours pale pink and a sort of sand colour. I also got a dress that was like something from the forties, flowery with little cap sleeves. As if that wasn't enough, I added two cotton blouses which I got for a song and a lovely long navy cardigan to hide my protruding bum. It was nice to having something new to wear when you were on holidays.

We rented an apartment in the centre of the town and toured round in a hired car by day. Alice did the driving because I never learnt. We saw Kate Kearney's Cottage and the Gap of Dunloe and the scenery was wonderful. The sun beamed down every day and at night we went drinking. I'd cut back on two of the tablets so allowed myself a few glasses of Guinness. The pubs were full of American tourists and Alice and myself joined along with them singing 'Danny Boy' and 'When Irish Eyes are Smiling' out of tune.

I sent postcards to Minnie and Angie and also one to Nigel though that stuck in my craw a bit. I knew he wouldn't even read it. He'd probably be too busy worrying how much I was spending on touristy nic-nacs from Hong Kong to give to my little fan club of friends.

Alice was a brilliant cook and we dined in for a few of the evenings. I felt back to myself in the nerves department and if I got an anxious thought I immediately put it out of my head. 'Deal with the head stuff when you get back,' I told myself in one of my endless pep talks. As for now, bring on the fun.

The night before we left, Alice suggested we go to a dance in a nearby hotel. With our tans we both looked very well and I wore my forties style dress. I put the cardigan over it to cover my bulges.

The place was packed and there was live music. Both of us were danced off our feet. One fellow asked me up a few times and wanted to make a date. He was attractive enough but not in the first flush of youth. An American, what else. I told him we were leaving the next day but gave him my phone number in Dublin. I didn't see any harm in meeting him some night. He was on a three-month tour of Ireland and would be in Dublin until 'the fall' as he put it.

Alice was amused at me. I told her I'd dated an American one time. His name was Charles J.P. Smith Junior. He wrote to the *Evening Press* looking for an Irish girl to correspond with. He said he loved music and the arts. For a while our letters flew back and forth across the Atlantic. He had a way with words and we became close through our shared interests. I used to type my letters at work when Fiona wasn't on the prowl. Every morning I watched for the postman, often missing the Dart if he was late.

At Christmas Charles sent me a basket of flowers through Interflora. A few months later he invited me to visit him and I said yes. I was full of excitement travelling over. I pictured myself swanning around Denver like something out of the TV series 'Dallas'. In the mornings I'd have an appointment at the beauty parlour, take the poodle for a trim in the early afternoon, maybe fly to LA with him for a concert, then take in a spot of gambling in Vegas. I'd throw huge charity functions and we'd go ski-ing in Aspen every year.

He met me at the airport. He was older than I'd imagined. He'd said he was in his fifties but he definitely looked nearer to seventy. If this was Junior, I thought, I certainly wouldn't like to see Charles J.P.Senior. He was smaller than me too. With his grey beard and grey eyes he looked quite scholarly.

We drove to his apartment which turned out to be a sheltered residence for older men. So much for ladies who lunch. It was drab and shabby but that didn't bother me as much as his personality. I was hardly in the door before he was having a go at me about my habits. Even folding my arms became a big no-no for him. He said it was a sign of inhibition, closing my body off like that.

When I developed a passion for chocolate chip cookies he lectured me on how bad sweet things were for me. When my hair fell over my eyes, which it did frequently, he told me I'd go blind.

He talked about his plans to come to Ireland and seemed to assume we were getting married. I wasn't consulted about this. It was as if it was certain I'd be champing at the bit to have Sir Lancelot take me off the shelf.

After three days in his company I couldn't wait to get home. The last bit of time with him was like torture for me. We both knew it was over but neither of us could muster up the courage to say it so we just went through the motions. I almost felt sorry for him as he left me to the airport. He was like a sad dog with his long face and trust-me eyes.

We continued to write for some time but after a while I began to feel trapped .I told him an old lover had come back into my life.

I got a real snorter of a letter in reply. He ranted on about how I'd misled him after all the money he'd spent entertaining me. He conveniently forgot to mention that I'd brought him an Aran sweater and paid for most of the meals we'd had out. He used to phone up and pass sarcastic remarks to me for a few months. Then I heard nothing more.

'I wonder what he's doing now?' Alice said to me as I finished my sad saga, 'I hope he got a girl who keeps her arms down by her sides and doesn't like chocolate chip cookies.'

The next morning Alice and myself made our way to Killarney railway station. When we got there I phoned Nigel. I hoped he'd pick us up in Dublin and drop Alice home but he sounded as sulky as ever. He said he had to go out. What else was new?

In the end we had to make our own arrangements. I could see Alice wasn't pleased. 'You'd want to think twice about that fella,' she said. Sometimes it took another person to say something before you saw it. After I was five minutes back in Dublin my spirits sank again. It was back to the old grind.

In a few short days I felt I'd never been away. I hated being back at work. Same old dreary routine. Fiona was off on two weeks holidays. That meant I had Leslie Smith, the firm's most recent recruit, watching every move I made - or didn't make. He was like a hen on a hot griddle and he pushed me to crack-up point. It was worse trying to pretend I was busy than actually being busy for this ambitious little whippersnapper.

Then one morning I got a phone call from Edward Skelly. Joanie was out sick and he wanted me to take his work. He knew Fiona was away so there was no way out for me. 'If you wouldn't mind taking those two tapes I'd be glad,' he said, 'They're extremely urgent.'

My heart went down to my boots. I had no problems with probate or conveyancing but litigation was like the other side of the moon to me. I wasn't one of those secretaries who liked a challenge. Stuff challenges. I knew it would take me the guts of the day to get through this stuff. No place to hide so I decided to lash into it.

I plugged in my earphones and started to listen to Edward's voice. He ran all the words into each other and it took me until eleven to get just one letter finished. No coffee break either, just soldier on. By lunchtime I'd done half a tape. No lunch for me today. He phoned me at 3.30 asking me to bring up what I'd done. When I presented him with three letters and a Notice for Particulars he looked at me as if I was a specimen at the end of a pin.

'Is that all you've done since morning?'

'Sorry, I'm not used to litigation.'

'It's nearly four now. Would you please do the Notice of Discovery? I need that before close of business today. Joanie will be back tomorrow so you can leave the rest.'

'I'll do it straight away.' In my dreams anyway.

'Please run off Discovery in the usual form, refer to file for defendant and plaintiff.'

Mother of God. Total double dutch to me. 'Usual form'. What did that mean? I phoned Sandra and she told me to refer to the precedents. It took me twenty minutes to find where they were and another twenty before I found the one I needed.

I consulted the file and typed up names in the blank places. My phone rang. It was Edward.

'Is it ready? I'm due to meet somebody at five.'

'Almost.'

The sweat was pouring off me and my fingers were sliding all over the keys of the computer. At last I printed it out and just caught Edward as he was leaving his office. As I presented it to him his face fell a mile.

'Jesus, only one copy. You need three bound copies done on judicature paper. I take it you know what judicature is. There's a blue line down the side.'

Back to the computer. No judicature paper in my drawer. Downstairs in a mad gallop to the stationery room. Tore open a packet of paper and got the three copies printed. I was almost in tears at this stage, so much so that Sandra took pity on me and did the binding. My faith in humanity was restored, sort of.

When I got to Edward's room I could hear him on the phone to Mr Roberts. 'How many years is she here? Fifteen? Don't you realise Sandra could do that in her sleep?'

He hung up as I entered the room, not really bothered if I heard or not. He grabbed the documents from me and I was the little girl of all those years ago at school in Galway without my sums done as he looked it up and down. My exam report usually said 'Fair' or 'Could try harder'. Well I couldn't try harder than this, but it still wasn't good enough for Lord Edward.

CHAPTER 14

Joanie turned up the next day and I told her my tale of woe.

'I don't know why you get so worked up,' was all she said. She was right but the crazy thing was I knew I was going to be just as bad the next time, and the next time. You couldn't change what you were. I always felt one day they were going to find me out. Call me into the office and say, 'It has come to our notice that you've been inhabiting this building for fifteen years and haven't a blessed clue what you're supposed to be doing.' If that transpired I doubted if I'd have had a defence. I'd have had to enter a Guilty plea - or take the Fifth. (A fifth of vodka, more likely).

I went for a drink with her that night and unloaded all my frustrations on her. She listened but didn't contribute much. I envied her her casual disposition. She was in a much worse situation than me but let it ride over her. Just like her attitude to work. People were as good as they thought they were.

Towards the end of the night the chat turned to my impending nuptials. Or were they really impending?

'When are you tying the knot?' she asked me, 'Have you and Nigel decided on where you'll spend the honeymoon?'

'We haven't quite made our minds up but we're nearly there.'

There was no point telling her we hadn't even talked about it since I got back from Killarney.

Nigel went away for two weeks at the beginning of August. He barely told me where he was going, muttering something about a liquidation. I felt much better than I thought in his absence. No loneliness, no panics. Even work was bearable - almost. I lashed into lavish fries nightly and played Beethoven until the floorboards shook.

When he did come back he was in better form. The work went well and Brannigan was pleased with him. He told me he had a good chance of a partnership and we went for a meal to celebrate. He didn't bring up the subject of marriage but never mentioned Slim Trim either. You lose some, you win some. We also slept together, which meant I held out some hope for the future.

A week later he had an audit, this time in Cavan. He expected to be away for a few weeks but hoped to get back at weekends. It didn't bother me that he was gone. That should have told me something about our relationship but it didn't. I clung on like a drowning woman to a piece of wood.

On the first week he was away I had a phone call from Minnie. I hadn't heard from her for ages and I knew immediately she was upset. She could hardly speak to me; she just bucketed tears into the phone.

'It's John,' she managed to say after what seemed like an eternity.

'What's wrong - is he sick? Take a few deep breaths, Minnie.'

'I'm sorry,' she said, 'give me a minute.'

Sharp intake of breath and then she blurted it out.

'He's having an affair'. It was like a rock coming down on top of my head.

'I don't believe it. You pair are together too long. You're probably imagining it. Why are you thinking like this?'

'He confessed last night.'

'Oh Minnie, I'm sorry. Look, it's probably just a fling. An awful lot of men go through it. I have a friend and the very same thing happened to her. It burned itself out in a few weeks.'

'No, he said he loves her. What am I going to do? I can't tell the twins, not yet anyway. Do you really think it could be a temporary thing?'

'I'm sure of it. Keep cool. Don't let him see how upset you are, just act as normal as you can. How about coming up to me at the weekend? A break would do you both good. Nigel is away so we can talk.'

'I'll think about it. You're so good. Oh God, he's coming in. I have to go'. I heard a door bang and the line went dead.

I phoned Nigel to his hotel room but he sounded distant, He said he was working late. I told him about Minnie and asked if he could stay away this weekend if she decided to come.

His reaction to her news was very Nigel.

'I knew that relationship wasn't good,' he sniffed, 'look at the way she let herself go. You can't expect a man to stay with a woman who puts on that much weight.' He agreed to stay in Cavan for the weekend if Minnie came up.

I found myself thinking of how Minnie had ended up with John. I'd never particularly liked him but she was totally smitten. Fell into his arms the second he proposed. The wedding was a big affair. She was three months pregnant at the time and then had a miscarriage on her honeymoon. She was devastated when she lost the baby. It took two more years of trying before she had the twins, Gracie and Greta.

They would be about twenty at this stage. If there was a break-up would be so much worse now.

She'd met John when I met Daire, my first love. Where was he now, I wondered – Spain? America? Australia? I wondered to myself if he ever came back to Galway. I was afraid to ask Minnie. The past was the past. Nigel was my man now. There was no point dreaming about what ifs.

Minnie phoned again two days later and asked to come up. She sounded a little better but when I saw her she looked terrible

I brought her into our renovated kitchen but she hardly noticed it, I sat her down and fed her and then lit the fire. Even though it was August the heat was comforting. I opened a bottle of wine and let her talk.

'It's the end,' she said, 'It's not a flash in the pan. He said last night it was for keeps. He doesn't love me anymore.'

'People say things in the heat of the moment. Who is she? Do you know her?'

'She's a hairdresser from Rockbarton. Years younger than me. She's separated. No children.'

'Has he been seeing her long?'

'He didn't say but thinking about it I'd say a few months. Do you remember all those trips away? I wouldn't be a bit surprised if he was with her that time he was supposed to be in London.'

'I still think it could be a passing thing.'

'He said he loves her. I had a feeling for weeks and weeks. He changed. You know him and clothes. He went round in rags all the time but if you were to see him now you wouldn't believe it. Bought himself a new suit in Anthony Ryans and started wearing smart casual things too. To make himself look younger, I suppose. She's only thirty-two. What chance have I? I'm sure she's good-looking and thin.'

'You're worth ten times her, whatever she is. It'll blow itself out. What's important is that you want him back.'

She was fairly knocking back the wine and started to cry. We sat in silence for hours but then something would strike her all of a sudden and she'd go off in full flow about it.

'He kept using these trendy sayings like, 'I'm not going there.' When I asked him was he leaving me he came out with all this guff. It was like talking to somebody from an American sitcom for teenagers.'

'It has to be the male menopause. They all get like that after fifty.'

'He's only forty-four. Another thing - every second word out of his mouth is 'Hello' for a long time now. Not Hello like 'How are you doing', just Helloes put in all over the place. I should have copped on long ago. It's only now looking back I see all the little signs adding up.'

'Does he know you're here?'

'I'm sure he guessed I'd be with you He's probably delighted to be free to see her. I was tempted to go to the hairdresser place she works and give her a bit of my mind. The twins will be devastated. I want to keep it from them as long as I can Just as well they're in Australia, God love them, what they don't know won't bother them, the poor dotes.' '

'From the sound of it he's trying to recapture his youth. If I was you I'd go on with my life as best I could. Get out of the house. Stay here as long as you like if that helps. It sounds more and more like an infatuation to me. He loves you. He wouldn't be with you all these years if he didn't.'

'You do what you want. I won't go near you in the morning. Get up when you feel like it and we'll head into town if you're able. Spend the bastard's money and buy yourself a new rig-out. Maybe if you stay for a few days he'll start to miss you. I'm sure that streel of a hairdresser is only using him. At 32 she'll soon get tired of him, mark my words.'

She did that, bought herself a nice dress the next day and started to look better. That night she was in better form. She was sound asleep in the sofa when I got in from work on the Monday. Sleep was what she needed so I didn't disturb her. She woke late in the evening and I got her something to eat.

'I couldn't touch anything,' she said, pushing the plate away. When I woke at first I didn't know where I was. Then it all came back to me. It's unbelievable that he'd do this. Do you think is it my fault? I know I've put on some weight but everybody does at this stage.'

'How can you think like that? He has a fine big belly himself. Anyway, you're not off stravaging with some toyboy. You're far too good for him, Minnie, I've always thought it.'

'But I love him. I'll phone him. Now that I'm not around, maybe he'll feel different. Do you think that's a good idea?'

'If you want an honest answer, no. That'd be giving in. If you let him away with this he'll just walk all over you.'

'No, I'm phoning him. If this bitch thinks she's going to get my husband as easy as that she has another think coming.'

I left her alone. She must have been fifteen minutes on the phone. After she rang off I asked her how it went.

'He wants me home tomorrow. He says we need to talk.'

'Well I suppose that's a good sign. Maybe he's come to his senses.'

When I got in from work the next day she was gone. She left the sitting-room a total mess. She didn't even move the duvet upstairs. She'd left a paper bag on the table with a card. When I opened it I saw she'd written a note: 'Thanks a million for listening to me. I found this in a bookshop in Galway. I was going to keep it for your birthday but I'm giving it to you now.'

It was a book, *King of the Tinkers*, by Patricia Lynch. The exact same grey-green cover with a little hen on it. I'd searched for it for years. Everywhere I tried I was told it was out of print. Brian had won it in school for English when he was ten and gave it to me. He thought it was too childish for himself.

I adored that book. Michael Fahy and his mother the Widda Fahy. She'd knit jumpers and he'd make clothes-pegs out of wood. They lived in a snug little house beside a mountain. It was like a comfort blanket to me through the years of my childhood. What a present. I wanted to rush to the phone to thank her but she wouldn't be back yet.

Later I did phone. She'd arrived back to an empty house. I thanked her for the book and asked her how she found it. 'Just luck really. You were always talking about it when we were young. Then when we got to our teens it was *Jane Eyre*.'

'You're right. Both of them are still my favourites. I really appreciate this, Minnie.' I used to take out that book for the same reason I did my ABC routine - to relax me.

'Not to worry. In fact there's something else I remember from that time.'

'What's that?'

'Your favourite line from *Jane Eyre*.'

'You must have some memory.'

'*Reader I married him*. Am I right?'

'You are for sure.'

'I remember you going on and on about that line one day we were out Salthill together.'

'Did I? Do you know why I love it so much?

'I should. You've told me hundreds of times.'

'Let me explain it to you again. Jane was to get married to Mr Rochester and she dressed up in her finery, a beautiful veil so out of character for Jane. Rochester was as eager to get her to the church and she was so happy she couldn't say if the weather was fine or raining. Then just as they were being joined together in the church a voice spoke up and the ceremony had to stop. It was Mason, Minnie. He was Rochester's mad wife's brother. Grace Poole was only the nurse.'

'I know all this.'

'Yes, but the thing is they had to call off the marriage and poor Jane left Thornfield Hall and then after a time with St John Rivers she heard Rochester calling her in a kind of dream. Then she came back and he was blind and she just starts the last chapter saying 'Reader, I married him,' which I think is so beautiful, as if she's telling me personally.'

'You always were a romantic, loveen.'

'Maybe so but where has it got me?'

All the talk with Minnie got me thinking about myself. I wondered if I'd end up like my Uncle Bernie. with a house I owned that nobody ever moved into, the paint cracking on the walls and the wind whistling through it as children skipped up and down outside, peering through. At least Jane finally got her Rochester.

Bernie drove a hackney car and sometimes when I'd be in bed in the room behind the sitting-room in Glenamaddy I'd hear a loud knock at the door and he'd be called out to drive some unfortunate person to hospital or the asylum in Ballinasloe. He was tall and lean and always carried a crumpled cowboy book in his pocket. 'Have you any Westerns?' I'd ask and he'd always have one to give me. I'd take a peek at the last page to see if there was a girl in it. If there was I'd read it through, otherwise I wouldn't bother. I remembered gulches and creeks, lean men with weatherbeaten faces, blue faraway eyes and gold-haired girls called Cindy Lou.

Bernie almost got married one time. He was going out with a local girl, someone he cared for much more than he let on, but she went off with someone else. He'd bought a house, hoping the pair of them would move into it when they married. When it didn't happen the life seemed to go out of him. When me and Angie walked past, Auntie Eileen would say, 'There's Bernie's place,' and we'd go, 'It can't be. Bernie lives with granny.'

Even as children we knew not to probe. We'd peep in through the dusty windows, half-afraid and half-fascinated. Bernie himself of course never talked about it at all. He went even quieter than usual when she left him, buried behind his books. Afterwards he started to go on these long walks. He seemed to become an old man almost overnight. She married a fellow from out the country who had a farm and a herd of cattle. Bernie's house, meanwhile, stood empty for years. It made me sad to think of him shaving granddaddy every night and then off to his solitary bachelor bed. I picture him with a cigarette always in his mouth as he cradled a mug of black tea.

He died of lung cancer in the Regional. We all went down to visit him in hospital the week before. Brian and me sat with him one night. He had a mask over his face and looked so out of place in the clinical environment. I whispered to him that he'd soon be home and that I had a pile of Westerns to give him.

He smiled at me with his eyes. I was just sixteen but I knew he knew he was dying.

The heavens opened the day of his funeral. We huddled under umbrellas at the graveside looking out at the lake across the road. I noticed a woman in a grey coat standing alone. Afterwards I asked Auntie Eileen who she was and she said she wasn't too sure but she thought she was Mary Geraghty, the girl he'd loved.

'Isn't it a pity,' I said, 'they could have been so happy together.' 'That's the way,' said Auntie Eileen, 'that's the way.'

CHAPTER 15

Nigel came back at the weekend. He seemed exhausted and not in the mood to talk about anything. He barely asked about Minnie, which didn't surprise me.

I phoned her twice but got no answer. Maybe that was a good sign. Maybe they were away for a few days.

'Have you thought about holidays?' I asked Nigel when I thought I saw him coming back to himself, 'the summer is nearly over.'

'I'm too busy to even think that way. We'll consider it after Cavan.'

'Okay,' I said, 'after Cavan.'

We were already into September and he still hadn't said anything more about our proposed wedding.

They stopped asking me at work when the big day was but the question was on everyone's face each time they looked at me.

I had a letter from Minnie to say things were a bit better. John seemed willing to try and keep the marriage together. Big of him, I thought. 'Fingers crossed,' she wrote. I knew the crossing I'd do with that fellow. I'd cross his fingers and his bloody toes.

I kept stocking up on my wardrobe. Two blouses here, a skirt there, a green jumper with a zip, a long grey skirt which cost a bomb. Size 14 barely fitted me now but that didn't stop me buying. As for the tablets, I'd cut them down to half but I didn't tell Walsh because I knew he'd go bananas at me self-prescribing again.

Probably tell me to put a plate outside the door and set up my own practice.

Nigel had a break coming up the following week. I was hoping we could go somewhere together to patch things up but I heard him making arrangements over the phone one night and they didn't seem to involve me. Too much to ask that the little woman would get considered. Donegal was his choice, a luxury chalet, mind you. Some people liked themselves. He didn't ask if I could get time off to join him so I presumed he wanted to be alone. That was fine by me.

Just before he left I had a call from Minnie. Things were back to square one and John was staying out three or four nights a week.

'I know he's kipping up with that one,' she said, 'but I'm afraid to say anything in case I drive him out for good. I still haven't told the twins. I feel if I keep it to myself it'll go away.'

'Why don't you come up to me again?' I offered, 'Nigel is going to Donegal next week and I could take a day or two sick.'

'I don't know. I feel if I'm here I can see what he's up to. Not that it's doing me any good. He's acting as if I don't exist. I feel if I object he'll move out.'

'That's no way to live. The bed is here for you. We'll have a night on the town. Come on, Minnie. I'll put your name on the kettle.'

She finally agreed and I arranged to meet her at the station on the following Monday.

She'd lost weight, quite a bit in a short time. Because it was mostly from her face it made her look older. We went for a drink in town and then home in a taxi. She talked for hours and hours.

It was all John and what did I think she should do. I felt like telling her to boot him out of her life but I knew that wasn't what she wanted to hear. For good or ill she was nuts about him.

The next day I persuaded her to come to Bray on the Dart. I wanted to climb the Head but she wasn't up to that. Nothing would do her but to sit in a café talking endlessly about it all. Should she give him an ultimatum?

Did I think it better to turn a blind eye? Why was he doing this? Was she unattractive? Did I think it was the male menopause? On and on she droned, worrying the sore. I felt sorry for her but there was nothing much I could do.

I wanted to say, 'Where's your pride, woman? Tell him to take a long walk on a short pier,' but all that came out was, 'Give it time.'

When we got back to the house there was a message on the machine. It was from Tom, the American I'd met in Killarney. He was staying for another few months. He wondered if myself and a pal would fancy meeting him and his friend for a meal on the following evening.

He left his hotel phone number.

'Why not?' I suggested to Minnie, 'he was a really nice guy and I'm sure the friend will be fine. Let's meet them tomorrow - just for the craic'.

She didn't want to but I kept at her.

In the end she gave in and I phoned up Tom. We arranged to get together the following evening.

We met the two boyos at their city centre hotel. We piled on the warpaint till we were confident we could pass for two young(ish) doxies.

Clem, the friend, took to Minnie from the start and it was mutual as far as I could see. He was divorced for fifteen years and was full of advice on how to deal with marriage breakups.

Tom was quieter. He didn't say it in so many words but I felt he was married. They treated us royally and between the four of us we knocked back three bottles of very expensive red wine.

They insisted on seeing us home in a taxi. They were both over the sixty mark so I felt we'd have no problems with amorous advances. That's why we invited the pair of them in for a cup of coffee.

Nigel had a large bottle of whiskey and I offered them some. We all duly partook of same. Minnie got more and more squiffy and ended up sitting on Clem's knee. Myself and Tom cuddled up.

The mood was relaxed. I had the soft lights on and we were all pleasantly merry.

Next of all the hall door opened and in walked Nigel with a face that would frighten the crows.

'Excuse me,' he barked, 'I didn't know you were entertaining'. Then he made towards the stairs. I knew I was in for it.

'Nigel,' I called after him, 'this is a friend I met in Killarney. Himself and his pal have been entertaining Minnie and me. They treated us to a beautiful meal.'

I doubted it would pacify him and I was right. He gave a grunt and kept walking. I looked over at Tom and he was already on his feet saying it was probably time to go. I told him not to be stupid. I managed to get him seated but a while later Nigel put his oar in again, tramping down the stairs on some ridiculous pretext. Eventually I had enough of it and decided to call it a day. Tom gave me a wink at the door as if he knew what I was going through.

'Are you happy now?' I asked Nigel after the taxi took them away. I didn't expect a reply and I didn't get one.

Minnie and myself had to share my bed, my charming fiancé once again opting for the delights of the spare room. I wasn't looking forward to his grumpy face over breakfast but Minnie cheered me up. She was totally out of it on the wine. Left to it she'd have asked Clem to stay the night. She got a fit of the giggles and kept roaring with laughter all night. It was good to see her focussed on something other than her wandering hubbie.

She headed back to Galway the next morning. She had a whopper of a hangover but said the visit had really cheered her up and Clem had given her some sound advice.

'If he's to go off with Rockbarton,' she said, 'let him at it. It's a pairing made in hell'. I knew she didn't believe a bit of it but that wasn't the point.

Dying with a hangover, I stayed in bed all day. I managed to make a quick call to work. Marjorie said she'd tell Frosty I had the flu. I didn't lay an eye on Nigel all day. I soldiered in to work the next day. Fiona, as I expected, was having a blue fit. She didn't ask me how I was so I knew she suspected I was trying it on. It wouldn't have been the first time.

I kept the head down to keep her away from me and tried to ring Nigel on his mobile at elevenses. The old stick-in-the-mud had it switched off. I could imagine him drumming his fingers on his desk in temper.

I dropped into the park on the way home. As expected, the Right Honourable Jack was there in state.

'How's it going?' he beamed.

'Don't ask. I had a bit of a tiff with the boyfriend.' He screwed up his eyebrows.

'The course of true love and all that. Listen, you'd be much better off with that fellow you were going out with years ago. I said it before and I'll say it again, you two were made for each other.'

'That's ancient history. Nigel is my partner now. We're actually getting married.'

'Jaysus, not another casualty. And to think I thought you had sense once. Where were you the day they gave brains out?'

'Give over. I have enough on my plate without you bothering me. I have to be off, it's getting late.'

'You're only here and you're going again. Typical woman. I hope your marriage lasts longer.'

I shook my fist at him and he guffawed. Then he was gone, off to a prosperous-looking woman walking the other way who might give him a precious few euro for more cheap wine. I wandered round the streets in a daze. I was purposely delaying because I dreaded going home to Nigel.

Needn't have worried, because when I got to the house it was empty. He'd left a note on the table and can't say I was surprised when I read it. The curt tone was classic Nigel: 'I need to be on my own for a while. Staying over with Charlie. If and when I'm up to discussing things I'll phone you.' Whoopie doo. Nice billet doux after my taxing day. I wondered if he'd left my dinner in the oven. Hardly.

I considered phoning Charlie but thought better of it. Decided it would be better to give him a few days to cool off. 'Keep on never minding,' as Uncle Bernie used to say, 'All you can do in this life is keep on never minding'.

Nigel arrived home after three days. He was sitting at the kitchen table when I got in. 'You're back,' I said, trying to sound enthusiastic, but he just grunted. He nodded to me to sit down and I found myself getting nervous. It reminded me of the time Big Knickers caught me copying my sums.

He had his head in a sheaf of papers and there wasn't a meg out of him.

'I've been doing a bit of serious thinking,' he said finally. The oracle had spoken.

'And what have you decided?'

'To forgive you. I realise you were totally under the influence of that Minnie person. My God, has she no shame? A woman of her age up on top of that old fellow. I'm not surprised she has marriage problems.'

'It was harmless. They weren't doing anything wrong. It was just a bit of fun."

'So much the worse. They should both have zimmer frames. Anyway, I hope you don't see her again.

I'd also prefer if you didn't visit her. I certainly don't want her in our house.'

'But we're friends from school. We go back a long way.'

'Is our relationship more important than school friends? I sincerely hope so or we're in big trouble.' I couldn't understand the way he thought. The dogs in the street knew we were in big trouble anyway.

CHAPTER 16

One evening out of the blue Nigel announced he was going to Florida for the month of November. Just like that, no warning. Since we'd got back together we seemed to be sharing the same premises like lodgers. We ate together in silence and slept in separate rooms. I spent many evenings wandering around the house while he worked late, dipping into the vino to drive away my worries. But it really only made them worse when I sobered up.

'Florida for the whole month?' I said, trying to act casual. 'Maybe I could get off. I have some time due to me.'

'I'm afraid that wouldn't work. I'm actually going with some male colleagues. It's strictly men only.'

'What if I came for two of the weeks? I don't like being alone now that the evenings are getting dark.'

'You're a big girl now. The break will do both of us good.'

He was due to fly out of Dublin the following week so he started his packing a few days beforehand. He had two huge suitcases. I sat downstairs to keep out of his way. I'd washed and ironed at least twenty of his prized shirts. The room was like a laundrette.

For some reason, don't ask me why, I decided to bite the bullet and ask him where I stood with him. He was bustling around with that demented look on his face and I stood there blocking his path between two doors as he tried to pass by me with the address label for one of his bags in his hand.

'Not now,' he moaned.

'It's always not now with you.'

'I have a plane to catch, my darling.'

'That's a cop-out. You're always running away from confronting things.'

'If I am, you make up for me. You analyse us to the death every time you open your mouth.'

'I'm a woman, Nigel. We think differently. I'm insecure.'

'That may be so but why do you have to make a major scene out of everything?'

'A major scene? Jesus Christ, what next. Have you any conception of the way you can twist things to suit yourself? You're not a man, you're a robot. The world's only living heart donor.'

As soon as I said that I knew I'd blown any chance we might have had. And yet a part of me was glad I'd blown it. 'A living heart donor. So that's the latest, is it? It's all coming out now.' He smiled at me in a cruel way, as if I'd shot myself in the foot. He'd given me a gun and I'd used it to kill what we had, or pretended to have. Yes, that was it. Nothing was lost because there was nothing there in the first place. I'd stayed with him all those years not because I loved him but because I was afraid of being left alone. Better a bad marriage than no marriage: Granny's words would come back to haunt me.

He was out most of the time over the next few days but even when he was in the house it didn't make much difference. Every time I walked into a room he walked out. Before I knew it he was ready to go. You could cut the atmosphere with a knife.

He was like a man possessed on the day of the flight, phoning here there and everywhere and checking departure times on his computer screen.. Once I would have been walking on eggshells round him, doing anything to break down that brick wall, but instead of that I felt a funny sense of relief. When you give everything and it still doesn't work out you don't guilt-trip yourself. You just stand outside the experience, watching it unfold.

When the taxi-man honked I lay on my bed waiting for him to come in and say goodbye but he didn't. I heard his footsteps going down the stairs and then out the door. I didn't look out the curtains as I heard his luggage being put in the boot of the car, I just listened to the wheeze of the engine until it grew faint. Then I took a Xanex. I didn't feel depressed, though. It was as if it was all happening to someone else. I felt I was waking from a seven-year dream.

I thought of a night with Daire long ago as he stood in front of me with a rucksack on his back about to leave for the continent. He'd chucked in his engineering job for no better reason than he had itchy feet and I was giving out hell to him about that, telling him he was wasting the money his parents had slaved to earn to put him through Uni. It seemed so laughable now, mature me telling him he should hang on to the permanent pensionable job instead of haring off to France to scratch his bellybutton. As if I'd found the secret of life in a solicitor's office in Dublin 4.

It was the first of our many breaks. We'd get together for a while and it would seem great and then I'd think he wasn't the man for me and I'd tell him I needed a break. We both went out with other people but always found ourselves drawn back to each other like magnets. I wanted him and yet I didn't want him and the more available he was I seemed to want him even less. It was the way I'd always been, mad interested in someone and then as soon as they asked me for my phone number I'd get scared off and make up a false one.

I remembered him standing in front of me with his rucksack, quietly asking me to join him even for a few weeks. If I didn't like it I could come home and there'd be no hard feelings. He didn't have much money but we'd make out. It would be nice not knowing where we'd be from day to day. There were camping sites we could go to and some friends of friends. 'If you don't do it now you'll never do it,' he said.

I knew it was reaching make-or-break time for both of us but I couldn't go with him. My feet felt like lead, cemented onto the floor. I told him I didn't have that kind of jizz in me any more. He looked at me as if I wasn't being true to myself but he said nothing.

A man with a rucksack looked at me with pleading in his eyes, too disgusted to tell me what he really thought of me, a woman too fond of her comforts. Electric blankets, central heating and three square meals a day. I really thought life could be this simple, that if you arranged these things around yourself some man would come out of a magic bottle like a genie and round it all off for you.

The thought of sleeping in doorways didn't appeal to me then, or not knowing where I'd be on a strange continent, so I let him slip away. He wrote to me a few times, soul-searching letters first, and then just postcards.

When he returned to Ireland a few months later he asked me to marry and because I watched a woman hanging clothes on a line I refused him. What an idiot I'd been. Miss Upperosity destined for better things. Like wonder boy Nigel.

Now Nigel was gone too. Would he come back? I didn't know and in a way I didn't care. He was losing his power over me. I was fed up apologising for being alive.

The next few days passed in a blur. Memories of the good times flashed through my mind but they were few and far between. Maybe I was in love with love, I thought. I had to have a man in my life to stop me having to face the emptiness. It was the way I'd always been, ever since creating John as a child, spending hours talking to him when most other children were playing with their dolls. For a while Mammy and Daddy thought I had a screw loose. Maybe they were right.

I didn't go into my usual decline this time. Maybe I was well shot of him. He took so much out of me even when things were going moderately well I wasn't sure the relationship was worth it. Why did I try so hard when he gave so little?

I did my best to forget him and it was easier than I imagined. If this was the end, and it seemed like it, why wasn't I in bits? Maybe I was operating on my reserve, or else there'd never been anything there at all. Whatever way I was feeling it didn't stop me visiting the shops. I got a gorgeous red skirt, my favourite length tipping the knee and a classy-looking black top that really set it off.

I phoned Minnie one evening to see how she was. The minute I heard her voice I knew things were bad. It turned out John was definitely serious about the Rockbarton girl.

'It's unbelievable,' she sobbed down the line, 'he says the only way he'll stay here is if I let him have his freedom.'

'That's not on. Nobody could put up with that.'

'It seems I have no option. At this stage of my life I don't want to be left alone. The twins are doing their own thing. If he moves out I know I'll go to pieces.'

'No you won't. Look at me.'

'What do you mean? Are you having trouble with Nigel?'

'You could say that. He's gone away.'

'Oh no.'

'He'll probably be back, but not to me, I feel. He's gone to America for a month.'

'Everybody has rows, I'm sure ye'll get back together again. I must say you don't sound too upset about it'.

'That's the funny thing. I don't know why.'

'It's different for me. John and myself are together all our lives. I wouldn't want to live if he leaves me We've had children together.'

'Cop on to yourself, Minnie. He's not worth it. He has you on a string. Throw him out, the Rockbarton one will soon get fed up of him, mark my words.'

'That's easy for you to say. I'm afraid if I do he won't come back at all'.

'That's the power he has over you. You're making it too easy for him. I'm telling you, give him two months with that one and he'll come to his senses.'

'Maybe you're right but I'm not that strong. The twins are talking about coming for Christmas. I know I'm going to have to tell them.'

'Please God it'll be sorted out before then.'

'Maybe. Oh, by the way ,I had a letter from Clem. You know, the American guy.'

'How did he get your address?'

'I must have given it to him that crazy night. I'll never forget the face on Nigel when he walked in the door. Anyway he wrote a lovely letter and I've answered it.'

'That's the way to go, Minnie, keep writing. If John cops onto that he'll be mad jealous and he'll soon come back to you with his tail between his legs.'

'It's not romantic or anything. He's just a really sweet man.'

'You'd never know the way things might develop,' I said and she laughed. Then she was gone off the line. After I hung up I found myself getting worried for her, more worried even than for myself, which was saying something. Over the next few days I concluded all men were pigs. You could dress it up in other words but at the end of the day that's what it amounted to. And they were running the world. No wonder it was in such a state.

On Sunday I stayed in bed for most of the day and rose in the evening. I was tempted to go into the park again but thought better of it. I knew Jack would be asking me about myself and I was in no mood for going into things. Once or twice I felt sad about Nigel but it didn't last. I felt relieved to be getting him out of my system. I was sleeping well and walking into work any chance I got.

I left my engagement ring on because I didn't want any of the busybodies asking me questions. If I took it off they'd notice immediately. They'd give me the pitying looks and probably pass smart comments about me behind my back. Two-time loser in love, that kind of thing.

Fiona was in another one of her black tempers on Monday morning. 'The dead arose and appeared to many, ' she huffed when I walked in the door.

'It's only twenty past,' I said, 'I'm not late.'

'You're supposed to be here at a quarter past at the latest. Anyway, things are manic today. Would you mind starting immediately?'

She hardly gave me time to get my coat off before she started baring instructions at me. I was up to ninety with the typing when two of the symbols went missing from the toolbar again and I started to cry. I know she heard me snuffling but she said nothing. Eventually I went to the toilet to clean my face. I sat there for a good twenty minutes sobbing my heart out. What would I do? Lousy typist. No boyfriend. No marriage. No Nigel. Would he ever come back to me? Who cared. He was no good to me now. Maybe never had been.

I dried my eyes and went back to my desk. Fiona knew I was upset but that didn't stop her loading me down with work. I knew her form was to put on the pressure on or at when you were having personal problems. She saw it as therapy. Emotions, for her, were indulgences only permissible after five thirty or at weekends.

Things went from bad to worse for the rest of the day. After lunch I typed a long letter and forgot to save it. Then Fiona wanted to change it and I had to redo the whole thing. Luckily I still had it on the dictaphone. She kept asking me if it was ready. In the end I broke down completely. This time she reacted to my crying by telling me I could go home early. When I heard that I had to look out the window to see if there was a blue moon out. Either that or she was afraid I'd destroy the computer with my tears.

When I got home there was a message from Nigel on the answering machine. It was spectacularly direct: 'I will be writing to you.' That could mean anything, I told myself. Maybe he'd changed his mind. 'I will be writing to you.'

I played it over and over, trying vainly to convince myself he sounded friendly. Could a leopard change its spots? Hardly.

CHAPTER 17

November was a lonely month and it brought back a poem Mammy used to recite to me, 'No sun, no moon, no morn, no noon' it went, every line beginning with 'No', and then the last line was 'No-vember.' Even though it sounded negative, for some reason it always put me into good form thinking of it.

I hated getting home in the dark to the empty house so I left lights on all over the place. Every night I'd snuggle up with *Jane Eyre*, immersing myself in it like in the past. There was something about the language that was so simple and yet so moving:

'My first quarter at Lowood seemed an age, and not the golden age either; it comprised an irksome struggle with difficulties in habituating myself to new rules and unwonted tasks. The fear of failure in these points harassed me worse than the physical hardships of my lot, though these were no trifles.' I related everything Jane did and felt to my own little life, even when it wasn't directly relevant.

I took a few days off work after convincing Dr Walsh I had cramps in my stomach. I was probably his best patient by now. He could nearly afford to retire on my revenue alone. My own personal physician. Did he really buy all my lies or would it be too expensive for him to contradict me? I was practically writing my own prescriptions now.

When I turned up for work after my little break I was over the moon to discover Fiona was out with flu. I turned on my machine and played Patience instead of typing letters. I took an extra twenty minutes at the coffee break and went early to lunch and stayed late at it so the days sped by.

At home I kept watching for the postman in case Nigel wrote but that watched kettle didn't boil until the very day before he was due home. His letter was cold and to the point. He'd made some decisions. He'd meet me at the house on the Saturday after his arrival in Dublin to discuss his plans.

Thanks a bunch.

True to his word, he arrived on the Saturday afternoon. He looked well after his trip and was sporting a nice tan.

'You look well,' I said and he shrugged his shoulders.

'Could you sit down,' he opened solemnly, 'and I'll tell you what I've planned.' It sounded ominous.

He rambled on about lack of trust and my ballooning weight and then accused me of sleeping around with Americans in their dotage. The upshot was that he was telling me the relationship was over. In his accountant's voice he told me of the options we had. The grim picture looked like this: (a) I took over the mortgage of the house and refunded him what he'd paid into, it including the price of the extension. (b) He took over the mortgage and would refund me what he felt was a fair sum, bearing in mind that he'd paid the full deposit. (c) We'd sell the house and he would pay me what I was entitled to.

I panicked as this set of horrors that was put before me. I told him I never had a relationship with another man since we got together. If he wanted to leave that was fine but I wouldn't have him branding me a cheater or a flirt. I told him I'd bent over backwards to please him for nine years and got zilch gratitude for it. I was willing to be his skivvy, even his stick insect, but not branded a liar.

He listened to all this with mock-patience and then said, 'Are you finished?'

'I suppose I am. Why?'

'Because I have something else to tell you.' This should be good, I thought.

'I don't quite know how to put this. The truth is, I've met someone else. She's American.'

So that was it, another woman. Same old story. I was another Minnie.

'Really? I'm delighted to hear the news. A bluestocking, I'm sure.'

'There's no need to be like that.'

'Like what? All I'm saying is that I presume she matches up to your usual high standards.' Good old Nigel.

He certainly hadn't wasted much time. Exit nutty secretary, enter cheerleader from Junior High.

'We don't know each other very well yet but we seem to get on well together.'

'I'm sure you do.'

'Anyway, that's all I wanted to say. It might come to nothing but I'm telling you just in case. I wouldn't have wanted you to hear it from anyone else.'

'Perish the thought.'

'If you were interested, which I doubt considering your attitude, I could introduce you to her when she comes over here.'

'For what - a *ménage-a-trois*?'

'Okay, maybe I deserved that.'

'I'm sorry. I'm being a pain. Believe it or not, I'm glad for you. Forgive my bitchiness. It just takes a few minutes to sink in.'

'You're not being a pain at all. I knew you'd be dignified about it.'

My head started to pound with some unexplainable tension. I tried to think of something to say to him but no words came. I just wanted him out of the house. And out of my life.

'Thank you. Look, there are no hard feelings, are there?'

'None at all.'

He stood at the door shuffling around looking for his car keys. Job done. Ex-lover safely consigned to the dustbin of memory. All in all a good day's work. Dammit, he even got the accounts sorted into the bargain.

'Well I'll see you around.'

'No doubt you will.' (I was going to say 'Very round' but restrained myself).

He stretched out his hand for me to shake, like a client after brokering a deal.

'Let's still be friends, will we? You brought a lot of happiness into my life and I'm deeply sorry it didn't work out.'

'Oh well, that's life. Onwards and upwards, isn't that what they say? Anyway, let me know how it goes with your new partner.'

'I will for sure, and let me know what you decide about the house.'

As he made his way out I found myself starting to cry but I didn't let him see me, closing the door quickly. I don't know where the tears came from as I had no more emotion for him than a flea. It had to be everything happening together.

The next time he called I'd been out with Alice. I came home to find another one of his messages on the machine: 'Nigel here. I'll call again on Tuesday evening, say 9 p.m. and you can let me know what you want to do. If we decide on different things we'll have to talk again. I won't say what my preferences are until I hear what you have to say.'

It seemed to cement the finality of it all. There was almost relief at seeing the end in black and white. Now all that remained were the practicalities.

I wondered if I should ring somebody for advice. I knew I wouldn't have a hope in hell of taking over the mortgage with my extravagant habits. (How many houses could I have bought with the contents of my wardrobe?) I could hardly live on what I was earning and I was only paying half the mortgage at the moment.

The following week I came back from a walk and he was in the house waiting for me. D-Day. I offered him a drink but he said this was strictly business and he wanted to get it sorted out as quickly as possible.

'Have it your own way,' I said, 'I've been going over all you said and I'm thinking of going for you buying me out. How much would I get?' It was almost enjoyable, playing him at his own mercenary game. Monkey see monkey do.

'Obviously I'll be fair to you. I'm quite okay with that arrangement. I wouldn't have a problem meeting the mortgage on my own.' He said this with a certain air of assurance. Damn right, I thought. He'd probably have it wiped out within the year if I knew anything.

He rhymed off figures like the Chancellor of the Exchequer.

'So what's the bottom line?' I said. I was getting quite good at this, using fancy American expressions like 'bottom line'. He looked at me with a mixture of shock and a weird kind of respect. Was there a side to me he'd never seen until now, when it was too late to matter?

'Well, bearing in mind I've put so much into this place, I feel that if I buy you out for €50,000 I'll have been more than fair to you. Remember the extension was paid for by me, as well as the deposit.' I certainly did remember it. And if I didn't, guess who was going to remind me.

I told him it sounded very generous. Fifty thousand smackeroos. I'd be dangerous if I was let loose with that kind of money round the designer shops.

'Where will I live until I get a place of my own?'

'You can stay in the house for a while. I'm with Charlie at the moment, as you know, and he's invited me to hang on indefinitely. I was thinking of mid-Jan. I've pencilled it in my diary. It gives you a bit of breathing space. Does that help?'

I felt like saying, 'It's so good I feel like doing a hornpipe'. His generosity knew no bounds. I nodded.

'Good,' he said, clapping his hands together, 'I'll draw up some papers with my solicitor. We can both sign them next week and then I'll give you the cheque. I know this sounds very cold-blooded. I hope you appreciate I'm doing it to protect you rather than for any other reason.'

He didn't let the mask slip right through our little rendezvous. There was no way through that Rock of Gibralter. It was all so callous I felt like bursting out laughing. He was getting the new kitchen and me the Beethoven CDs. So what was going to happen to the TV? Maybe he'd take the set and leave me with the table. There were salt and pepper shakers in the kitchen cabinets. Would we share these? How about the box of matches on the mantelpiece? 28 matches each and toss for the box. As for the mirrors in the house, I told him he could gladly take all of these because he'd used them more than any other single item and I was sure he'd get full value for them.

He gave a hollow laugh when I said that, then shook his head as if I was descending to a childish level. Maybe I was but he certainly spent more time admiring his gorgeous physique than he did looking at me. I could imagine Nigel dying in his own arms. I kidded him once that I could imagine him shouting out his own name during love-making. He wasn't amused then either.

He shook my hand before he left, the final insult. I found myself wondering if my cheque would arrive marked 'To Whom It May Concern'.

He must have known what I'd go for if he was pencilling arrangements in his diary. That made it all into a sham. He only pretended to offer me a choice. It was like a Trojan horse. But what did I care. As far as I was concerned I'd be rich, at least in contrast to the years gone by when I always found myself in trouble with the bank. Friday's wages were usually gone missing by Monday morning after some not- so-clever jiggery-pokery with my Visa Card.

Maybe I'd ask for a month off work next year. God knows I was long enough in the place. I thought I might take a trip to the States. I owed Angie a visit for ages and she was practically hoarse asking me over. I could finally get to see the country where all the dotty fat people on *Springer* came from. I'd probably embrace them like long-lost friends.

It would be hard not to love people who actually made me look skinny.

CHAPTER 18

I phoned Alice to meet for lunch the next day and to tell her the news. All she kept stressing was that I wouldn't have a roof over my head and that the money would walk if I didn't watch it.

'Remember,' she advised me, 'you won't get a mortgage on your own and if you rent a flat it's money down the drain.'

She was so stuck in her ways. 'I can rent a place,' I said, 'I'll still have my salary, remember, as well as Nigel's windfall.'

I pressed her to have a brandy, telling her we had something to celebrate, but she wouldn't be swayed.

'It's a bit like Job's consolation,' I said. 'My world is falling down around me and I'm laying into the gargle. Nero fiddles.'

'We're so different. Jekyll and Hyde for sure. I can see the money disappearing like magic once you get your hands on it.'

The papers were signed a few weeks later and Nigel presented me with my cheque. When we left the solicitor's office I asked him could I treat him to a drink for old times sake but he declined.

I flipped at this. Maybe it was all the repressed emotion of the past few months but I totally lost it. I found myself pulling the engagement ring off my finger and flinging it at him. 'We've finalised everything else,' I roared, 'you might as well have this as well'. I don't know if he picked it up or not because I turned on my heel and walked away. The look on his face was worth the price of it

I walked back to work crying uncontrollably. When I got to the office it was obvious by my face that something was going on. When I looked at myself in the mirror I thought I could have been in make-up for some play with all the mascara that was smudged on my cheeks. Fiona was as vile as ever but I gave her as good as I got. She didn't know what hit her. The worm was turning. It was sink or swim for me, kill or be killed.

When I got home that evening I felt strange. It was as if nothing could touch me. When you've been kicked hard enough it's like everything goes into the one trough. I didn't know if I was getting stronger or just indifferent but whatever I was I welcomed it.

I phoned Minnie but she sounded dismal. Things were just as bad with John and she barely saw him now. The twins had cancelled the Christmas visit because they were invited to Switzerland with some people they met.

'I'm glad for them,' she declared in her typical generous fashion 'Since they're not coming home I'll tell them nothing. If they knew the truth they'd be home in a shot.'

Not those two selfish lassies, I thought to myself, but you just didn't say something like that to a doting mother.

'What do you think of my news?' I asked after she'd emptied herself of her own.

'If it's what you want I'm pleased. I never liked him and you're well out of it.'

'€50,000, Minnie. Can you believe it?'

'It was well earned, I'm sure. But mind it. Remember you have to get somewhere to live.'

'You're just like Alice. Can you not be glad for me? I never had €5,000, let alone €50,000. It's like winning the Lotto.'

I stayed out of work for the next two days to let the shock sink in. I went into town and bought myself a new winter coat for €600 and a little black dress worth every penny at €850. It was a novelty for me to be able to write cheques and not worry about when the next payday was. I treated myself to a new hair-do in a place I'd never dare go usually. The bill was huge because I got blonde highlights but it was worth it. Now that my weight was more static I looked my best. I'd gained over a stone but I was tall enough to carry it. Swanning round town with my new hair-do and the beautifully expensive coat, as Auntie Eileen would say, I wouldn't call the queen my aunt.

When I went to work the next morning Fiona cut me dead on the stairs. There was no comment at all about my being sick but then that was nothing new. She lived, ate and breathed the job and I accepted that. But just because she didn't have a life outside it herself, did that give her the right to stop me having one?

I did as much work as I could manage in the morning and then went for lunch. Afterwards I wandered round the shops and bought myself a pair of leather boots. They came right up to my thighs and looked really well with my new coat and the short plaid skirt I was wearing under it.

I was a little late back and Fiona's face let me know in no uncertain terms she was aware of the fact. I was hardly seated before she said she'd like me to stay after work because she wanted to talk to me.

I didn't let it bother me too much because I was so preoccupied admiring my boots. I went up to Joanie's room to show them off and stayed gabbing to her for about fifteen minutes. By 5.30 I'd completely forgotten Fiona the Snow Woman wanted to speak to me. I was just heading out the door when she came out of her office and signalled for me to go in.

'Would you mind coming in for a moment,' she said. She wasn't hostile now, just more official - which was nearly worse. I felt a sinking feeling in my stomach.

Herself and Leslie Smith were seated behind her desk. Both of them looked as if they'd just got a bad smell. Leslie cleared his throat before delivering a speech that had obviously been worked on.

He meandered on about my timekeeping, my poor work, my atrocious attendance record. He said he was shocked to see me the day before, having rung in sick, parading down Tara Street looking like the Queen of Sheba. He pointed out that I had many years of good service with the company but things had gone just that little bit too far. He was now giving me a verbal warning and if I didn't pull up my socks after that I'd get a written one as well. A third infringement would mean they'd have no choice but to let me go.

My mouth went dry as I listened to this. I just sat there paralysed, saying nothing. If Fiona sprouted a second head I doubt if I'd have been more surprised. Was this my thanks for fourteen years of 'Yes sir, no sir, three bags full, sir'? When I started to work for Fiona I was in awe of her. I'd known she was a bitch but I had a certain amount of respect for her. If she said 'Jump', I'd have replied, 'How high?' It was only in the last few years I saw her for what she really was. Maybe she heard me backbiting her and this was this was all about. Revenge for the tea-room chit-chat.

I don't know how long I sat in the hot seat as she laid into me. I can't even remember leaving. It seemed hours later when I sat on the Dart wondering how everything I touched in life seemed to turn to ashes.

I had my rights. I could have them for unfair dismissal. There were any number of places I could think of that might be interested in taking up the case of a long-suffering secretary down on her luck. Let them see how it felt to be at the receiving end. Okay, so my attendance record was cat but that in itself wasn't a hanging offence. For years I was your model typist. Did that count for nothing? Long before that cursed cursor came into fashion I could type faster than any of the secretaries. I knew how to sew up Wills with green ribbon long before computers came into fashion. I knew the whole spiel off at the end of the Will without anybody having to tell me. In fact I typed it out regularly for new girls in the office: SIGNED SEALED AND DELIVERED by the said blah blah in the presence of us both present at the same time who at his request in his presence and in the presence of each other have hereunto signed our names as Witnesses.

None of the computer whizzes knew that off like I did. I was once the prize secretary and now I was something to be flushed out with yesterday's rubbish. Was this the face of business in Celtic Tiger Ireland? If it was, give me back the mangy cub of poverty any day.

Over the next few weeks my head was a muddle. I ran into Jack one day and poured my heart out to him.

'I'm in big trouble at work'. I said, 'they almost gave me my notice.'

He took a swig out a bottle of cider he had cradled in his shabby old raincoat.

'What if they did,' he said, 'you're long enough at it to take some time off for yourself. You could join me here in the park.'

'We'd make a nice couple all right.'

Part of me wanted to sit down beside him watching the world go by. Who needed to spend their life stuck at a computer, day in day out? Was it for this my mother huffed and puffed on Christmas Eve night all those years ago? Nothing for her Christmas dinner but rice with a bit of jam on it, all so she could produce a mouse operator.

'Why don't you get out of there before they throw you out? Visit your doctor and go on the sick. Make an excuse about a bad back or something.'

'Maybe I will.'

'How is your relationship going, by the way? He said, changing the subject.

'I'm afraid it's over, Jack.'

'What? I don't believe it. Are you still living at the same place?'

'Until January. He bought me out and that's how I have the few bob. Listen,' I said, 'that coat is in bits, would you let me get one for you?'

'My coat is fine. I'm not into fashion.'

'I was just thinking of keeping out the rain. Look, take that.' I handed him twenty euro and made off before he could refuse it.

'Good on you,' he called after me. No doubt he'd go straight to the off-licence for another few bottles of cider. Maybe he was right. Maybe to be in a permanent state of drunkenness was the only way to get through this life.

I hadn't a clue where I was headed but I felt it would be a bad move to ask for advice from anyone. I knew Alice would try to influence me to stay put. Too much change wouldn't be good, she'd say, because I was just out of a relationship and would need a salary coming in. Minnie would have been too preoccupied to say anything at all.

Then I remembered Angie. I knew she'd have my welfare at heart. I had to wait a few hours to phone her because of the time change but she answered immediately.

'Is there something wrong?' she said, sounding distressed, 'it's only 7 a.m. over here.'

'No, I just want your advice about something.'

'My advice?'

'I'm afraid Nigel and myself have split up.'

'Oh no. You poor thing. After all those years. What happened?'

'It's too long to go into. In a way I'm relieved. I know you'll find that hard to believe'.

'I thought you two were like Siamese twins.'

'For a while we were but then it all went wrong.'

'Did it happen suddenly?'

'Not really. We've been having problems for years.'

'Why didn't you tell me?'

'What was the point? I felt we'd either get over them or we wouldn't. I didn't want to tempt fate by talking about it all. Anyway, what good can talking do. He made his decision and that's it.'

'So it was him who left.'

'I'm afraid so.'

'There are plenty more fish in the sea,' she consoled, the comfortable cliché that didn't really put balm over the wound.

'That's for sure. And I'm the woman to ferret them out.' If I said it often enough I might end up convincing myself.

'You are and all.'

'Anyway, to make a long story short, I don't feel half as bad as I thought I would.' The truth of it was, I felt a million times worse. Not because I loved him but because I was so long a part of a couple. I knew in my heart he'd done me a favour by leaving me but I didn't want to admit that to myself, at least just yet.

'How are you fixed financially? Did he rip you off?' We were getting down to the nitty-gritties.

'He bought me out of the house so I'm quite comfortable that way.'

'Good for you. I know you probably don't want to hear this but it's better it went wrong now than later on.' More common sense that I really didn't want to hear.

'I suppose so. By the way, did I tell you I'm also thinking of leaving the job?'

'My God, you don't do things in half-measures, do you?'

'Maybe one thing led to the other.'

'What are you planning to do with yourself? As you know, you're more than welcome to come out here if you want to. We'd put you up for as long as you liked.'

'I know that. Thanks, Angie. Maybe later. So you think retiring is a good idea?'

'I wish I could do it myself. You're still young enough to change and if you have money from the house you can afford to look around for lots of other things.'

'That's what I wanted to hear.'

The following day was the one I'd set aside to break the news to them all at work. For about five years I'd thought on and off about how I'd handle this kind of decision but now suddenly it didn't seem to matter one way or the other.

As soon as I got to the office I went straight into Fiona. I told her I'd been going through a bad patch, that my relationship had ended and that I was on medication. As a result of these things, all in all I felt it better to give it a rest.

'But you're part of the furniture!' she exclaimed.

'Yes,' I replied, 'all cracked and ancient.'

She didn't get the joke.

'Okay,' she said, 'Well I suppose you know your own mind and to be honest your mind hasn't been on your work for a long time. Maybe a change will be good for you.'

I knew she'd be indifferent to my decision. She was far more interested in the super-confident brigade, the Marjories and Sandras - with the added bonus that they were also young. I could never be in their league, my years of experience counting for little in her eyes.

She talked for a long time about my years there and I felt a sudden wrench of fear, as if it wasn't so much release I had ahead of me but the removal of all the routines I took so much for granted. We finished by her asking me could I stay on till Christmas. She also said I'd be getting a lump sum of about €15,000 for my years of service. All my financial boats seemed to be coming in at once - but none of them could cover up my emptiness and fear.

I told the girls at coffee break. Joanie gave me a hug and Marjorie and Sandra told me I was damn right. Rita and Mairead just looked bewildered. I didn't mention anything to Leslie Smith or Edward Skelly but I noticed the pair of them sniffing round my desk in the afternoon so I presumed they sussed something. Fiona probably blabbed out everything behind closed doors and swore them to silence. They looked at me as if to say they didn't think I had it in me. How audacious of me to deign to have a life outside their empire of dullness. .

I felt like I had ten thumbs all day. Typos in every other line, dropped files, and at one point nearly a full cup of steaming black coffee almost dunked into the fax machine. I was shivering with excitement, the same kind of excitement I had in Galway when Daddy would call up to the school for me and tell Big Knickers we were going for a drive out to the Silver Strand. My forthcoming freedom was like a sinful pleasure. It was like something you weren't meant to have. As if your future had to be forever inside these walls, typing affidavits for people you never saw because that was simply the way things were.

Part of me felt I was getting out of jail but another part made me feel I'd have too much time to brood over the break-up with Nigel - and even Daire. Hanging round the house might bring strange thoughts because I wasn't used to it. Ever since school I'd been in some form of gainful employment, however humiliating. I'd served my time as a wage slave since I was seventeen.

I tried to fill my mind with upbeat thoughts. I was getting out of Alcatraz. It was December already and I'd only have one more Christmas party. After that I would be a free woman. I could get used to that.

My nerves were up and down like a fiddler's elbow. Part of the time I felt almost elated with the prospect of my new freedom and all the money I'd have. Other times, mainly late at night, I'd be scared stiff of the same freedom. I knew some people blossomed in retirement but just as many withered on the vine. Especially single people. People who had nobody to share their freedom. People who got dumped.

Seeing as it was going to be my last office party I decided to go out in style. I spent almost €1,000 on a formal outfit. It looked like a simple black dress but you'd know immediately it was a designer outfit. I bought sparkling silver sandals and a very pricey little evening bag. The party was always dull but I guessed they'd give me my going-away present so I justified my extravagance like that. Anyway, I'd also be getting the €15,000 lump sum. Knowing that made me spend even more. (Not that I needed much encouragement).

I phoned Minnie a week before Christmas. I hadn't told her I was leaving until now. I thought she'd be surprised but it didn't seem to have much effect on her. John was officially living in the house with her still but he was missing 90% of the time.

'Can I ask you to do me a big favour?' she said, her voice expectant.

'What is it?'

'Would you stay with me for Christmas? He'll be out all the time. The twins won't be here after all. It would really help me if you came.'

I didn't even stop to think before accepting her invitation. I hoped to myself that John wouldn't be around because my last experience with him was something I didn't care to repeat. The prospect of Christmas in Galway was appetising as I hadn't spent one there since we left. I could have gone to Alice, or indeed Angie in the States, but the fact that Minnie wanted me made all the difference.

I did very little work for my last days in the office. I felt I was already gone from the place. Fiona and Leslie were more pleasant than usual, probably because they were glad to be seeing the back of me. Mr Roberts seemed genuinely upset. I thought that was ironic - the man I knew least of all. Skelly looked at me as if I was some strange creature from another planet. He genuinely seemed to think I'd have hung on in the job until the Alzheimer people came to cut me out of my chair.

Like some other people in the office, he was entitled to think I was surgically attached to it by this stage.

CHAPTER 19

I met Sandra and Marjorie for a few drinks on the Big Night. They asked me if I was excited but I couldn't honestly say I was. The truth of it was, I did feel quite tense. I sat up until 4 a.m. the night before I left, sweating over my farewell speech. It went like this:

'I want to bid you all a fond farewell and to thank you from the bottom of my heart for your beautiful magnificent fantastic present. I've worked with this firm for donkey's years and I'm very sad to be leaving.'

(Cue long pause)

'Well actually that's not totally true. The truth of it is, ladies and gentlemen, that if I stayed here one more second longer I'd go out of my tiny little tree and in jig-time you'd find me in one of those dark ugly buildings with a lot of people in uniforms patrolling the grounds with guard dogs even uglier than themselves.

And now, friends, let me tell you a little bit about the woman you think you've known for fourteen years, the one who sits pert behind her desk and never says boo to a goose, nor indeed to a gander, or talks back to bosses.

This little mouse of a woman who has been your colleague for 14 years and whom you may see as an open dreary book. .

But I do have secrets to tell. To wit:

I wish to inform all here present that I cannot, will not, and care not to ever use a binder. I have dreamt about my binder, had nightmares about it,, woke up in the middle of the night in cold sweats fantasising about chopping it up into tiny little pieces and feeding them to the ducks on Stephen's Green. Put plainly, folks, I think it's the most awkward contraption on the face of the earth and I now proclaim to all of you that I am pathologically unsuited to using it, punching holes in the documents I put inside it, and snapping down the blessed thing afterwards with the prongs. I resolutely refuse to make any apology for this unforgiveable lapse. So you can all stuff it up your collective behinds.

Let's see - is there anything else? Oh yes, most of the time my mind is a million miles away from this pathetic little apology for an office that I work in - I use the word 'work' advisedly - even though when you look at me I have this deep and meaningful expression on my face that suggests I will have a nervous breakdown if the next urgent Contract is not put to Tender so all the fat cats I work for can bring their kids to Tuscany in June. At such times, my friends, what I'm usually thinking about is the moss green top I'm going to purchase at Marks & Sparks at lunchtime, or pinchy pains in my feet that make it difficult to position myself comfortably under the grotty little piece of decayed wood you call my desk.

I might also add that my typing skills have gone to pot since about 1995. Before we went computerised I got more tipp-ex on my clothes than my letters, I've spilt 65 cups of half-drunk coffee into my filing cabinet per year (no, sir, it isn't time that's yellowed the files after all!) and the number of times I've sent letters to wrong addresses has caused the local postman to have a mild stroke, from which he is said to be now recovering at a nursing home in Malahide, thank you for enquiring.

Neither could I ever do algebra, geometry, or turn the heel of a stocking. Also, I constantly lose symbols from toolbars, mix up files dealing with constitutional law and tort, think my hard drive is something Nigel uses when he's trying to crash a yellow light, and firmly believe we'd all be better off using quills like they did in the time of my good old friend Charles Dickens, Esquire.

Is there anything else? Oh yes. Sandra - please take a bow for the many times I ran to you after losing said symbols and instead of telling me to cop on to myself you came over to me, put on a lovely friendly yexpression. and told me you'd love to help but were up to your tonsils. For that, Sandy, much thanks. Beneath that tough exterior lurks a heart of - well, stone actually.

While I'm at it, I might as well tell you some other things about this loyal trusted senior secretary you see every day of your lives that you think knows her onions. Not!

Basically, I think you're all a bunch of unmitigated horrors with not enough brain cells between you to fit into the bellybutton of a household gnat. Most of you make the fellow who comes in to take out the bins look like Einstein and yet you go round the place as if you're splitting the atom, saving the world, or at the very least curing cancer. While I'm thinking to myself, you couldn't cure bacon.

Well that's about it, so while the night is still young, even if we aren't, let's raise our glasses in a collective toast:

'Here's to you and here's to me, May we never disagree If we do, To hell with you, here's to me.'

SIGNED SEALED AND DELIVERED BY THE ABOVE NAME IN THE PRESENCE OF:

Okay, so it was a bit snotty but what could they do to me now. Lock me up? (They should have done that years ago). Report me to the Labour Court? Come round to my house and stuff threatening missives inside my letter-box? No, I'd have my solicitor (oops!) onto them like a shot.

To hell with it, I'd give it to them all good and proper, right between the mince pies. Now all that remained was to see the funny looks on their faces as the mouse finally roared. But would I have the guts to deliver it in front of everyone?

I hated people making a fuss of me. In fact I'd have much preferred to slink into the sunset with a few quid and maybe a BT token than all the attention. I knew I'd have to perform later, to be as falsely polite to people I didn't like as people I didn't like would have to be falsely polite to me. When I said this to Sandra she exploded with laughter.

'You must have come down in the last shower. That's what we do every day of our lives. In every office in the country people lick up to one another to get through the day.'

'Maybe so, but knowing it doesn't make it any easier.'

The two ladies were in ecstasies about my dress. My hair also turned out particularly well, and I had a good week beforehand, practically free of funny sensations in my legs, arms, front torso or back of same. So I was in tip-top condition for the night.

They'd booked a section of a hotel bar for me. Skinflint Smith had splurged out for once. It would have stuck in his craw to do so. It was like prising blood from a stone to get him to contribute to anything. He was the only man in the office who was said to leave a pub with more in his pocket than when he went in.

Balloons hung from the ceiling, surrounded by bunting. Food and drink were piled high on the tables and the walls decorated with fond messages of farewell. If I wasn't careful I might have found myself thinking they actually cared for me.

'I could have worked more effectively in this atmosphere all through the years,' I told Fiona, 'Balloons bring out the best in me.'

'Come again?' she said. She looked at me as if she wanted to feel my forehead, as if I was in a fever. She tried to plaster a smile onto that corporate face but it wasn't easy for her, .

People filtered into the room in twos and threes, some of them delighted for me, others resenting me being the centre of attention. The drinks I had with the girls helped me not care either way. I also spotted some faces from the past, probably dredged out of a crumpled notebook Fiona kept in a drawer. The Chosen Few.

Mr Purcell turned up. That surprised me as the joke was he only went to state functions since he retired. Skelly was there with some cronies from the Law Society. All they were missing were the tilted wigs. Either I'd made a very big impression on these people a long time ago or they'd go anywhere for free booze. (I suspected the latter).

Other than that it was the usual suspects. Mr Roberts flitted in and out as usual. If you didn't look at him you'd hardly know he was there. Sandra used to say that if he was drowning, his whole life would flash before him and he wouldn't be in it. She gave him a horrible time and would continue to do so because he took it. That was the really sad thing.

I sampled a few salad sandwiches but they lay in my stomach like cement. Joanie told me to keep shovelling them in to act as blotting paper for the gargle. She had the inner track on all such ruses so I took her advice.

Sandra and Marjorie went into rhapsodies about my dress again, probably because they couldn't think of anything else to say to me. I was tempted to tell them about the conversation I overheard that day but didn't want to put a damper on the night. Sandra had her mobile in her hand - she probably took it to bed with her -and was busily texting someone, probably her boyfriend. She started to giggle as she showed me what she was writing: 'How RU? Dullsville here. CU soon. Keep bed warm 4 me. Luv Sandy.' Not too diplomatic considering this was my big night but that was Sandra.

Marjorie started on about the al-Queda. It used to be Robbie Williams. She was going through her Serious Phase. She wanted to get a discussion going about Barack Obama but nobody was interested. Sandra told her to shut up and have a look to see if there was any 'talent' in the pub. So much for the 'Luv' message. I could see her in a few years, settled down in a fancy house in the suburbs, power-dressing and going for the Main Chance. From playing footsie to studying the ftse index. Marjorie was a bit the same. They were well met. But if they had a disagreement, look out. Two explosive forces. The good thing was that I wouldn't be there to see that any more. Joanie could update me on developments in my absence. My Deep Throat.

She told me she'd give her eye-teeth to be in my position but that she didn't have either the courage or the money to 'break for the border'. Sandra told her to stop the sensible talk and let her hair down. So easy to let your hair down at twenty. Not so easy when you're married to a man trying his best to kill himself. But Joanie said none of this. She was a lady.

Rita gave me a necklace. It was silver with a blue stone. She was more subdued than usual. I saw her having words with Leslie Smith at one point and wondered if she was in the wars again. Mairead, as ever, looked as if it was her time of the month. Maybe she was worried about what the expenditure for the night would do to the stability of Petty Cash.

I drank too fast and it went to my head. After a while I found myself actually flirting a bit with Ed Skelly. He was at least fifteen years my junior but I was so squiffy I had no objection to being a cradle-snatcher for the night. He got pink in the cheeks at my overtures – it was a bit of a contrast to my general office behaviour - but I didn't let that stop me.

'How is that affidavit of attesting witnesses doing?' I asked him and he guffawed nervously.

I was on neat vodkas now. Seeing double and feeling single. I knew I'd pay for it in the morning but how often did people leave a 14-year-old job?

'You'll be over in the office photocopying your bum next,' Marjorie warned me.

'The A4 sheets wouldn't fit it all,' I told her. Mr Purcell gave me a look when I said that. He must have thought I'd had a personality bypass since my mousy days with him. Give me time and I'd be under the PC with Skelly, having close encounters of the 24th kind.

I went into the Ladies to empty my bladder and who was there but Joanie, doubled up on the floor an bawling her eyes out. I sat down beside her, the pair of us like two bag ladies, feet splayed out all over the place. We decided we'd set up a Woman Only club and bar accountants, heavy drinkers and solicitors from it. After a few minutes the pair of us were in convulsions. Mairead heard the noise and came in.

'Jesus Christ!' she screamed. The look on her face was priceless.

'Take that poker out of your arse,' Joanie told her and Mairead turned on her heel and stomped out. It was as if I'd found a soul-mate. I never realised there was bad blood between herself and Mairead.

'We didn't need to go to Lourdes to get the cure,' I said, feeling quite happy with myself that the night was on the road.

'I wish we could stay here,' she said, 'I need to talk to you.' I told her to drag me away from Fiona as soon as the formalities were finished.

After the meal Fiona stood up and gabbed on about how I was now a lady of leisure and might be able to take up a hobby, or even go back to my abandoned novel. I'd forgotten she knew anything about the bit of writing I'd done when I first started in the job. My so-called novel had been from the dim and distant GPO days. It was so long ago it might as well have been written with a quill as far as I was concerned. I was no longer that woman, starting out in life with every new day a rich shade of expectation.

Afterwards Joanie winked at me to come over to her. She was cradling a naggin of whiskey, halfway between tears and laughter as she tried to sit on a seat with her dress half off her. When I got over to her she put on a solemn expression.

'I'm going to leave the hubbie,' she said, slurring her words.

She used to say that at every Christmas party but I reckoned she'd stay with him, suffering his bad moods and endless bouts of drinking until she was too old to do anything about it. I wanted to put my arms round her and tell her to get out while she still could but I wasn't sure if she could survive on her own. Even though he was a disaster zone, she was dependent on him. Rita had a theory that she was a masochist, addicted to men who made her miserable. I knew it was a bit more complicated than that.

'You're great the way you keep going,' I said, 'you're always in such good form.'

'I have to be. If I started to think about my life I'd go mad.'

'Is it as bad as that?'

'It's worse. He's a timebomb waiting to explode. That's the only way I can put it.'

'I couldn't stay in that situation,' I said.

'I don't know how I've waited so long. I love him. That's the sad thing. He's the loveliest man I ever met. If only he could get off the booze. But I don't blame him for it. It's a disease. That's how I see it. It's the only way I can cope.'

'You're right. Grab at anything you can to keep you going.'

'That's why I couldn't give two figs about this shower here tonight. They know sweet feck all about life. Getting the letters typed is their definition of heaven. Money money money. It's all so crazy. If they lost their health they'd know the difference.'

'We're all a bit the same, though. You don't know what you have till you lose it.'

'That's for sure.'

'What's his own health like?'

'I don't know. He tells me nothing. I don't even know what medication he's on because he hides it. Along with his whiskey bottles. He could drop dead any minute as far as I'm concerned. That's what I live with. That's what drink can do to you.'

'Jesus, Joanie.'

'Anyway, will you have a refill?'

For a second I thought she was joking but she meant it. It was ridiculous but I had to take my hat off to her. If you couldn't beat them, join them. I wanted to stay with her but I was dragged out onto the floor by some junior solicitor from a firm down the road. I only knew him to see and he was probably about half my age. I struggled to break away from him but Joanie told me to give him a swing. The room swam in front of me. It brought back Galway again. Teddy-boys, winkle pickers and slicked-back hair. Limbs I hadn't used in twenty years were called into action until I collapsed in a heap on the floor. Clearly, my body was trying to tell me something. I crawled over to a seat to catch my breath.

'I see we have a new Isadora Duncan,' Fiona said. God love her, she was trying her best. Syrupy Sandra had a few tipples, unusual for her, and vowed she'd miss me 'like crazy'. Sure: now tell me the one about the three bears.

Fiona looked more miserable than ever as everyone started to let off steam. Drink did nothing for her so she was always going to be ᵉ poor girl at the feast, watching everyone get footless and ᶦng it all up. She hated it when people had fun. In the office she break it up with a snotty look but it wasn't so easy here. ᵈd-conquer strategies hadn't much effect when the people ᵛying to divide were too drunk to know you were trying to

ᵉ her disapproval of me as I stumbled around the ᵃlltalk with strangers. She would have seen it as ᶜ Maybe, but I didn't want to be high if it meant ᶠor the evening.

ᵛere such a party animal,' she said to me at

' I shot back. It just came out and I was ᵘldn't believe I called her by her first ᵘrteen years to break that taboo. ᵉing intimidated by her when it

ᶜhe said, and suddenly I felt

ᵐy arm round her, a

ᵉ weren't normal

ᵘld
ᵉ if I
, you
ᵃt the
ᵘ. And
ᵃy eyes
ᵃll the
ᵃ had souls
ᵃ to slip down
ᵃared out my
n her handbag
ᵉ called 'a small
rs on them.
ᴼ lump sum. The
ᵐekeeping but the
til my next shopping
lie Smith grabbed my
ᵒoked out at the sea of
roof of my mouth as I
prepared speech when I
at the school play where
ᵈ, I believe.' Now, as then,
ᵒld her not to
ᵉ it or not I
, and to
ᵘt was
ᵈse's
my rescue. She must have
ᵘnk is the message,' she said
ᵉre guffaws. I felt sick with
ᵒ my seat.
ᵈ at least have said thanks.'
ᵉ consoled, 'everyone is too drunk
ᵉpare a speech last night but it was
ᵉd

'What he needs is a miracle,' Sandra said. She knew it all. Of course Sandy invented sex - like all of her generation. God help her boyfriend. She always struck me as being a man-eater. .

'Where do you see yourself in five years time?' she asked Marjorie, slurring her words.

'Not in this dump anyway,' Marjorie replied. 'It's an open secret round Dublin that anyone who gets out of here goes up in the world.'

'You could hardly go down further!' Sandra said, delighted wit herself.

I found myself fantasising about a world where everyone wo talk this honestly without the dutch courage of booze. Imagin could go in to Fiona every Monday morning and say, 'Jesus look like death warmed up today. What were you up to weekend? Oh and by the way, that dress is horrific on y Nadine is a royal pain in the neck.' Imagine if we had X- and could see into people's souls. It would break throu bullshit and hypocrisy.

And then I wondered if people like Marjorie and Sandr at all. If they had, it seemed like they had holes in them

As the night neared its end, Marjorie's dress started from her shoulders, exposing her ample bosom. She name and said, 'Jesus! I almost forgot.' She rooted and to my amazement presented me with what sh going-away thingie': two little mugs with cuddly be

Finally, The Establishment announced itself.

They gave me a silvery watch and my €15,0 watch might have been a dig at my poor t money would set me up for life – or at least u spree ended.

'Speech! Speech!' everyone shouted. Le arm and dragged me up to a little podium. I faces and froze. My tongue clung to the searched for the words. Where was my needed it? It was like all those years a *all I had to say was, 'I believe, oh my G I couldn't do it.

Joanie was* the one who came to *seen me go white. 'Everybody get d through the mike and there w embarrassment and shuffled back

'Janey,' I said, 'You'd think I cou 'Don't worry about it, love,' sh to notice anyway.'

'I'm useless, useless. I did p a bit bitchy.'

'Stop putting yourself down. You're wonderful, just a bit shy. Anyone would dry up with that lot gawking up at you with their eyes out on sticks.'

'That's not the point. They set up this spread.'

'Bloody right they did. After you giving the best years of your life to line their pockets.'

I slurped another cocktail and then everyone sang 'For She's A Jolly Good Fellow' to the background of fake tears. As I sat in a corner feeling sorry for myself, Leslie, to my amazement, came over and planted a wet kiss on my lips. 'That's for refusing to bore us with bullshit about how wonderful we all are,' he said. For a joke I told him I wouldn't wash my face for a week and for one mad moment I think he took me seriously. Rita always told me he had a God complex. Why was it that the people who had least to offer in life always had the most flattering opinions of themselves, and vice versa?

After he was gone I thanked Joanie again for pulling me out of a tight spot.

'If you mention that again I'll hit you,' she said. 'One favour you can do me is to stop putting yourself down all the time. God knows, there are enough people who'll do it for you anyway.'

'It's always been a fault of mine.'

'There you are, at it again!'

'Maybe I do it to stop other people doing it.'

'It doesn't work that way. It only makes them worse. Believe me, I've been there.'

'I have this thing of wanting to be liked all the time. I feel if I criticise myself it will have this effect.'

'I don't know how you lasted so long here with that attitude.'

'Maybe it's just as well I'm going.'

I told her I was amazed Fiona left before the presentation, and without saying goodbye to anyone.

'What would you expect from a pig but a grunt?'

'You really think she's that bad?'

'To be honest with you I feel more sorry for her than anything else. As far as I can see she's seriously depressed. Depressed about her pathetic life and about the fact that some of us are having fun here. The little power she has is nothing tonight. In a pub she's just the same tuppence hapenny as the rest of us.'

Joanie used to call her 'Hitler in knickers'. Now she didn't even have her Third Reich or her Gestapo. It was our night. The peasants were taking over the palace. The rest of them had to crawl back into their forced identities in a few days but not me. I thought of the message on a poster I had once: 'Today is the first day of the rest of your life'. I'd never believed it before now.

We sank into our drinks as the lights went down. Some disco music came on and a few stragglers from the other end of the bar started to inveigle their way into our party. A friend of the barman tried to chat me up. Not very subtly. 'What would you like for breakfast?' he asked. 'Not you anyway,' I snorted back.

Joanie said she wouldn't have thrown him out of the bed for eating peanuts. 'Yuck,' chorused Sandra and Marjorie. Marjorie thought he looked like The Elephant Man. She would.

The legal brigade filtered out, tipping me on the shoulder and wishing me all good things. Their duty was done. One more casualty of the work force out on her ear, unable to take the pressure. Making way for the youth. I could already see them on Monday, shovelling all the keepsakes from my desk into the nearest wpb. Out of sight out of mind. Only as good as your last letter. All the years of typing and phone calls and faxes and eleven o'clock chats and rushes from the Dart and panic about lost files and learned-off probate speeches and angry clients and gossiping behind closed doors and promotions and demotions and elbowing for promotion and pretending you didn't care - or pretending you did - all wiped out in a few hours of drunk goodwill and mouldy cheese sandwiches.

Fifteen minutes later it was over. I was no longer an employee of Purcell, Fennelly & Co. Die cast. All that remained for me now was to live my future like I'd planned it. Easier said than done.

I took a last look round the room. Crumpled party hats, butt-filled ash-trays, boozy smells, dead, tired faces. Why hadn't I gone years ago?

I staggered out into the night, tottering on my drunken feet, and fell into the first taxi I saw. I don't remember the journey home, except for a few watery buildings whizzing by and the taxi-man saying 'Easy there, ma'am,' as he helped me out of the car. I felt about a hundred. God only knows what age I looked. If I could only buy a picture in the attic with my windfall.

I had visions of myself kneeling round the toilet bowl at 4 a.m. with my head inside it, vomiting my guts out and begging God to put me out of my misery and let me die. How many parties from my teens had ended like that? Age was supposed to bring sense. What part of the lesson had I missed?

The door kept revolving as I tried to get the key into it. When I got inside I put a wet cloth on my forehead because I thought I was going to faint, another massive phobia of mine. I collapsed on the bed in a heap, falling asleep in my clothes.

The next day I woke up feeling a million chainsaws were having a hooley inside my head. In vino headachitas. Even my hair hurt. (I thought of daddy's story about the man with the sore eyelash). I walked around the house trying to remember what I'd said and who

I'd said it to. Every few minutes brought a new 'Oh no, I couldn't have'. But I knew I did. Again and again. Thanks be to God I didn't have to face them again. I thought of Leslie's kiss and rubbed my hand frantically across the part of my face I remembered him violating. Sorry, Leslie.

Joanie rang, apologising profusely about getting in too deep about her husband.

'What husband?' I said, and she laughed.

'So it's like that, is it?'

'I wish it was. Every now and then I get a flash of the night and wish I didn't. Sometimes you're better off not knowing. When I was younger I used to get black-outs. They were easier to deal with.'

'Stop it, will you? You were the life and soul of the party.'

'That's what worries me. Anyway, one slight consolation is the fact that I don't have to face the Blessed Trinity again.'

'What do you mean?'

'Skelly, Purcell and Smith.'

'The Three Wise Men. Why? What did you say to them?'

'I don't know, and I don't think I want to either because I know it wasn't good.'

'What do you care. You can meet any of them on the street now and give them the two fingers if you like.'

She was right. They were just people now, like me. I could sit in a rubbish bin in Mountjoy Square all day if I wanted and they couldn't say boo to me. I looked at myself in the mirror and thought: I better not go outside for a month or I'd be arrested.

It was two days before Christmas and I was unemployed, almost on the street and without a Significant Other.

'Here's to the New Year,' I said to myself, raising an imaginary glass.

CHAPTER 20

The next few days passed in a blur of inertia. I sat around the house watching back-to-back soaps and waiting for the phone to ring. I kept looking at it almost willing it to ring, as if I was hypnotising it. And yet I wasn't even sure who I wanted to hear from. I'd cut myself off from one life and was waiting for another one to begin. I seemed to want it to happen almost without me being a part of it. I felt outside myself, a specimen being observed by some long-haired scientist without emotions, I was both the scientist and the case study, not even sure if I wanted a relationship with a man or not, drifting along in a kind of fog. Where was I going? What was the rest of my life going to amount to? Hardly much. I felt like a supporting actress in a bad TV movie.

To pass the time I comfort-ate, feeling disgusted with myself afterwards. Drink had the same effect. Maybe I was too immature to have given up work. I was hardly out of the place and already the honeymoon was over. Purcell, Fennelly & Co. suddenly didn't sound all that bad. It had, if nothing else, saved me from myself for a decade or so - a considerable enough achievement. But there was no going back now. I'd crossed the Rubicon without a safety helmet. Next stop The Old Folks Home.

I spent the day before Christmas Eve in town. It hadn't really registered with me that I was no longer a working woman. No doubt I wouldn't realise it until the day the office opened after Christmas, or when I got my first surly letter from the bank manager telling me my account was in the red.

I bought a large bottle of Chanel No 5 for Minnie and a fuzzy blue jumper that would suit her colouring. I picked up a shirt and tie for John just to have something. On the spur of the moment I got an overcoat for Jack and a warm tartan scarf.. The poor old devil was out in all weathers and the rag of a thing he was wearing wasn't worth a tinker's curse to him.

He was walking up and down the pathway of the park when I spotted him. It was too cold to sit down, even for him.

'How goes it?' he opened, as ever.

'Not too bad. I came to wish you a Happy Christmas and to give you a little present.'

He looked at the coat with a snotty expression.

'Try it on,' I said, it's pure Donegal tweed, great for keeping out the cold.'

'I told you before, I don't need a coat. I'm perfectly happy the way I am.'

'Take it in the spirit it's given. It's just a little gesture for old time's sake.' I hated coming across like Lady Bountiful because he was more of a friend to me than anything else.

'What are you doing here anyway?'

'I just dropped in on the off-chance you'd be here. I'm going to Galway in the morning.'

'It's well for some. Travelling on our tod, are we?'

'I'll be staying with an old school pal.'

'Nice one.'

'Look, can I do anything for you at all? Would a few bob help you to have a half-decent Christmas dinner for yourself?'

'Keep your money' he said walking away, 'but I do appreciate the kind gesture. Enjoy yourself.'

'Are you going just like that?' I called after him.

'Don't worry about me. I'm fine. By the way did you read up on Bram Stoker?'

'Who? Oh yeah, not yet but I will.'

'Pull the other one,' he shouted after me.

'Please take the coat,' I called, but he didn't show any reaction.

He looked sad and old lumbering away through the trees. I began to feel guilty going back to my warm house and the lovely prospect of Christmas in Galway.

I treated myself to a hot whiskey before going home to bed. The pub was jammed with ossified revellers. I got chatting to a bunch of girls and ended up getting merry myself. We all wished each other Happy Christmas through a haze of smoke. When I was going out I left Jack's expensive coat and the jolly tartan scarf on a bar stool. Hopefully somebody who needed it would wrap themselves up in it and have a warm Christmas.

I stumbled home to bed. The girls came with me and I invited them in. I left them in our quote unquote Beautiful Kitchen and set the alarm for eight a.m. in order to be sure of catching the train. Before going to bed I told them to feel free to guzzle anything they wanted from Nigel's cabinet.

I woke a few times in the night and heard singing coming from downstairs but when the alarm went off they had all gone. I was relieved they'd cleaned the place up. There were quite a few empty bottles in the bin but it was Christmas. Nigel could restock his expensive wines and brandy when he moved back in.

It was a cold crisp Christmas Eve. Not cold enough for snow but there was some frost on the rooftops and the footpath was slippy. I had a large suitcase and a smaller one and had booked a taxi to bring me to the train.

When I got to it it was jammers. I knew I was lucky to get a seat so I didn't leave it the whole way to Galway. All the happy people going home for Christmas. It was refreshing to me to be part of that. I'd spent so many of them in Dublin.

I got chatting to a couple from Bearna. They'd been in Dublin shopping for their children. Two boys and a girl who all still believed in Santy. It turned out they knew a man my father worked with. Jim Delaney. I found myself relating the funny story about him.

'Tell us, Daddy, tell us about Jim and the false teeth.'

'Well once Jim came back from his dinner and called in Miss McLean. 'Would you mind giving them a rinse?' says he, taking out his dentures, 'I had strawberry jam for my dinner and it's stuck in them.'

The Bearna pair enjoyed that. 'That'd be Jim all right,' the husband remarked.

Jim Delaney, He was the only person Daddy ever heard of that used to get a pain in his eyelash.

Ha ha ha. Strawberry jam and a pain in his eyelash.

By the time the train reached Galway I was feeling quite well in myself. All traces of the hangover were gone. I got my cases and made my way out of the station. The sun was shining here as in Dublin and people were being met off the train.

I knew Minnie would still be working so I had some lunch. I wandered round the shops and bought a few bits and pieces for Minnie: a warm scarf and matching gloves with fur trimming, and a gorgeous silk nightie. I picked up a pale blue dress for myself. It came to just below the knee and really flattered my figure.

I called in to the chemist where Minnie worked. It was packed to the doors with people stocking up on last minute presents. Men who probably never bought perfume before in their lives were deep in chat with the sales ladies and young girls were sniffing at after-shave for their boyfriends. Minnie was surrounded with customers but managed to give me a wave.

When she had a free moment she told me I could sit in a little room at the back of the shop. She said she'd be off in an hour's time and we could make our way home in a taxi. As she was putting on her coat old Donnelly, the chemist, gave her a kiss on the cheek. Then he presented her with what was obviously a bottle of wine in a dirty seasonal wrapper.

'Moneybags gives me the same crap every year,' she groaned when we got outside, 'a bottle of the cheapest supermarket plonk. But I suppose I should be grateful for small mercies. Come on, let's get home. I just want to sit down and put my feet up.'

She'd made a big effort with the house. There was an artificial tree in the window and she'd actually cleaned the kitchen and hung up some decorations in the sitting-room. There was a big Santa doll on the wall and tinsel and holly everywhere. You could hardly see the furniture with all the trappings.

I knew this wasn't really Minnie, that she'd put on the spread for my visit.

'You've really gone overboard on the decorating, Minnie,' I said.

'Don't be ridiculous,' she said, 'I do this every year. Anyway, it's good to have you.' I dreaded that she might have a fancy present for me. What I'd gotten her was harmless.

I left my things in her spare room and put on a cup of coffee for both of us. When we finally sat down I asked her about John.

'Don't even mention his name. I haven't seen him since Sunday last. He plans to spend Christmas in Rockbarton.'

'I hope my coming isn't behind that.'

'No way. I think it makes him feel less guilty knowing I won't be on my own. Anyway, what good would it be having him here? He never talks to me anymore and he never stops going out of the room to text sweet little nothings to his lady love.'

'That's terrible, Minnie. Have you seen her yet?'

'No, but Teresa Duggan told me she saw them dug into each other at the pictures.'

'So Teresa knows.'

'Everybody knows.'

'What does Teresa think of her?'

'Very good-looking. Very young. No surprises there.'

'Well whatever she is, she's not a patch on you.'

'Thanks love. Look, there's no need to *plamas* me. I know how serious this is. I try to get him to talk to me but all he says is that if I don't lay off he'll move out.'

We cooked the ham she'd got and sat up late eating sandwiches and drinking beer. Outside we could hear the carol singers: 'Silent Night', 'Away in a Manger', all the old favourites. Listening to them it was as if the last forty years hadn't happened. I was still that skinny little girl in O'Leary's Lane, not able to sleep with the excitement of what would be lying on my bed the next morning. Before midnight my father used to light a candle in the window. When Minnie did the same it brought back memories of all of us kneeling round it to light the baby Jesus home.

I told Minnie we always did that at home, with Daddy saying 'Go mbeirmid bheo ar an am seo aris.'

'So did we. I think all our mothers and fathers did. I've carried it on. The twins had no time for it and John was usually legless in the corner but I always light it.' Seeing the candle flickering in the window made me sad. Mammy, Daddy and Brian all gone. Angie out in the States and me with no home to go back to, spending Christmas Eve with a woman who was without her husband and her children. I didn't want to upset Minnie by breaking down. We gave each other a hug, a rare thing for us to do as we weren't part of the touchy-feely generation. Then I took out her presents.

'This is the bit I was dreading,' she said.

'Go on, open it,' I urged, 'it's just a few bits and bobs.'

When she saw the perfume she went all the colours of the rainbow.

'I thought we had an agreement about no presents,' she said.

'I wouldn't call that a present. I picked it up for a song in Eyre Square.'

'That must have been some song,' she said, 'Not 'Five Little Pennies' anyway. But I won't give out to you. What's done is done. I'm afraid all I've got for you is some cheap sweets.'

'I don't want anything from you, Minnie, I can't stress that enough.'

She sheepishly handed them to me.

'They're lovely,' I said, trying to sound as enthusiastic as I could, 'Black Magic were always my favourites.' I unwrapped them immediately and offered her one before stuffing two into my own mouth. A few minutes later we were almost half way into the first row. I pulled off the paper to get onto the ones I liked best on the second row and she started laughing.

'I used to do that as a child,' she confessed. A few moments later she went out to the kitchen, coming back with the bottle of Donnelly's wine.

'You don't get much free off that bugger,' she said, 'we might as well make the most of it. Besides, it's Christmas.' Not that we needed an excuse.

I felt drunk almost from the first drop. To hell with everything, I thought, I was just going to let the moment take me. We regaled one another with all the old yarns. It was as if boyfriends or husbands or even children were the last things on our minds. She put the radio up so high it seemed about to break the sound barrier and we sang along with Elvis and Perry Como.

'We'll be hoarse in the morning,' she said. I told her I was that way already. She began to get giggly on the wine but after a while she started to talk about John again and her eyes welled up with tears. That was my signal to put the bottles away.

'It's bedtime for little girls,' I said, taking her hand. But she resisted.

'I want to finish the bottle,' she snapped, 'Jesus, I'm entitled to some fun in this crappy universe.'

There was no talking to her so I let her fill another glass. She filled one for me too but the mood was gone off me now. It had grown quiet outside and the room was swimming before me with what I'd already had. In the corner the small tree looked a bit pathetic surrounded by all the decorations. How many wives were sadder than Minnie tonight, I wondered. How many were deserted or beaten or unloved? How many were sleeping in refuges for broken hearts? How many were widowed?

How many pretended to love men they'd stopped loving? Wine always made me think too much.

'Minnie, if you take any more you won't wake up till Stephen's Day,' I warned as she got to the dregs of the bottle.

'Who cares,' she said. Her eyes were sleepy now so I went over to her and took the drink from her hands. This time she didn't resist. I led her up the stairs and she went willingly but when we got to the landing she fell and started cursing. I brought her to her bedroom and put her under the covers without taking her clothes off. I knew she'd be asleep in a matter of minutes.

'Happy Christmas Jim Bob,' I called to her before turning off the light.

'Happy Christmas Mary Ellen,' she called back faintly. And then I heard her snoring.

CHAPTER 21

The next thing I remember was the Christmas dawn creeping in through the windows. I got up early so I wouldn't disturb Minnie.

I decided to go for a long walk. Something guided me in the direction of Palmyra Park where I was born. . In my mind it was Christmas morning over forty years ago and my mother had just delivered me into the world. She told me when I was a little girl that I was the most delightful Christmas present she ever got. It was bitterly cold and there was snow on the ground until late January. It must have been hard with no central heating, just open fires and fuel if you were lucky enough to be able to afford it.

It started to rain after a while so I sheltered in the Jesuit Church. Until I was fifteen I would have been here with all the family for Christmas Mass, then home to the excitement of Santy's presents. 'Mammy,' we used to say, for weeks before Christmas 'when are you putting up the decs?' Then the excitement of coloured paper chains and a real tree. There would always be a special birthday cake for me from Mrs O'Leary with 'Happy Christmas Birthday' written on it. There were treats for all of us but I had my own special cake every Christmas.

I watched two little girls in the church with ringlets in their hair, just like me and Angie. Here I was alone, envying them. But no, I wasn't really alone. I had Minnie waiting for me. For her sake I was going to make it a good time.

I walked past the Columban Hall and remembered Brian taking part in a school drama. He played a mouse. For years I used to dress up in his mouse costume. Mammy had sewn it for him with long ears and a thin tail. Where was it now? Probably ended up in some dump in Artane. Myself and Angie danced in that hall in our Irish costumes. Once I won a medal for second place in the Slip Jig competition. I still had that medal somewhere. Before I left Fairview I decided I'd gather all my stuff and not leave it for Nigel.

The house was quiet when I got back. Minnie was still in bed. She'd got a small turkey. I put it in the oven, got the potatoes ready and turned on the telly. *The Sound of Music* was on. Julie Andrews trilling away in the Swiss Alps with all the children in tow and not a bother on them about the war.

Two hours later and still no sign of Minnie. The turkey was small and would be ready in an hour's time. I went to call her.

She was lying staring at the ceiling. She'd obviously been crying but I pretended not to notice.

'I have the dinner on. Maybe if you had a shower you'd have an appetite. If you stay in bed you won't feel like eating.'

'I'll be down soon,' she whispered.

She didn't surface for another three hours. I kept the dinner hot and sipped a few glasses of wine. She finally came down in her dressing-gown.

'Can't you eat something, Minnie? You'll be sick if you just keep on drinking.'

'I'm sorry but I wouldn't be able to keep anything down the way I'm feeling.' I knew what she meant. How was it that everything seemed so much worse at this time of the year? All the lonely people dreaming of Christmases past.

She drank the best part of another bottle of wine and then fell asleep on the sofa. I had a few glasses myself too. We must have made a sorry pair on that Christmas Day. The phone rang once but Minnie said to leave it. We were both in our beds by nine o'clock - a bit different from the days in St Mary's Avenue when all the neighbours would come in. None of us would be tucked up in dreamland before two in the morning.

I cleaned the place up on Stephen's Day. To my surprise, Minnie was down and dressed before twelve. She apologised for ruining my Christmas but I told her she didn't ruin it, she made it.

'We've hardly talked at all,' she said.

'We don't need to talk. We know each other too well for that.'

'You're right. We're like two old crocks. The blind leading the blind.'

'Speak for yourself!'

We had our Christmas dinner a day late but it was doubly sweet for that. In the evening we lit the tree and watched some more television. There were back-to-back Disney films for the children followed by lots of people in woolly jumpers singing with great gusto. All that was missing was Daniel O'Donnell..

The twins phoned and said they'd been ringing the day before. Minnie made some excuse that herself and John had been with the neighbours. 'God love them,' she said after she came off the phone, 'they were worrying about me yesterday.'

'Have you still told them nothing?'

'I keep thinking if I don't that things will come right.'

We had a visitor after tea. When I opened the door I recognised Teresa Duggan immediately. She still had the gingery hair and the mean little mouth. We pretended to be pleased to see each other.

She said she'd come to cheer Minnie up. She plonked herself on the best seat beside the fire and started to rattle on like a clock. She hadn't changed much. Minnie offered her a drink and she said she'd just have a small drop of whiskey. I knew what her small drop meant. She'd be here for the night.

'How are you coping?' she asked Minnie when she was well oiled, finally emptied of her own dull news.

'Bearing up, I suppose. Yesterday was a nightmare but I'm managing. It's great the two of us being together.'

'Weren't you great to come all the way from Dublin,' she said to me, 'Are you married now or what?'

'No,' I replied in a dead voice, 'but I'm having a wild affair with a guy fifteen years younger than me.' Might as well be hanged for a sheep as a lamb.

'Is that so? Fair play to you. You always were a great one for the men.'

'And yourself?' I asked, knowing full well that her husband had left her years ago.

'Oh, I've given all that up. I enjoy my own company. I can come and go when I like.' Minnie was too hungover to drink but myself and Teresa fairly lashed into it. She really made me angry because every so often she'd say to Minnie, 'God love you, it's a terrible blow.'

'She'll be fine,' I rasped after the fifth time.

'Of course she will. I don't want to upset you, Minnie, but would you mind terribly if I went to John's girl for my hair? I don't want to but there's no choice down here'. I couldn't believe what I was hearing.

'I don't think she could do much with that ginger mop,' I put in, and her face went all the colours of the rainbow.

'I beg your pardon?' She was aghast.

'I said your ginger mop is behind repair.'

She blinked twice as if she couldn't properly take in the words. I could see her little face starting to twitch.

'Well at least I don't dye it like you do.'

'It's a pity you wouldn't. It's a sight on you.'

'Look, I came here for Minnie's sake. We've been friends for years. While you were gallivanting up in Dublin, who do you think kept Minnie going?'

'Oh, will ye stop fighting,' Minnie interrupted, 'for the season that's in it.'

'Sorry, Minnie love,' Teresa said, 'but that one is too rude for words. I could tell you something about the same lady and it might put a stop to her gallop.'

'Tell it away,' I invited.

'No, I gave a promise to you years ago and I don't break my promises.'

'Go on, I'm letting you break it. Spit it out.'

'Well all right. I heard you missing your Confirmation question so I did. Remember that day when the bishop was examining us at the altar? I was next to you and I heard you missing. Remember going home you gave me half a crown and I swore I wouldn't tell anybody? Well I didn't.'

'So what? It doesn't bother me if you put it on the internet.' The way she said it, it was as if I murdered children or something.

'Oh indeed, you weren't always so airy-fairy. I kept that secret for years.'

'Thanks. I'm eternally grateful.'

She sat on for another half an hour and every chance she got she brought up the Rockbarton one's name.

You could see she was getting some kind of sick kick out of it. When I couldn't take any more I said 'All right, so I missed my Confirmation question. Well at least I didn't blame somebody else for something I did in third class.'

She sat down again, her face even redder than her hair.

'What do you mean by that insinuation?'

'Oh for God's sake will you both shut up with your insinuations, far from them you were reared,' groaned Minnie.

'It's no insinuation. I saw you doing your wee-wee on the floor. You didn't open your mean little beak while Sarah Gavin was being blamed for it.'

'I did no such a thing. I never in my life wet the floor. Minnie, do you hear what's being said of me?'

'Will the two of you shut up, for God's sake. Two women over forty years of age fighting over wee-wees and Confirmation. I need to go to bed, I can't take any more of this.'

'Teresa,' I said, 'maybe it's better you go.'

'How dare you throw me out of Minnie's house! Minnie, would you prefer I leave?'

'Well maybe it would be a good idea. I'm just worn out. Thanks for calling. I really do appreciate it. I'll give you a ring tomorrow.'

Teresa stormed out, muttering about wee-wees and the downright nerve of some people. I hoped I'd softened her cough for her.

'Good riddance,' I whispered as her footsteps dwindled into the distance.

'Ah she's not the worst,' said Minnie, 'She means well.'

'I don't agree. She wants you to be like herself, hardened and alone, but you'll never be that way. I made that up about the wee-wee, by the way. It was Sarah Gavin. I just did it to get at the bitch.'

'That was cruel of you. She'll be demented over that.'

'Let her. Sit down and have one drink before you go to bed.'

'No I couldn't. Put out the lights now, will you.'

'Of course.'

'Goodnight, and thanks again for the lovely presents.'

'They were nothing.'

I heard her crying in the night and didn't know whether to go in and try to comfort her. In the end I decided she'd rather be left alone. Was my situation much better? I had no man, no home to go to and no job either. Ah well, we never died a winter yet.

The drink must have knocked me out because I didn't wake until 1 p.m. the next day. Minnie was gone to work and I knew she wouldn't be home until evening. I cleaned up the place, went out and got some steak and two more bottles of wine. I lit the fire when I got back and was sitting down eating some chocolates when I heard the key in the door.

'Minnie, that's great. They let you off early.'

'It's not Minnie, it's me,' said a voice. Bold as you like, in walked John.

'Minnie is at work,' I said coldly to him, 'Would you like something to eat?'

'No, I just need to get some clothes.'

He marched upstairs and I heard him clattering around in the bedroom and then in the bathroom. He had a large suitcase with him. He took so long he must have filled it. He came down the stairs as if he was running for a train.

'Where's the fire?' I asked.

'Sorry I have to rush. Will you tell Minnie I'll be in touch?'

'Why not have a drink?' I thought that if I managed to engage him in conversation I could knock some sense into him.

'Right so. Put us on a cup of coffee, will you?'

He was never a man for please or thank you. I remembered how ignorant he was with Minnie. She'd spoiled him rotten and now he was walking out on her. For her sake I tried to be as friendly as I could.

He was wearing a denim jacket with matching trousers and the hair was styled in the out-of-bed look. His delightful lady friend had probably done it for him. It almost made me vomit to think of him romping with that slut.

'Did you enjoy the Christmas?' he asked casually as he sipped his coffee.

'Hardly one to enjoy with the state of poor Minnie.'

'Hello, did I ask about the state of Minnie?'

'Hello yourself. What are you doing to that poor girl? She's worth ten of you.'

'Is that right now?'

'Look John, I know we don't get on but Minnie is shattered. Why are you doing this? Is it the male menopause or something?'

'I've met somebody I love. I didn't plan it. Shit happens. You only get one chance at life and this is mine.'

'I heard she's years younger than you. You and Minnie had a lifetime together. Think of the twins, what will it do to them.'

'The twins are grown young women. They'll cope. Anyway, I have to go now. I have an appointment.'

'With your hussy of a girlfriend, I suppose.'

'I don't have to listen to this crap! No wonder you can't hold onto a man with a tongue like that.'

A moment later I heard Minnie's key in the lock. When she came in her face was ashen.

'You're home,' she whispered to John, her face lighting up in hope.

'Hello, Minnie. No, not really. I've come to collect some of my stuff. I didn't intend to be this long. I'm late already. Look, I know it's bad of me to rush off but.' He stood up awkwardly.

'You can't go just after me coming in, John. Please. Have a cup of tea at least.'

'I'd love to but I can't.'

'It's me you're talking to, John. Jesus, a cup of tea wouldn't kill you. There are some things I want to say.'

'I'll go out,' I said.

'No,' said John. 'Look, Minnie, this isn't the time or the place. I'll ring you. That's a promise. It's better this way. Both of us know that.'

She put her head in her hands as he went towards the door. He stopped for a moment after opening it but she didn't look up. Then it clicked shut.

Minnie just sat there sobbing. I wanted to go over to her but I felt too awkward. She didn't move for a long time.

'Your voices were raised,' she said finally, 'what were ye talking about?'

'Not much. One word borrowed another. He wasn't here long.'

She dried her tears.

'I know you mean well but would you please keep out of it?' I assured her I would.

The next day was December 28. I made my mind up that I'd go back to Dublin. I'd hoped to stay to see in the New Year but Minnie needed to be left alone. Before I got the train I left her a note. I advised her to keep on not minding and that things would work themselves out. I added that if she told the twins I was sure they'd be a great support for her.

The journey to Dublin seemed endless. The train was practically empty because most people were off until the New Year. A pang of loneliness came over me as I thought of what I was going back to. Christmas had kept me going in a way but now the changes in my life seemed huge. I'd taken so much for granted. I felt like I'd been standing on a Chinese mat surrounded by colours and designs and now somebody had given it one large hoosh and I was spinning through the air.

I got a taxi easily. It was just after three in the afternoon when I arrived at the house. It was freezing when I opened the door but then I remembered I'd turned the heating off. There were no Christmas decorations, just a cold bare soulless house. Even the kitchen looked clinical. There was no food in the fridge but I could hardly have eaten anything anyway.

I found a one bar-electric fire upstairs and plugged it in. It would be a few hours before the place heated up. I had two more weeks here and then Nigel would throw me out. I supposed I should start chasing up apartments to rent but there probably wouldn't be much in the papers until after the holidays. Maybe I'd leave off looking until early January.

It was too cold to go out walking. I wondered was Jack out in this weather in the bit of a coat he had. If he was, he was crazy. I looked in the drinks cabinet but it was bare. Then I remembered the girls from the night before Christmas Eve. They'd fairly lashed into the booze. I made a note to refill it before Nigel took over. He counted every bottle he had and would make a big to-do if anything was missing.

I tried to concentrate on television but all the Christmassy programmes were still dragging on, making the whole festive spirit like a bad joke to me. I phoned Angie for a chat but there was no reply and I didn't bother leaving a message. I went to bed early but couldn't sleep. I spent the night making plans for my new home. Maybe a new job would come too, or maybe even a new man.

. I woke early and decided to go out. Moving around was my only option. Otherwise I'd work myself up and end up parading down to the doctor.

Some shops were open and a few stragglers headed for work but most people were still in their beds, full to the neck of turkey and plum pudding. I thought of cross children and toys scattered on floors. Toys that just a few short days ago had been hidden in dark wardrobes and for one short day had given a little pleasure.

What was Christmas all about anyway? One-parent families up to their necks with moneylenders. Young girls worrying about drunken moments they'd spent with Mark from Accounts at the office party. Lonely old men and women being thrown out of hostels until the day got dark and then wandering the streets, huddling up in doorways to get in out of the rain. Happy Christmas people.

I did some shopping to tide me over the next few days. I gave Alice a call but she was entertaining her sister and the family. 'Come over if you like,' she said, 'you're more than welcome'. But I didn't want to interfere. In an empty house in Fairview a spinster woman of 45 sat down to eat alone in the season of goodwill, 2002.

The dark days at the end of the year dragged on and I found myself missing Nigel. Good old Jekyll & Hyde me. I had to admit we'd had some good times together. I thought about phoning him but I knew there wasn't much point.

Instead it was him who phoned me early on New Year's Eve.

'Hi, just checking if you were there.'

'I'm only back from Galway. I had a good Christmas. How about yourself?'

'So-so. Do you realise I'll be moving back in next week?' He was right to the point as usual.

'Don't worry, I'll be out of here by then.'

'I don't want to sound cold but I need the house from that date.'

'I know,' I said, 'you told me.' And then I hung up. Not like me to be so assertive. Maybe it was a start. Beware, feminist on the loose.

I spent all of New Year's Eve on my own. Minnie phoned to wish me a happy one. She hadn't seen John since Stephens Day.

'I just want it to be an ordinary day. It's finally beginning to sink in that he isn't coming back.'

'None of us knows what the future holds,' I said, 'Take care of yourself. Happy New Year, old friend.'

'And to you.' Then she added with a giggle, 'Teresa Duggan sends you her love as well.'

'I'm sure she does. Give her a kiss for me.'

'She's still going on about not wee-weeing on the floor. You've driven her crazy with that comment.'

'She was crazy anyway.'

I was in bed by ten. I heard bells ringing and bangers going off at midnight but covered my head and didn't let myself think about anything. It was the end of the old year and, hopefully, the end of the old me as well.

CHAPTER 22

I looked at a lot of apartments before I settled on a one-bedroomed one on the Howth Road. It was convenient to town, just down the road from where I'd spent the last seven years, and also near my old home in Artane. The rent was expensive, €1,200 a month, but I was still comfortable in the bank and decided to go for it.

I was to move in the following day so phoned Nigel to ask if I could stay an extra night.

'That's not convenient at all,' he snapped, 'can't you stay with one of your friends?'

'What's one extra night? I can't move in to the new place till tomorrow. I'll have all my stuff ready to roll and then I'll be out of your life for good. Is that too much to ask?'

'All I'm saying is that it's putting me out. Is there no way you can arrange things a day earlier? I gave you plenty of notice.'

'Jesus, one lousy night and you're acting like I'm asking you for the Crown Jewels.'

'All right, all right. I'll need the main bedroom, though. Hopefully you can use the other one.'

'That won't be a problem.'

I had all my bits and pieces in plastic bags the day before I was due to leave. Not many possessions really. Some CDs and photographs, a few birthday cards from Daire tied up with a blue ribbon, tattered old pages of type wrapped inside a green folder. My famous attempt at a novel was there as well, the pages all mildewed and dog-eared now Maybe I'd give it another go sometime.. A matchbox with a small stone covered up in cotton wool. Daire had given it to me years ago. We were sitting on a bench down by the canal. He'd pretended to be Richard Basehart from *La Strada*. There was a scene in that film where the Richard Baseheart character tells Gelsomina about a stone he carried round with him. He used to look at it every time he had a problem. It was like a comfort blanket to him. In time it became my one too.

I bought some fillets of steak, one of Nigel's favourite dishes. I made an apple tart as well, using my mother's recipe, and even bought two candles. A bottle of red wine and a new tablecloth rounded off the picture. A crazy part of me had a little hope that maybe if we got together tonight we could patch things up. Who knew? What was there once could return. If he was willing to try again things could be different. More time together, more closeness.

Everything was ready when I heard his key but he seemed to have somebody with him. Was he afraid to face me alone out of some unusual guilt? Had he brought Charlie and his wife?

when they started on about their workloads in the coffee-room. I tried to hide my disinterest but it wasn't easy. Marjorie thought I was getting above myself but it wasn't that. It was almost like I wasn't there, as if I was having an out-of-body experience. I couldn't connect with anyone. For the first time in my life I actually wanted to get more work to stop myself looking at the clock.

I only lasted a day. By 5.30 I made up an elaborate excuse about something sudden having come up.

Marjorie knew I was lying but I didn't much care. I took the money and ran. At the door Fiona told me not to become a stranger. Some hope.

If I couldn't be a member of the workforce with any success anymore, I decided to throw myself into the world of leisure with something approaching passion. Let them eat cake. That was me: born to shop.

I felt I needed an image overhaul. Most of my clothes were of the secretarial type and this had to change. I togged myself out with trousers, casual blouses and warm cheerful jumpers. My office suits lay collapsed in a little lump in one of the plastic bags I'd shoved behind a door. I pictured them moaning and groaning and telling each other, 'The cheek of your woman. The day will come when she'll be glad to squeeze her out-of-shape tummy into us.' For so long they'd been cock of the walk, presenting themselves for duty day in day out. Now all they could do was huddle up and think of better days. I felt I never wanted to see them again.

The clock was another irrelevance. Once the most important item in my bedroom but now I didn't even bother plugging it in. How treasured, once, were those seven minutes between when the alarm went off and I pressed the Snooze button for a stay of execution before I rose. Now morning and afternoon were almost interchangeable, my day beginning simply when I wanted it to.

I often walked past the old house in Artane. Again I thought of my confidante Jane Eyre:

'Now I can recall the picture of the grey old house of God rising calm before me, of a rook wheeling round the steeple, of a ruddy morning sky beyond.'

There were children playing in the garden one evening and I imagined a whole new family growing up there. 'I hope you're being kind to your granny,' I said to them and they gave me a strange look.

It was good to be able to walk up and down streets I'd known as a school-goer and a secretary. I didn't need to hurry my footsteps now for fear of what a boss or nun would say to me if I was late. I could saunter along and say 'Stuff your job and stuff your Deeds of Conveyance, I'm a free woman now.'

In the mornings I'd loll in my bed listening to the radio. I got a perverse delight every time the Dart was delayed or the traffic clogged up for two hours in Fairview. I imagined Fiona stuck on the Merrion Road drumming her little painted nails on the dashboard in temper, brimming over with road rage, downtown- Fairview-style. I pictured rows of secretaries with plump little tummies caged inside pinstriped business suits scuttling down the steps of Pearse Station or wobbling through the cobblestones of Trinity on their spindly-heeled shoes. They'd curse as they checked their watches, scared out of their wits that some horrible boss on the prowl for latecomers.

When I rose out of the bed I'd make a cup of tea for myself; the performing seal that had been me seemed a million miles away. I thought back to all my office years, so recently ended and yet so irrelevant to me now. I'd been there so many years, and yet knew I'd feel decidedly ill at ease now if I was to even inhabit the place for a moment in my old chair.

I pictured myself going back to the office in disguise. I decided in a mad part of myself that sometime in the future I'd present myself as a client and make an appointment to see Fiona. My disguise would be so good she wouldn't recognise me. I'd tell her I wanted to sell a mansion down the country and that I also wished to purchase a place on the Vico Road right next to Bono's house. The bitch would spend hours labouring on my case because she'd know I was loaded. She'd have my replacement bring me coffee and chocolate biscuits and when everything was prepared I'd remove my disguise and say, 'Fiona, you make me sick'. On the way out of the premises I'd give your woman Marjorie a punch into the nose and her posh accent would get lost in the shock.

By the middle of February I could feel spring in the air. Crocuses were popping up in the park and I saw some early daffodils in a garden at the end of the road. February brought back memories of Lent and going to Mass in Artane Church every morning. Going off sweets until Patrick's Day. A brief time long ago when I thought I'd join the nuns. I'd seen myself in darkest Africa taking care of all the little lack babies. Some nun I'd have made.

'Excuse me, Reverend Mother, I need to get into town to buy a moisturiser and a blue mascara to match my eyes.'

I continued to give myself treats in the clothes department. If I liked a blouse or a pair of trousers I'd buy three sets of them. I saw a gorgeous blue jacket made in Denmark. I got two of them to have one on hand while the other was being washed. I stocked up on CDs and always had a bottle of the most expensive red wine in the house. Sometimes I thought I should check the balance in the bank but that was never my style. Easy come easy go.

Would I ever change? Hardly at this stage. I kept telling myself next year I'd draw in my horns in the buying department but if push came to shove I doubt I had the interest to carry it out. My key-ring even said 'Born to Shop' and it seemed to sum me up, through fair weather and foul.

When I was on my best behaviour I'd give myself these pep talks about no more clothes, no more looking into shop windows, no more fantasising. It was very easy late at night when you were tucked up in bed far from the malls but when you found yourself in them, and gazing at this gorgeous designer job in Powerscourt Centre or Wicklow Street or the Kilkenny Design, the best laid plans of mice and men – and women - went by the board.

I knew I was a hopeless case. If I continued the way I was going it wouldn't be long before a big duck egg would represent my credit balance. What a pity there wasn't some organisation that could help me. Was there such a thing as Shopaholics Anonymous? I could ring it when the temptation got too much. 'Excuse me, I need help. I'm sitting in a cold sweat with my cash card in my hand looking at a dress that I'd die to wear but I can't afford it. What should I do?' 'Now listen to me, anonymous shopper,' a stern voice on the other end of the line would say, 'Do you realise there are people starving in Iran and Iraq? Or on your own doorstep? Think of the less well-off. And think of your wardrobe. Isn't there enough in it?' Answer: Yes, yes, a million times yes. In fact if I try to squeeze another garment into it the wood will have to expand to accommodate it.

But I'd still succumb to temptation. As soon as the sun rose the next day and I'd be down there large as life, first in the queue and my mouth full of saliva with the excitement. Heart going da-dum, da-dum dadum as I got inside the door. Surely no alcoholic could experience the same glee in front of a frothy pint?

It was short-lived, though, like all elation. I'd put on the dress, get fed up of it within the hour, and then tear it off me and curse my impetuosity. A kindly traveller would call to the door and more out of rage at myself than Christian charity I'd give it to her. She'd look at me as if I'd just given her the keys to heaven and I'd just shrug. Maybe she'd be doing me a favour. More wardrobe space and the next week, or even day, I'd be on the rampage again. Or a copy of 'Family Album' would land with a clunk on the floor after coming through the letterbox and I'd gobble it up. Just when I thought I was cured.

I might even find myself writing letters to the non-existent Shopaholics Anonymous. 'Dear SA, I'm your worst patient. Worse than the worst. Incurable, in fact. I buy things I don't even need. I must be like those dipsomaniacs who guzzle liquor when it makes them sick.' Could you throw up an item of clothing? You could certainly throw it off you.

On a good day I'd be able to say 'I've been clean for three days now, three days and twelve hours and fifteen minutes, but I'm still in that cold sweat.' And the good people from the organisation would write back to me and say, 'Hang in there, worst patient, one day at a time is our motto, just keep wearing the old stuff, the clothes you don't like as much as that fool's gold in the windows where the models make it look so gorgeous but you know in your heart as soon as you put it on your less than ideal body it won't be quite the same.' Hmm. Maybe they mightn't be allowed be quite as blunt as that but I'd take the point.

Surely I wasn't such an idiot that I didn't realise any garment would be there next week. It wasn't like a rare book or a painting by Caravaggio. Of course all logic went out the window when you had Shoparexia Nervosa. You simply didn't think in those terms. It was as if clothes were the meaning of life, the only road to happiness. it. Maybe when I was bankrupt I'd end up like Winona Ryder, cruising department stores with scissors to cut off the price tags. Fennelly & Co could represent me in court.

'Your honour, this lady has been a character of exemplary virtue for thirty years before this, er, momentary lapse'. No. Simply wouldn't work. I couldn't pay the fees Winona did. I'd end up in the Joy surrounded by my wondrous robes. Or else I'd be in striped pyjamas breaking stones. That'd put manners on me all right. From feast to famine.

Don't be too hard on yourself, I'd say to myself. Start next year on a new slate. Or would I? Maybe it was like the diets: always in the future tense. As everyone knew, the verb 'To diet' could only be conjugated in the future. 'I will diet, you will diet, he will diet, she will diet'. And the same went for stopping shopping. 'I will stop, you will stop, he will stop, she will stop.' Meaning they wouldn't. The shallow comfort of time.

It was all so absurd when you considered the real problems people had, like sickness or bereavement or even redundancy. And here was me feeling the world would fall down around my feet if I didn't use my Swipe card to get my greedy hands on the latest creation. And then just as quickly trash it. Women -the logical species.

Instead of ringing any organisation, fictitious or otherwise, I decided what I really needed was to get my mind off myself. The clothes thing was just a symptom of something else, probably self-loathing. So the whizz kid psychologists said, at any rate. Or maybe they were covering over a deeper need. Maybe I simply wanted to be a part of a couple. If this was true, could I admit it to myself? Should I have been in Dateline Anonymous instead?

hanging out of her mouth. I confined her to the garden for her smoking but she'd disobey me and puff in the house if I nipped out to the shops.'

'I suppose it's hard to give up the smokes when you're addicted,' I offered.

I felt sorry for the poor creature of a wife, the life she must have had with this tulip.

'Life is hard, my dear, but that doesn't mean one shouldn't try.'

'Do you mind if I use your toilet?' I asked. I was at screaming point now with the wine churning in my stomach.

'Be my guest. It's at the top of the stairs. Give me a shout if you get into trouble.'

Peach toilet, peach toilet paper, peach tiles, peach towels, peach bath. Maybe his poo was peach too. When I came out of the loo he was standing there like a sentry.

'Your toilet is only gorgeous,' I mumbled.

'Thank you, my dear, I clean the whole place three times weekly, and on the other four days give a quick flick round the place.'

'Well,' I said, 'it's getting late, I should be going home. There's no need for you to drive. I'll get a taxi.'

'Don't fret yourself, my dear. Before you go I'd like you to see this.'

For a small skinny bit of a fellow, not in the first flush of youth, he was stronger than I thought. Without warning he shoved me into a bedroom. Peach everywhere; duvet, carpet, even the wardrobe. And a peach lamp next to the bed.

Lovely, but I must be off now.'

He grabbed me by the knees and before I knew where I was I was stretched out on his bed. He yanked off his trousers and I could see a little pair of peach underpants from out of which stuck his two little sticks of legs. He pulled at my jacket and tore at my skirt. Off rolled my elastic panelled panties. He was all over me like a man possessed. My legs were flaying about and I gave him one hard kick into you-know-where. He let a roar out of him and I grabbed my jacket and pounded down the stairs. My skirt and panties I left on the bed. I could hear him screaming 'You bitch!' after me.

Outside it was raining. I legged it down the street, terrified he'd follow me. I hadn't a clue where I was but it was somewhere in the suburbs. The jacket barely covered my bum. Thankfully I'd grabbed my handbag as I ran down the hall and out onto the street. I finally came to a taxi-rank and luckily there was one available.

'The Howth Road,' I panted.

'You're a long way from home,' said the taxi-driver.

I sat hunched in the back seat looking out at the rain. The taxi-driver coughed through the static, checking in with his boss. He tried to engage me in conversation about some strike that was coming up as we stopped at an intersection but I just sat there watching the lights change from red to green. As we passed Fairview Park I was tempted to ask him to let me out so as I could cry on Jack's shoulder.

We got to the apartment and I signalled the driver to let me out. I was so relieved I gave him a huge tip.

'This is far too much,' he said.

'No,' I told him, 'it's not half enough.'

He's probably still looking at me.

CHAPTER 25

The experience with Box 101 made me cop onto myself. I knew things could have ended badly for me if I hadn't been able to hit him where it hurt. Having had as much drink consumed as I had was crazy at my age and to go voluntarily into a stranger's house was certifiable. I didn't even know where he lived but it must have been quite a distance judging by the length of time it took to get home in the taxi. I decided to make a serious effort to cut down on the drink and to stop looking up the personal columns.

March and April were sunny months, unusual for so early in the year. I took long walks on Dollymount Strand and met Alice now and again for lunch. There was a routine in my lack of routine, so different from all the years of slavery behind a mouse.

One morning I set the alarm and jumped out of bed as soon as it pinged at 7.30. I dressed myself with care and raced down to the Dart. It was just as crowded as it had always been and Flying Elbows Man got me right in the eye. Somehow it didn't bother me as much as the 75 people on their mobiles, texting each other to beat the band, their fingers going a mile a minute. Did nobody talk to each other anymore? It was just faceless people on the other end of a text: 'Hi. I'm stuck at Harmo. Signal failure.' Their faces all looked dead. Nobody talked with their mouths anymore, just their fingers. I imagined two people on the same seat texting one another instead of talking. 'Hi. Weather awful, isn't it?' 'Yeah but at least dry.' A mortal sin would be a sentence of more than five words.

At Pearse Station I got myself two Crunchies from the sweet machine and sat on a bench watching all the crazed ants racing by. Set expressions on their worried little pusses as they thought about symbols and binders and contracts and mergers. Sit on, dearie, I told myself, what's your rush.

The red-haired man was still behind the counter of the corner shop.

'I'm in no hurry,' I told him, 'serve that gentleman first.'

The gentleman in question almost knocked me as he demanded his paper and Granny Smith apple.

'I see you're keeping to a healthy diet,' I said

'Excuse me?'

'I said good on you with the healthy diet. And how are you this Monday morning, Mr Skelly?

'Oh, hello it's you. It's late, you know. Well after twenty past.'

'So what?'

'I beg your pardon?'

'I said so what.'

Suddenly it dawned on him. He muttered something and disappeared like a bat out of hell.

'And have a nice day yourself,' I shouted after him.

'We haven't seen you in a while,' said the red-haired fellow, 'Have you changed jobs?'

'I've given up completely. Now could I have a brown scone and two butters?'

'On the house,' he chirped.

I sat on the steps of the office munching my scone and enjoying the scenery. I pictured all the trusty secretaries inside in their cubbyholes doing their binding, answering phones, photocopying and frantically banging keys like there was no tomorrow. Food never tasted so good. I sauntered round Stephen's Green until lunch time and then dropped into Bewleys for a bowl of soup. I meandered home and treated myself to a large bag of chips and slept like a baby that night.

The next morning I had a long letter from Minnie. John had moved out for good and was living in Rockbarton now. The twins had come home for a week and were upset but they were young and had their own lives to lead. They were now back in Australia. Some selfish bitches, I thought. They were gorgeous little children. I'd been like an auntie to them until they reached their teens. Gracie was my godchild but I'd spoiled both of them. The way I distinguished them was to tell myself Gracie was graceful. (Greta was a bit clumsy, like me). The last time I'd seen them was for their 16th birthday. They'd suddenly changed into a right pair of stuck-up madams and barely acknowledged my existence. Minnie had been such a good mother to them, often leaving herself short so they could be dressed in designer gear. There was nothing more hurtful than a thankless child. It was sharper than a serpent's tooth. I think Shakespeare said that. Anyway good riddance to both of them. (I said that).

Minnie said she missed John every day and still had a hope that maybe he'd come back to her in time. She finished by announcing that she was still in touch with Clem from America. He was a lovely man, she said, and they'd been on the phone to each other a few times. It was a relief to me that she still had an interest in making contact with another male of the species. He'd be much too old for her, of course, but it was encouraging that she was still keeping in touch, whatever came of it.

Easter arrived with a lot of fanfare but now that I was free from work it didn't make much difference to me. I was on a permanent holiday. I thought of happy days when this time of year meant getting into ankle socks and O'Learys home-made ice-cream on sale. On Easter Saturday night, for old time's sake, I went to midnight Mass in the local church in Artane.

It was a beautiful night and you could see the stars. Not what you'd expect from an Artane sky, which was normally covered by a thick grey smog. The bright stars reminded me of coming from a Ceili in Inis Mor with Daire. We'd danced all night. The Siege of Ennis, Haymaker's Jig, Clare Set. Afterwards we walked along by the shore, his arm around me.

I remembered the far-off days when Lent was Lent and you didn't dare disobey its dictates. All of us would parade over to Mass on this night and then home to Mammy's big fry-up at two a.m. We'd all have a lie-in the next day. Easter eggs for Angie, Brian and myself was the highlight.

I went home to the apartment. Too tired to make anything to eat, I climbed into my lonely bed. I was still wide awake by dawn but didn't see the sun dancing the way Angie and myself had one magical Easter morning in Galway.

After the holidays I contacted Alice and she invited me over for a meal. She cooked a lovely dinner and made an apple tart for me to bring home.

'Any luck with a job?' she asked after we'd eaten.

'Not really. Then again I haven't been looking.'

'You should, you know. Your money will run out. Besides, it's bad for you to be doing nothing.'

'What about yourself? You retired, didn't you, and you seem comfortable enough. Honestly, Alice, I don't think I could face another job. Not just yet anyway.'

'I'm older than you, remember, and I've a good pension. Why not join a walking group or something? You seem to be very in on yourself. I've given up ringing you. I was amazed you actually contacted me. It's bad to be so much alone.'

'Maybe sometime but not now.'

We discussed holidays and she told me her sister in London would be glad to put the two of us up anytime. She was unmarried as well and out all day. Her flat was very central.

'That sounds interesting. Are you sure she wouldn't mind both of us coming?'

'Not at all. So why not make arrangements?'

'Yes, maybe sometime soon.'

'No, not sometime soon. Let's plan it now. No time like the present. Two weeks time and I won't take no for an answer.'

'Oh Alice, I don't know.'

She kept hounding me and finally we settled on the first week in May.

That night lying in bed I began to think about what she said. Had I really got in on myself? The one trip I'd taken in weeks was my wonderful experience with peachy Gerry Greene. Maybe that had a bigger effect than I realised.

London would be buzzing in early May. If Alice's sister was anything like herself she'd be welcoming.

Anyway, what had I to lose? I could buy some clothes over there and maybe even go to a club with the pair of them. Who knows, I might meet a Reginald or a Walter and settle down over there.

Planning for the trip gave me a lift. Even if I didn't pick up some nice clothes over there, what was to stop me having a look round town first? I couldn't go to London looking shabby. Summer was coming and I needed to update my wardrobe.

My hair had gone very straggly as well so I booked myself into one of the best salons in town. While I was there I got a facial and my nails done. Waltzing round town on a Tuesday afternoon planning my trip was just the tonic I needed.

I also went shopping for other things. I got a new Leonard Cohen CD to remind me of the Daire days. You could have your Westlifes and your Britney Spears. Nothing could substitute for the old favourites. In some ways he gave me as big a buzz as Beethoven. It was hypnotic listening to those soulful melodies at the dead of night. You felt he was in the room with you, sharing your loneliness. Or a flake of your life…

While I was wandering round the video department I spotted the old version of *Jane Eyre* and bought it as well. For a treat I got a bottle of wine and phoned for a pizza. I wallowed all night in Rochester and Pilot and Grace Poole and Blanche Ingram. The bleakness of the moors and the coldness of Lowood Institution. The grandeur of Thornfield Hall and Jane so meek and small and full of raw passion and heartbreak. No modern-coloured version could ever capture it the way Orson Welles did. I fell asleep in the chair after watching it, drunk on my indulgence.

Alice and myself sailed for Holyhead on May Day. The weather was terrible. Gale force winds. It was dicey if the boat would sail or not but eventually it left East Wall two hours late.

Alice was a bad traveller and spent most of the crossing huddled up on a couch in the passenger's lounge. Amazingly enough, I hadn't a twinge of nausea at all. It must have been only on terra firma that I was a shivering jelly.

It was a good feeling to be wandering around the ship. Treated myself to a large bottle of Chanel No. 5 in the duty free. I even went out on deck for a while just to get a good blow into my lungs. There were a few hardy people like myself battling the raging wind.

It seemed no time at all till I saw Holyhead approaching. I made my way back to Alice. She was covered up under her coat and didn't look at all well.

'Alice, we're nearly there.'

'Leave me alone,' she proclaimed, 'I'm dying.'

I got her sitting up and from then on it was rush rush rush until we found ourselves sitting in a train carriage en route to London. We both slept all the way.

Euston Station was bulging with rushing bodies being vomited from trains. English voices called out platform numbers and trains for Manchester, Liverpool, Edinburgh, Leeds. So much of a hubbub when compared to Pearse Station. Alice knew her way round so we got a taxi to where her sister Mary lived. We got there just as Mary was leaving for work. The flat was the top portion of a house. It was old and a little depressing. I fell into bed and conked out until the following morning.

Mary had gone to work when we surfaced the next day. I only got a quick glimpse of her. She was fifteen years younger than Alice and didn't look a bit like her. Alice was small and verging on the plump side, while Mary was tall and thin as a rake. She'd moved out of her own bedroom for us so the two of us had to share a bed. I knew Alice for such a long time that this didn't bother me at all.

We had a quick breakfast and took the tube into the city centre. The last time I'd been in London was almost twenty five years ago. I'd gone with Daire for a long weekend. We'd booked into a 3-star hotel and had a ball for ourselves. We spent a whole day in our plush bedroom, only surfacing for a late dinner. I was so young then, and so happy. We saw all the sights, sat in Hyde Park listening to the speakers on the Sunday morning, went to the Tower, St Paul's Cathedral, the works. When we were leaving, we discovered the breakfast was extra. We had a tight squeeze making up the money, budgeted to the last slice of bread. In the end, what with other hidden extras and all, we had to travel on the train and boat with just one bar of chocolate between us. We were in love, we told ourselves, we didn't need food. It worked too. Funny the way love feeds the body. But where was that love now? Had he married? Strange that he never came home.

Alice and myself arrived back at Mary's flat late in the evening. How two sisters could be so different amazed me. Mary was a total snob and had this awful put-on English accent. She worked in Harrods but I told Alice they should spell it Horrid instead.

She took great delight in telling me about ten times that she didn't know how anybody could spend their life in Ireland.

'It's the dirt over there that gets me,' she groaned, 'and the ignorance.' I felt like saying, 'If it's ignorance you're looking for, check out the nearest mirror.'

Her accent was the thing that got me the most. She probably lost her own one as soon as she stepped off the boat. Irish emigrants were often the worst anti-Irish snobs.

Because we were her guests I had to be polite and say nothing. Alice seemed to worship the ground she walked on. Luckily she was at work most of the time so we didn't have to see much of her.

The days flew by. Alice and myself went to a show on our own because Mary wasn't free. She seemed to have a hectic social life. I bought some pricey clothes, permitting myself the indulgence because we were on foreign shores. In one very expensive boutique in Knightsbridge I tried on a blue floral dress. It was a bit matronly I felt but my decision was made for me when the shop assistant gushed, 'You could wear that dress going to tea with the queen.' Little did she know that was enough to make me scarper out of the place minus the said dress. I also chose a Waterford crystal vase for Mary to let her see some real Irish beauty.

Towards the end of our stay she asked would we like go to a club. She was a member and could get us in as her friends. Alice didn't really want to go but in the end she agreed.

I took particular care with my appearance and wore a grey silk dress I'd bought on Bond Street. I felt quite jaunty heading out for the night.

It was a dark basement of a place and Mary had to sign us in. We got ourselves a table and I ordered a bottle of wine. There was music playing and a few people were dancing. I noticed a fellow staring at me. He looked quite handsome so when he came over and nodded towards the floor I got up to dance with him. It was a slow one.

'Trendy place,' I said.

He just nodded.

'Do you come here often?' I continued when he didn't make any move to talk.

He smiled and put his hand to his mouth. It was then I realised he was dumb. The dance ended and I smiled and carefully mouthed 'Thank You', not knowing whether he could read my lips or actually hear.

I made my way back to the two ladies and didn't say anything to them about him. The music started up again and he was over like a shot.

'You've made a hit there,' said Mary. I could see she was raging that she was left sitting. It was hard work trying to smile and nod at him. I felt sorry for the poor devil. I thought it must be awful not to be able to speak, but fair play to him for socialising anyway. After a while I got worn out mouthing things at him and pointed to the Ladies. Hopefully he'd be gone when I emerged.

Not so lucky. He was literally waiting to pounce when I stepped outside. Again he pointed to the floor and again I smiled and got up to dance. When the dance ended he signalled towards the bar and put his hand to his mouth to signify a drink. I agreed to have one with him. At the bar I asked him what he wanted and again he pointed to his mouth and waved his hands about. By a process of elimination - red or white, dry or sweet, French, Australian, South American, Italian - I was able to order him a dry white Australian wine. I had a glass of French red myself. He didn't make any effort to pay so I reached into my bag and gave the money to the waiter. He didn't need my help to drink it, though. He slugged it back, and then another, with Miss Moneybags doing the honours.

'I'm here on holidays,' I said and he smiled.

'Do you see my two friends over there?' I continued, 'One is Alice, she lives in Dublin. So do I. Her sister works here in Harrods. You know Harrods, don't you?' He smiled again.

'I used to be a legal secretary,' I said, miming typing. I added 'It's better than being an illegal one, I suppose'. He smiled again. I couldn't think of anything else to say. I didn't want to be rude but obviously things weren't going anywhere. I was glad when the lights came up and the place started to close.

'Thanks for the dance. It was nice to meet you.' Then I got my coat and headed over to join Alice and Mary.

As we were making our way out the door I looked across at him and my mouth opened in shock. There he was nattering away to another fellow to beat the band. I went over to him and stood at his table.

'You're talking!' I said.

'So you noticed. That was observant of you.'

I couldn't understand what he was up to.

'Why did you do that to me?' I asked and he laughed again.

'That's easy. I knew you wuz a bleedin' Paddy the minute you opened your gob.' There were guffaws from his friends all round the table.

I felt as if my stomach had been punched in. I went back to the girls, unable to speak.

'I thought he'd be seeing you home,' Mary chuckled.

'He wasn't dumb,' I said to nobody in particular, 'He said he was dumb but he wasn't.'

'Said he was dumb? Talk about an Irish one,' Mary laughed, 'What do you mean?'

'The man I was dancing with. I thought he was dumb.'

'I could see you making funny signs at him. I didn't know what was going on unless it was some new hip-hop dance routine.'

'He pretended he couldn't talk to fool me.'

'Why?'

'Because I'm Irish, I think.'

'Because you're Irish?'

'He thinks the Irish are thick and wanted to prove it.'

'I think he succeeded,' Mary put in. 'Who's the real dummy here?'

'At least you got asked up,' said Alice, trying to take the harm out of it, 'that's more than Mary and myself achieved.'

'Come on,' said Mary, 'let's get out of here. I've got work in the morning. You pair of lazybones can lie on'. Neither of them seemed to realise how shocked I was. Bleedin' Paddy. I was in a daze all through the journey home. The taxi sped along through rainy streets. Wipers swishing back and forth. Alice and Mary chatting to the driver and I was barely aware of the drone of their voices. A bleedin' Paddy. I really knew how to pick them.

'Cheer up,' Alice said, giving me a poke, 'it's not that big a deal. It was quite clever of him actually.'

'Clever. I certainly don't think it was clever.'

I couldn't wait to get home and hide my head under the covers. I thought back to another time I'd made a fool of myself Years ago I'd been in love with a gay man. I refused to believe it about him and maybe he did himself too. Both of us were struggling with the idea. I felt if we didn't think about it, it would go away. He was tortured by it and maybe that's why he went out with me.

After an office drink-up one night I met him with his boyfriend. They invited me back to their flat and I was so besotted with my buccaneer I went. The flat was arty and they had candles lighting. Next of all Andy - that was his name - got candle-grease over his trousers. The friend said they'd go to another room and iron it out with brown paper. They left me outside and, being the dope I am, I waited and waited. Eventually the penny dropped that they were in bed together. 'Where were you?' my mother said when I finally got home, 'I was nearly ready to send for the guards.' I wanted to say to her, 'Don't worry, mammy, I wasn't up to anything. I was part of a *ménage-a-trois* but the other two fancied each other like mad and plain Jane was left in the corner.' Somehow I doubted she'd have understood.

'Penny for your thoughts,' Alice asked but I told her she'd be wasting her money.

'Cheer up,' she consoled, giving me a poke, 'it might never happen.'

As soon as we got in the door I ran upstairs and bawled into the pillow. It was as if the build-up of all the other stuff was hitting me together.

'Don't worry about that fellow, Alice said, 'it's him that has the problem.'

'It's not just him, it's everything.'

'You mean Mary? Don't let her get to you either. She doesn't mean to be so hard. She left Ireland over a broken romance twenty years ago. He married somebody else and she was devastated. There's no harm in her really.'

'You always see the good in everybody, Alice' As for me, I felt it was a turning point. It was the last time I'd play the Good Samaritan for a while. Why was I always so slow to see things? It was as if a piece of my brain was missing. First my experience with   Mr Peachy Green and now being made an eejit of by a smart racist.

Neither was I forgetting the fact that I'd spent nine years of my life with a man who was my polar opposite. The delightful Nigel. A man who dropped me like a hot potato the day he decided I represented more debits than credits on his emotional balance sheet.

Why hadn't I seen any of it sooner? Was I forever destined to chase after the carthorse of life like a demented sparrow? I was going nowhere fast.

CHAPTER 26

Back in Ireland I continued to ruminate about the fact that I seemed to be jinxed with men. Occasionally they'd approach me in bars but nothing ever seemed to happen. None of them were exactly spring chickens and mostly they wanted to talk about their young days. There was a gardener who told me all about his late wife, a retired army man whose wife had left him, a travelling salesman who'd been married three times. From the gamey eye of the last I knew he wouldn't have said no to a quickie tumble with me to add to his collection of trophies. He flattered me, telling me I had the bluest eyes he ever saw but I knew he'd have been more interested in something lower down.

How come other girls met sensible men with good intentions? Where did I go wrong? I hadn't wanted much out of life but I blew what I was given.

Daire and myself could now have been celebrating our fifteenth wedding anniversary if I hadn't been so stupid. We'd have had a big family, I felt. Five children, the names I'd picked out becoming real people. Three girls with ringlets in their hair like Mammy used to do for me and Angie. Trophies in every part of the house from Feis Ceoil an Iarthair for the hard reel they'd have. Sally. Caitlin and Shauna for the girls. The two little ladeens, fair-haired like their Dad. Tim and Tom. Too late now for this dreaming. Biological clock beyond repair. Tick-tock tock-tick.

I hadn't had these thoughts for years. With Nigel I'd never contemplated having a family. I couldn't picture him changing nappies or bringing Tim and Tom to Croke Park to cheer on their home county or any other county.

With Daire it was different. Was he married now, I wondered, or living in America? Had he children of his own to bring to the ball game? Buddy, Junior and Mary Lou?

I could ask Minnie if she ever saw his sister. She could enquire for me. On second thoughts, no. I wouldn't want him to know I still cared about him if he was with some other woman - or even if he wasn't.

Out of boredom I answered a few ads for temporary typing jobs but was never even called for interview. I thought of doing some charity work and remembered a woman I'd met years ago who did that sort of thing. Her first name was Anna but I couldn't remember her surname. I rummaged through a torn old notebook where I kept numbers and found her one there so I rang it up. Amazingly she answered. She was in her sixties when I'd last seen her but she sounded full of pep. She remembered me immediately. We had a great chat about old times. At the end of the call she told me to come along the following afternoon to the shop she worked in and she'd sort me out. When I got there she welcomed me like a long-lost sister.

She also introduced me to the two other ladies in the shop. Josie and Phyllis were grannies. We had good craic together sorting through the bags of clothes that came in. Some of the stuff looked as if it had been around since the World War - the First World War.

A pair of long johns arrived in one day. They were so worn they reminded me of something from a cowboy film. As I looked at them I could just picture Randy having a shave after a hard day on the range while pretty Mary Jo sang to herself in her wooden tub, her modesty covered by bubbles.

I donated some oddments from my own wardrobe. Like myself, they'd seen better days. I also bought quite a few snazzy bits and pieces. I got a gorgeous blue coat with a velvet collar and a swing to it that looked like something out of a 1940s film. I pictured the owner, now probably in her eighties, crossing O'Connell Bridge and maybe being snapped by a photographer, the coat swishing as she strutted out in style. Maybe she was in a nursing home now and might look at that snapshot and remember happier times.

I worked in the shop three days a week and the routine suited me. In between customers Josie had us all in stitches with her stories. One day she regaled us with her views on sex. She claimed she never enjoyed one minute of it even though she'd borne ten children. 'I'd prefer a nice cup of tea and a cuddle any day,' she said, 'and as for all that puffing and panting I see on the television, to my mind the lot of them look to be in deep pain. If that's fun, they're welcome to it.'

Anna was quieter than Josie but she became a great friend to me. She was a real inspiration. She was in her early seventies and had had some serious illnesses in the past. She'd had a bypass operation six years previously and a hip replacement after that. She suffered from arthritis in both knees as well but she hated talking about anything like that. She related very well to young customers, advising them about what suited them, as though she was a teenager herself.

One evening I invited her back to the apartment and cooked a meal for her. She got quite tipsy on two glasses of wine and started to tell me all about herself. It turned out she'd worked as a waitress for over forty years in Clery's restaurant. She hadn't had a huge salary but she was frugal in her ways and saved enough to buy a small house in Marino.

Under the influence of the wine she told me about the love of her life. He'd been a bus driver and when they met he was married. I was surprised to hear this because I'd assumed she was as pure as the driven snow. They had an affair for over thirty years. He married very young and had two children but himself and his wife had nothing in common.

They met, of all places, in the Vincent de Paul doing voluntary work. I asked her if it was love at first sight.

'For me it was. Terry took a few weeks before he realised what was happening. I gave him a bit of prodding before he realised how crazy he was about me.'

'It must have been sad that you were never really together.'

'What does together really mean, though? I know a lot of married couples who are together all day and yet they're not, if you know what I mean. We mightn't have lived together but we had some great times. And fabulous holidays.'

'But how did you get away?'

'His wife was big into choral singing and was always off here, there and everywhere. Over to Wales, down to Cork, gone all the time. The kids were reared so he was free quite a bit. Petra was the wife's name. Strange name, strange woman. I don't know why she ever married Terry. It certainly wasn't for love. '

'Do you still see him?'

'No, he died three years ago.' She began to cry and I went to put my arms round her.

'That's terrible, Anna. In a way, life passed you by. If you'd gone out and met somebody else you could have married and had a family.'

'I wouldn't change one day of it.'

I walked home with her and thought about the way my own life was going. I was in love and threw it there. What wouldn't she have given to have had my choices?

She returned my invitation and invited me back to her house for dinner one evening. The house was like herself, small and homely. She had a little patch of a garden and she showed me all her shrubs and bushes, including an exotic-looking flower that came from a holiday they'd taken in Cyprus one year. She'd made a delicious stew and afterwards the two of us sat in her garden talking. Out of the blue she asked me what age I was.

'Forty-five,' I confessed, 'Over the hill, in other words.'

'I wish I was forty again. Or fifty or even sixty. Go away with yourself, you're still a young woman.'

'Maybe, but everybody seems to be well settled at my age these days. If they're not they seem to have a problem. The kind of men I meet anyway.'

'I hope I never settle. It sounds like what you'd say for a cake when you take it out of the oven. Have you no man in your life?'

'There was one but it's finished now. Sometimes I wonder if I scared him off.'

'That's not the attitude to have. Think about the future. Life is for living. Get out there and look for your mate. There's a sock for every shoe, you know.'

'My mother used to say that.'

'She was right.'

I got her talking about Terry again and she asked would I like to see some photographs. They were mostly holiday snaps - their stolen moments on mainly foreign shores. She was able to tell me where every picture was taken and even remembered the particular person she asked to take them. A young boy in Spain, a woman with a stick in Cyprus, an Asian couple in Morocco. He seemed like a friendly man, always beaming for the camera.

I picked up a cutting from a newspaper that was in among the photographs.

'It's his death notice,' she said, filling up, 'Read it if you like.'

I folded out the crumpled page to see the words.

'Coffey, Terry, November 2001, dearly-loved husband of Petra and father of Jack and Con. House strictly private.

'That's very sad, Anna. Could you not even go to the funeral?'

'I went and visited the grave afterwards. I think she knew about us and it never bothered her . Anyway,

He's waiting for me up there. If what we did is a sin we can be in hell together.'

After that we went for drinks once a week and she visited me often. I felt I'd known her all my life so there was nothing of an age barrier. Women could relate to each other when it came to emotions and feelings; we were all sisters.

I talked to her about Nigel and she never offered advice, just listened.

'Were there any other men in your life beside this Nigel fellow?' she asked one evening as we sat in my kitchen drinking tea and gorging ourselves on a chocolate cake she'd brought.

'Yes, the love of my life, I suppose,' I said flippantly.

'Where is he now?' she enquired.

'Away. He could be married for all I know.'

'Maybe he's not. Why don't you try and find out?'

'Too late now, Anna,' I replied 'Have another slice of cake. It's a mortal sin, but gorgeous.'

There was a serenity about Anna that I envied. Looking at her life from a worldly point of view it seemed she had very little. No husband, no children, a modest house. Yet she had loved and been loved. A few hours in her company always made me feel more cheerful.

The next day I got round to phoning Minnie. She sounded in better form. John was still living in Rockbarton. The twins were still in Australia and she was working lights out. She was still hopeful he'd come back to her when he got the other woman out of his system but she didn't sound desperate anymore.

'Do you ever hear a word about Daire?' I asked when she was finished on John's escapades, 'Maybe you don't even remember him.'

'Of course I do. No, not for ages now. His sister moved to England and I don't know anybody else who'd have known him.'

'Don't worry about it, I was just wondering.'

'Maybe you still care about him.'

'To be honest I do actually. I didn't realise it at the time, and then Nigel came along.'

'You never really had anything for that Nigel guy, did you? I'll make a few enquiries. Maybe somebody would know.'

'You're a dote, Minnie'

A part of me was afraid she wouldn't find him but another part of me was afraid she might. '

CHAPTER 27

June was a lovely month. I still hadn't got a job but was now working four days in the shop. For a time I'd been good in the health department and was more relaxed generally. Anna and myself had become very close. The other two women had husbands and grandchildren so didn't have much free time to socialise.

She had a small car and we drove to Glendalough and all over Wicklow. One weekend we went to Wexford for two nights. Sometimes I felt like the old dame accompanying her. She was game for anything.

'We'll have to find a sexy young fellow for you,' she said almost every time we were together.

'I think you're the one will find the fellow,' I joked, 'you have much more jizz in you than I'll ever have.'

'Cop onto yourself, girl. You have to put yourself about. Nobody is going to fall down the chimney, you know. Why don't you go to one of those club places? There's a tea dance I used to go to on a Sunday afternoon. I'm past it now. My knees couldn't hold me up even if I did get a partner but if you want I'll go with you some evening.'

'A tea dance, what's that?'

'It's an afternoon get-together. Mostly ballroom dancing. Can you waltz?'

'Believe it or not I can.' Yet another of my hidden talents.

'There you go. I'll pick you up next Sunday at four. Wear your best outfit and I guarantee you we'll find a man for you.'

She was at the apartment at 3.45 and I had to rush to be ready. I settled on a denim skirt and a green blouse I had got in London.

'You look gorgeous,' she said, 'you're sure to be grabbed up. You'd pass for thirty.' It was gratifying to be told I was young. The truth of it was, I felt like a hundred most of the time. The place was hopping. Men and women in their later years were swishing round the floor like whirling dervishes. Others sat at tables sipping drinks. Not tea either, as I'd expected. We were hardly seated before a dapper little gent came over. He was dressed up to the nines and sported a red handkerchief in his pocket. How will I get away from this fellow, I thought. He was seventy if he was a day.

'May I have the pleasure, my dear?' he asked, curtseying. I was about to drag myself up when I saw it was Anna he was asking. That put me in my place. 'It's so kind of you to ask', she said, 'but I'm just here with my young friend. My knees are very bad with arthritis so I can't dance, I'm afraid. But thank you.'

'That's too bad. You're such a fine looking woman. May I join you anyway?'

'Certainly,' said Anna. The two of them proceeded to chat and I felt like a spare part. . I told them I was going to get a drink and offered to get them one each as well but they both declined. I was making my way back with my own drink when a youngish fellow tapped me on the arm. He was tall with brown curly hair and looked quite attractive.

'Can I have this dance?' he asked.

'Yes. Just let me leave my drink with my friend.'

'Mind that, Anna,' I said when I got to the table.

She was laughing her head off at whatever joke her friend was telling her and hardly heard me. I got out on the floor. It was an old time waltz and he whizzed me round like an old hand, 'What brings you here,' he said, 'aren't you a bit young for this sort of place?'

'I came with my friend from work. She's an elderly lady.'

'That was kind of you.'

'Not really. She's a wonderful person, an example to all of us. But what brings you here? You're not exactly in your dotage yourself.'

'I love dancing, particularly old time stuff. There's nowhere else to go for it nowadays. I'm Bill, by the way.'

The dance ended and he asked if he could join me. I pointed out where Anna and her pal was and he went over to ask if he could get them a drink. The four of us sat chatting and drinking. Every so often Bill asked me up to dance. Anna and Fred, her friend, just sat and laughed. Fred was a retired butcher and was quite saucy in himself. Anna was up for it too. The stories were quite smutty for such an ageing pair. Bill seemed decidedly solemn. When we were dancing at one point he said, 'That lady you work with, quite vulgar isn't she? As for the man, he's positively disgusting.'

'Anna is a pantomime. She's been through so much. It's brilliant she can still laugh. Fred seems harmless. They might as well knock out a bit of fun if they can. It beats sitting in an old folks home looking into space.'

'Obviously, but I hate dirty jokes. Particularly from older people. It's what you'd expect from adolescent boys.' Talk about a prude. Just my luck. Anna and Fred were talking about all four of us going for a bite to eat. Bill didn't seem interested in that but offered to drive me home. Since I thought Anna might like to have a chat with Fred, I agreed.

He barely spoke the whole way home. I finally got out of him that he lived in Terenure with his elderly father who was blind and that he worked in a men's clothing shop in Camden Street. I got this information by asking more questions than the Gestapo. He didn't ask me anything about myself. 'Are you hungry?' he said eventually, 'Is there anywhere in particular you'd like to go for a bite?'

'I'd be happy enough with a salad. If you like I can make one up for both of us.'

'Are you sure? I'm afraid I didn't bring much money out with me. That'd be just what the doctor ordered.' Scrooge as well as Prude.

When we got back to the apartment I whipped up the salad and opened a bottle of vino. He asked did I own the apartment and what was the rent. 'Expensive,' I told him. That was as much information as he deserved. (More than he'd have given me in the same circumstances, I imagined).

'You work with that old lady, you said. Surely she's too old to have a job.' So now I could add ageist to tightwad and puritan. He was hardly Bachelor of the Year.

'We both do voluntary work. It's great fun.'

'Voluntary? You mean no pay? But how do you live - have you a full time job?'

'I left it after twenty long years.'

'Surely you're a bit young for that. What age are you, early forties?'

'Forty-one actually,' I lied.

'That's far too young to be taking time off work. You must have plenty of cash to be able to afford this place.'

'Not really. I'm just taking a break. Tell me about yourself. Here, have another little drop of wine. I know you're driving but you've only had half a glass.'

'No, I don't take chances. Well there's not much to tell really. I like my job. Actually I'm the manager. Have you heard of us - Murphy & O'Callaghan Fashions for the Discerning Gentleman?' Fashions for the Discerning Gentleman? What century was he from?

Can't say I have, but then I wouldn't know too much about men's clothes. If it was women's now that's a different story.' And how.

'Do you spend a lot on clothes?' Was the Pope a Catholic? I could see by his face he would be disgusted with anyone who wasn't thrifty so I mumbled something about being careful with what I spent.

He was heavy going. That's why what happened next seemed so out of character. He'd finished his meal and came over behind me. Next of all his hands were sliding down under my blouse, I could smell his aftershave. It was heavy and overpowering and maybe that's why I let myself succumb to him.

In two minutes the pair of us were on the floor, puffing and panting. I'm sure the old woman downstairs must have heard us. I couldn't describe it as love-making because the art of making anything takes time and this was all over in jig time. What was all that about, I thought, as I tidied myself up. He spruced himself up in record time as well. I would have liked him to sit on and talk but what was the saying, men are from Mars and women from Venus.

There must be a lot of quick sex on Mars, I thought. (To go with the chocolate bars, maybe).

'I'll be at the dance again next week,' he said, as if we'd done nothing more intimate than sharing a cup of tea.

'See you there at the same time?' I was so stunned I nodded. Then he left, banging the door behind him.

And so began a pattern. Every Sunday Anna and myself sallied forth. She'd become very close to Fred. They'd gone to the pictures a few times together and he'd come to her place for a meal. She really was a woman who needed a man in her life and I could see a glow in her face that hadn't been there before. She got her hair restyled and told me one day that Fred and herself were planning going on a bus tour together. Maybe in July when there were cheap offers for golden oldies.

She was delighted I was continuing my meetings with Bill. She never commented on what she thought of him, being far too polite to do that.

Every Sunday afternoon he was at the dance before me and would immediately claim me as his partner. We'd dance and then he'd drive me home for our frantic fumblings. Afterwards he'd rush off and I wouldn't hear from him or see him for the rest of the week.

One such Sunday I asked him could I call up sometime to see him managing his shop. He got quite angry with this and said he couldn't stand mixing business and pleasure. I wasn't sure how I felt being defined as pleasure. In any case he left it clear that he didn't want me anywhere near his workplace.

I don't know why we continued to see each other. We had nothing in common and I believed he didn't even like me. Nor did I particularly care about him. We danced well together but we rarely had anything to say to each other. It was emotionless and yet we both continued to keep it going, probably due to the lack of anything else of note happening in our lives.

After a few weeks I realized I really didn't know anything about him. His surname was Shannon. I looked up the phone book many times to see could I find a Shannon in Terenure but there was only one and the initial was J so I had no way of contacting him from Sunday to Sunday. It frustrated me that I had to confine myself to these meetings.

On a Sunday that Anna and Fred were away I made my way to the dance but there was no sign of Bill. I sat at a table and kept watching the entrance but he never appeared. I thought it pretty shabby of him because he would have known I had to come on the bus.

On the way home I got off the bus before my stop and called into the park. Jack was sitting on his customary perch.

'All dressed up and nowhere to go,' he taunted.

'I was to meet someone but he never showed up, the louser.'

'That's too bad. Why don't you phone him?'

'I don't have his number.'

'Nothing you can do then, unfortunately. Is he a friend or a lover?'

'Neither really. We just spend some time together.'

'No law against that. By the way, where have you been? I haven't seen you in a while.'

'The voluntary job keeps me occupied.'

Anna arrived back to work on the following Monday. She had a great week with Fred. They went to West Cork and stayed in a 4-star hotel. There were bus tours every day as well. Fred was a brilliant comedian and had the whole bus in stitches with his off-colour jokes.

'He invited me over to meet his family next weekend,' she said, 'I'm really looking forward to that. Terry will always be the love of my life but it's great to be getting a second chance. Meeting his family is something that makes me feel he's proud of me. Not that Terry wasn't, but Fred is a widower and there's nothing to be kept secret. I feel like a young lass again.'

I was thrilled for her. Maybe a bit jealous, but only a small bit.

'He says I'm his older woman,' she laughed, 'I'm 76 and he's just a toy boy of 70. I said I'll teach him a few tricks.'

'Why not? You're the best-looking older woman I've ever seen.'

'How about yourself and Bill. How is that going?'

'He didn't turn up last Sunday and I have no number for him. I'm beginning to think there's something shady about him to be honest with you.'

'Maybe his dad wasn't too well. Doesn't he live with him? Next week we'll go to the dance. Fred can't go on the Sunday because one of his grandchildren is in a school play but you and I will go. I bet there's a reasonable excuse.'

As the week dragged on I got more and more worked up. Maybe it was the fact that he seemed to be playing hard to get that made him so important in my life. He had my number so I kept checking the phone for texts to make sure it was working. By Sunday afternoon I was in a frenzy. It seemed the only important thing in life was that he'd be at the dance.

He was. All smiles, he approached us immediately. He was quick to get a drink for Anna. Then he swept me onto the floor. When we finally sat down to join Anna I asked him about the week before.

'Sorry, something came up.'

'Was it your father? '

'Yes. He had a bad stomach.'

'Has he been blind since birth?'

'Yes, blind since birth.'

'Hey, you two lovebirds,' Anna piped up, 'I'm exhausted. I have a date with Fred tomorrow and was up till all hours last night.'

'If you're making your way home, maybe we should be off too,' Bill said to her, 'I didn't bring my car, so you can drop us off.' He was so rude I almost told him I'd go off with her on my own. He hadn't even addressed her by her name. I knew Anna could see how bad-mannered he was but being the perfect lady she just smiled and headed off to get her car.

The three of us drove in silence towards the apartment. Same story, me making all the conversation and Lord Tom Noddy acting as if Anna and myself were his servants. She gave me a look when we reached the apartment but said nothing and drove off. When we got inside I asked him was he hungry. Not surprisingly he said yes. I had steak in the fridge and made him a meal. Once the meal was swallowed he made a wild grab for me again as if we were in a war zone and I fought for breath under his big weight. It was as if I was another meal to him. No sooner was he finished with me than he stood up to leave.

'Bill, before you go, there's something I want to ask you. Does your father always have to come first?'

'It's not that he comes first. He has a disability.'

'I do appreciate that. It's just you should think of yourself as well. You deserve to have a life too you know. None of us are meant to live our lives totally for another person.'

I could see by his face he hadn't heard a word.

'I'm sure you're right but I can't delay now. By the way, are we okay for next week - same time same place?' I tried to hold onto him, grabbing his sleeve as he made for the door.

'Could I meet him your dad? Anna has met Fred's family. It might do him good to have a bit of company.'

'No, you can't. He's a recluse. Never socialises. He suffers from chronic depression.'

'I'm sorry to hear that, Bill, but maybe I could come and talk to him. Sometimes a man will talk to a woman.'

'Thanks but no thanks. That wouldn't be on. I've got to go now, it's getting late. See you.'

After he left I got the old sinking feeling again. What was wrong with me? I'd spent nine years I didn't even like, never mind love, with one man and it looked as if I was starting to repeat the same pattern now. Obviously he didn't want a long term relationship. 'If it's Sunday it must be the Howth Road' was how he saw me.' I probably came a poor second to the steak.

CHAPTER 28

The summer dragged on. There was a dead heat in the air that sapped my energy, making even the simplest tasks a chore. Anne was still going strong with Fred. He stayed in her place a few times and she was invited to all his grandchildren's parties. She looked radiant. She was such an unselfish person I knew she felt sorry for me. She tried to bolster me up by saying Bill was probably a dutiful son and that his father wouldn't be around forever.

One Saturday she was taking two of Fred's grandchildren to see a film. It was an afternoon show and as Fred wasn't free himself she invited me along. The children were little dotes. Harry was eight and little Maisie just five.

We bought them treats before going into the cinema. I was about to get ice-cream when Anna grabbed me by the arm. 'Come on, the film will be started,' she urged.

'Take it easy, Anna, we have fifteen minutes yet.' Then I saw him. Bill. He had a small boy by the hand. What was going on? My heart was racing. I started to walk towards him when I saw a woman approaching him carrying a bag of popcorn. She was younger than me by quite a bit and very attractive.

He turned around suddenly and saw myself and Anna. For a moment he seemed to be going into the cinema but then he turned and walked towards me. 'We need to talk,' he said.

'You're certainly right we need to talk,' I replied.

'It's not what it looks like,' he said, sounding like someone from a bad film.

'Are you married?' I said, 'Is that your wife?'

'Yes but our marriage is finished,' he said.

'Finished? So that's why you're taking her to the pictures – with your son.'

'As I said, we need to talk. I live with her but the marriage is dead. We don't – '

I started to walk away from him. 'Come on, Anna,' I said, 'Let's get out of here.' I can't remember the drive home in the car, only Anna banging her fist off the steering wheel.

'You're better off without that two-timer, as my mother used to say he's no better than butter.'

'It's okay, Anna,' I said, 'Honestly, he didn't mean anything to me. I half suspected anyway.' When we got home she wanted to come in but she had the two children and I sent her back to Fred and his happy family. 'Don't let him get you down,' she said, 'He's not worth it, keep telling yourself no better than butter.'

'Don't worry, I couldn't care less,' I assured her, and I was telling the truth this time.

I never saw Bill again. He was just another smashed dream. Or smashed illusion. Anna did her best to get me out in the next few weeks but I hadn't the interest. After this latest experience I felt it was time to settle down to spinsterhood. Maybe there wasn't a sock for every shoe, maybe some spare socks wandered the world weeping for another shoe, maybe some of us were meant to paddle our own canoe, like Jack. I wasn't heartbroken over Bill. It was my pride, I told myself, pride that he'd led me on like that. Here I go again: Nigel Mark Two.

Maybe giving in gracefully was the answer. I should become a woman who acted her age. Buy little runner shoes and wear a track suit. Let my hair go grey, develop a salt and pepper look and zip round the place, happy as Larry in my solitary state.

I probably wasn't the couple type. I was once, though, with Daire. That was a long time ago now. You just get one chance in life. I'd been too young to appreciate it: My sock had fitted so cosily into his shoe. I found myself wondering if Minnie had got any news of him. If she did she'd have let me know. Better let it lie.

If I didn't think too much I was fine. I occupied my time with the shop to keep myself busy. I also had some evenings out with Anna. As time went on she grew even more radiant and me even more dowdy. She was glowing from her Fredness.

Even though I'd resigned myself to a single state, I didn't want to become a pity case. I still treated myself to nice clothes but bought older woman's stuff now. The hair I'd let go back to its dirty fair colour mixed with streaks of grey. I didn't bother anymore with highlights. I had plenty of little crow's feet round my eyes and with the clothes and the dull hair, which I now wore pulled back in a bun, I looked much older than my years.

I hadn't been in touch with Alice for some time now. She'd left a lot of messages on my machine but I didn't feel up to talking to her. Jack was always available in the park and I'd often go in and engage him in chat. No matter how much I rambled on about my various problems he never lost his patience with me. In a way I think my crazy life amused him. Maybe, I thought sometimes, I should have set up house with him in a tree in the park.

I no longer cared about anything. I was in a state of total resignation about all that happened around me. My symptoms became a thing of the past, no pins and no needles, no numbness in my hands and my heart functioned without any sudden jumps. It was months since I'd visited the doctor with any of my famous ailments and fears.

One morning in the middle of September Anna didn't show up at work. Usually she would have phoned me so by twelve noon I was bothered. I tried to phone her but her number just kept ringing out. Then I phoned Fred. He said she'd been fine when he left her the night before. When Phyllis came in I told her I was going to nip round to see if she was all right.

There was no reply when I rang the bell but her milk was on the doorstep so I knew something was up. I called into her next door neighbour, who had a key, and we went in together. As we climbed the stairs I knew something terrible had happened. The house was too quiet.

She was lying on the bed and I knew immediately she was dead. I went over to her and stood there in a state of shock. It seemed like a long time elapsed with the two of us just standing there. I knew I was making the other woman uncomfortable but I was rooted to the spot. She tried to talk to me but I couldn't reply. I can't even remember what she said. It was like it was all happening to somebody else. I couldn't believe Anna was gone. She had more life in her than anyone I had ever known.

Eventually we rang for an ambulance. A few minutes later I heard the siren. As soon as it stopped at the door I looked out and saw Fred coming in as well. He was sobbing and shaking all over. He poured himself a whiskey from her cabinet and gave me one too. Left to it I knew I could have finished the bottle.

Anna's funeral was small. She told me once she was an only child so I wasn't too surprised. Fred came with his family, the small grandchildren all spruced up with ribbons in their hair. Josie and Phyllis from the shop came as well, and a few neighbours. Somehow the pathetic little gathering looked all wrong. I felt there should have been thousands there to mark such a passing.

She was buried in Glasnevin, where her parents were. Fred and the family invited me back to their place afterwards. We toasted her with tea and sandwiches and afterwards I went home, my emotions all over the place.

When I started to cry I couldn't stop. I felt almost sadder than when I lost my mother. How had she kept going when so many things went against her? Sharing her lover with another woman. No close family to confide in. What else did I not know?

I spent the next few days living on tea. The phone rang a few times but I ignored it. It was a full week after the funeral before I had the gumption to pick it up. When I did, it was Fred on the line.

'How are you?' he asked, 'I was wondering would you feel like meeting for a chat. Nobody knew her like you did. I need to talk to somebody, to share the memories.'

We met in town and had a few drinks. Both of us talked about the cheerful happy Anna we'd known, how much she'd graced our days, how she'd say 'Get up and grab life and don't sit staring into the fire.' I could never imagine her feeling sorry for herself no matter how many horrible cards life dealt her. She always saw the glass half full.

It seemed to cheer both of us up to talk about her. We agreed we'd meet at least once a fortnight and do it all again. II called into the chipper on the way home and had my first decent meal since she died.

A little traveller girls was standing outside the chip shop. She held out a paper cup and I gave her a few bob.

'Thanks missus,' she said with a cheeky grin.

As I walked home I thought about Anna's life and how she'd gone for things uncompromisingly without any self-pity at all or any feelings of being past her sell-by date. Even at her stage of life she'd been open to meeting Fred and had got some happy hours from doing that. And then the work in the shop, crippled with arthritis but still hanging in there.

I was 45, not 70. I started to take long walks, went back and had my highlights in and did a bit of therapeutic buying of clothes suitable for a youngish woman.

I arranged to meet Alice more frequently. She still needled me about getting a job but I didn't want to get into boring office work again. The world hadn't stopped turning since Fiona went out of my life. The sun still came up each day even though I sat at home like a vegetable.

I had a long letter from Minnie. The twins had invited her to come and stay with them in Australia for a month and had paid for her ticket. She seemed stronger. The only news of John was that she'd decided to go for a legal separation. 'No use in flogging a dead horse,' she wrote, 'and as for Rockbarton, she's welcome to him.' It was good to see her so upbeat and thinking about herself. She was still corresponding with Clem and he'd invited her to Florida. 'Maybe I'll go after all,' she said, 'I have the month off for Australia and I think if I put it to them at work. They'll allow me two weeks later at my own expense. If they don't I'm coming in with an Uzi to help them change their minds.'

Clem and Minnie. He must have be at least twenty years older than her. But then again maybe a bit of male company was what she needed. I phoned her and told her to attack life with a vengeance.

'You sound better in herself,' she said, 'Any news of Nigel?' Why was it the two things had to go together?

'He's totally out of my life.'

'I'm sorry to hear that.'

'Don't be. Maybe when you come back from your world trips you might drop up to Dublin for the weekend. There's plenty of room in the apartment and we could have a good old chinwag. I'd be thrilled skinny to see you.'

October was unusually cold but I always loved this time of year. Spring was raw with a harsh light and you had the feeling you were meant to be full of sap and up and at life, like it or not. Winter coming in meant long dark evenings with rain and wind lashing at the windows and you were perfectly right to snuggle up by the fire and read to your heart's content.

I took out *Jane Eyre* again, sinking myself into it. It was like being wrapped in an old quilt in bed in Galway when you'd codded your mother into giving you a day off school. I felt like Jane at the beginning of the story, hiding away in a window ledge, surrounded by the thick curtains:

There was no possibility of taking a walk that day. We had been wandering in the leafless shrubbery in the morning, but since dinner the cold winter wind had brought with it clouds so sombre, and a rain so penetrating, that further outdoor exercise was now out of the question.

Jane was such a little mouse of a girl, pale and insignificant in comparison to the Reed children and yet she had the strength of a lion and was so feisty against all the cruelties life threw at her. Intellectual girls talked about Emily Bronte and *Wuthering Heights* but solemn strong passionate Jane was always my favourite. For me Charlotte had created the epitome of a real man in Rochester. Cathy and her Heathcliffe seemed like tormented spirits to me. Give me the flesh and blood of Jane and Rochester every time.

I thought back to the days of Mammy and Daddy, Brian, Angie and me a little family to ourselves, the five of us saying the five decades of the rosary, and our grannys and grandaddys safe and well too in Galway and Cork, all of us in our safe havens and everything right with the world outside.

CHAPTER 29

A few weeks later I had a letter waiting for me from a solicitor. It was to say Anna had made a Will and had divided her house between myself and Fred. I was totally shocked. I'd only known her a few months and she was doing this for me. The solicitor enclosed a copy of the Will. She said she was bequeathing her house to her two good friends who'd brought such pleasure to her life.

I phoned Fred and he told me he'd got the same letter. He was deeply shocked as well.

'I feel I don't deserve it,' he said, 'I only knew her a few months.'

'Yes, but she got such fun out of your time together. She loved your family. You made her feel part of it. She never had that. As for me, I really don't know why she considered me. I never expected this in a million years.'

'You gave her more than you know,' he said, 'She worried about you. She told me once you were the daughter she never had. Having a friendship with you made her feel needed. We could all do with that.' We were beginning to sound like the Mutual Congratulation Society.'

The solicitor told us the house would be worth over €250,000 because of its location even though it was small and in need of modernisation. I'd be receiving half of that huge amount. Never in my life had I anything like that kind of money. Fred would be able to help his family and would be giving treats to his grandchildren as well. I thought of sending something out to Angie. With her big family she could always do with help.

I met Alice for lunch and told her.

'Put a deposit on a house,' she said, 'It will be your place and you won't be throwing good money after bad living in it.'

A mortgage wasn't really me. A trip to America would have been more my style, or even a world cruise. Maybe the best thing would be to do nothing, like all those Lotto millionaires. Sit on it and then decide. A donation to charity, a bit to Angie, something to Alice and Minnie and then sit tight. I still had quite a bit in the bank from my lump sum, not to mention Nigel's pay-off. A woman of means. Let the good times roll.

Now that I knew the money was coming to me I had no need to look for work. I continued in the shop and enrolled in a creative writing course in the local community school. I often thought of returning to my novel with my old friend Bridget Small. God love her, she was like a remnant from a forgotten past now. I wondered how she was getting along with her mouses and seals and lady supervisors and imaginary husband John. Maybe with a bit of luck I'd resurrect her.

I felt the course might set me thinking that way. At the very least I should be able to drum up a short story on the strength of it. Unless all that free time had turned my brain to cabbage.

I knew nobody could teach you to write but the discipline of being there every week and producing pages with a gun to my head might get me up of my ever enlarging bottom.

I wrote a story about a lonely spinster woman who obeyed all the respectable rules of life and then one mad evening she had a few drinks and, like those ladies you saw in films who pulled down their hair and cast off their spectacles, became in her mind a laptop dancer. A bit like Bridget Small really – or myself. Maybe every writer could only write about themself when you came down to it.

The people in the course were a likeable bunch. After being asked to comment, as we all had to for each other, they said my talent lay in humour. To my own way of thinking the story had been sad. Maybe we were all our own worst judges.

The teacher was a thin wisp of man going bald on top. His nose was like a little pig's snout turned up as if it was trying to get a peek at his tiny grey pinpricks of eyes. During what I called half-time, when we consumed tea and biscuits, he told me that I should keep it up and definitely work on the fun aspect of my creativity. He said if I wished I could bring him any work I had at home and he'd give me an opinion and perhaps help me. And so began my friendship with Harry Browne.

The course went on for eight weeks and during that time I had something to produce every week. All short stories. Too short for publication, though. Harry encouraged me all the way and after the third or fourth week we went for a drink when the class finished. He lived with his mother and had never married. In age I put him in the late fifties.

He'd taught English in a girl's secondary school for thirty years but had taken early retirement when he found himself spending more time trying to keep the pupils quiet than filling them with the riches of Virginia Woolf and Emily Dickinson. He never had anything published himself but had an eye for good work. One of his pupils had gone on to get two books published. That was his proudest achievement because he had given her great help at school. She never acknowledged his influence, he told me one night over a cup of tea, and this devastated him.

'You'd think when she was thanking every human being she had ever come into contact with, she could have put in a little mention of Mr Browne. I recognised her potential when she was just sixteen.'

'It seems a bit cruel, but people forget easily. Eaten bread is soon forgotten, isn't that the expression?

'Very true. Very true. Anyway I think I've found something special in you too. Basically the class consists of bored housewives, young fellows who haven't a clue about writing and you. You can make it, they won't. I also think you should develop the piece you wrote about the middle-aged couple. Very poignant indeed. It would make a marvellous novella. In a slim little volume it could appeal to a select readership.'

I was bucked up no end by this. He had, after all, taught English. I imagined myself at book signings all over the place. I'd arrive in a flurry with ten minders and a secretary to hold my coat. I'd be dolled up to the nines and radio and television scouts would be only leaping to get me on air. The more Harry praised me the more I lapped it up.

'Pardon me,' I imagined myself saying as I wafted down Grafton Street, 'I'm a writer.' Little insignificant secretaries would nudge each other and go, 'There's your woman off the telly, you know, she wrote a book. Too intellectual for me to read but I believe it's a best seller.' They'd recount the sighting in their Offices. Crabby old solicitors would say, 'She worked here one time, you know.'

I was cock of the walk for those days of October and November. One day I called into the park, not having seen Jack for a long time.

'So you finally condescended to pay me a visit,' he said grumpily. He looked even worse than usual. His pale face was sunken and his huge eyes were like black holes in his head. Time seemed to be

'I've been busy writing,' I said, sounding very important in myself.

'Is that so? What are you writing, may I ask?'

'An attempt at a novel, believe it or not.'

'Excuse me?'

'It's time for me to do something with my life. I feel I've wasted years in that office. Maybe this is my chance to fly.'

'I hope you don't forget your old friends if you do.'

'No fear of that, Jack,' I replied, stuffing a 50 euro note into his pocket. This he accepted with his usual cheeky grin.

The more I attended the writing classes the closer I got to Harry. I invited him to the apartment a few times and cooked a meal for him. He was fussy about his diet and told me to grill his rashers slightly and to remove the skin from his fried tomatoes as it tended to stick to his dentures. 'No fried onions for me,' he ordered as I was about to throw a few on the pan.

'They repeat on me, so they do.'

'So they do, so they do.' I answered, proud of my quick wit.

'I beg your pardon?'

'You know, repeat. So they do, so they do. Do you get it?'

'I'm not with you.'

'Repeat. I'm repeating like the onions'. For some reason I thought my joke extremely funny and laughed until the tears streamed down my face. Of course the onions probably didn't help either. Harry just stared into the middle distance, probably wondering what daffy woman he'd hooked up with. Most of the time we discussed my works of literary genius which I was now churning out at the rate of knots. Having him comment on them made me feel on top of the world. I was so starved for any sliver of praise that I hung on his every word.

'I feel like a fat housewife making her Christmas cake in September,' I told him, 'You know those types of organised women. Not that I'd have a hope of making a Christmas cake. Anyway she buys all the ingredients, the nuts, the raisins, cherries, flour, almond for the icing, little santies to put on top, a nice drop of whiskey. She slurps it into the baking bowl and whisks and stirs, singing 'White Christmas' in her flowery apron.'

'Christmas cake? What do you mean?'

'All the ingredients spread out before her, the thick creamy mixture coming together in the bowl and then she puts it in the oven and it doesn't rise. Or it rises in parts and sinks in others. Or parts of it are moist and parts like dry porridge meal. There's something missing. It needs to be just moist enough and just dry enough. Do you understand what I'm trying to say?'

'As far as I'm concerned your stories are masterpieces. Any fool can make a Christmas cake.'

'Well I can't, Harry.'

'That's because, my dear woman, you are an artist, a creative person with talent by the bucketful.'

'Do you really believe that?'

'Would I say it if I didn't? I'm long enough teaching English to recognise quality. But cooking has nothing to do with art. Sometimes it takes nine months or even longer to gestate inside the writer. Give yourself time. You're too hard on yourself. It's like a baby being born.'

'I hope mine goes the full term.'

'Why wouldn't it? And I'll tell you another thing. I'll be there for the delivery myself. No prouder midwife than me.'

'The way I feel these days I could have triplets inside me. Big bouncing ones that keep me awake all night with their kicking. Did I tell you I could be at the computer until four in the morning? It's taking over my life.'

'And so it should. Writing is a compulsion. A true artist will forget to eat, to sleep, to wash or dress. You have all the hallmarks, my dear. Joan Didion used to sleep in the same room as her books because she thought of them as living things. So indeed did John Steinbeck.'

'You're such an encouraging person, Harry. You really give me belief in myself.'

'The talent is there, but as I said before, stop all this story lark. Develop an overall plan, work all your characters together and blend them into a novel. Hey presto, before you can say Bob's your uncle, your creation will be on a shelf. As the old Chinese proverb says, he who does not create, destroys. Create, my dear woman, create, you have it in you.'

I pictured him arriving at Holles Street with a babygro and flowers for Mamma and the pair of us carrying my masterpiece home in a Moses basket where it would sleep warm and cosy inside its rich-coloured velum covers. But knowing me I'd probably miscarry within the month.

CHAPTER 30

One evening after the class he asked me if I'd like to visit him and meet his mother. For a moment I began to wonder was he reading more into the friendship than just pupil and tutor but then I thought he was obviously a confirmed bachelor and was just being friendly.

They lived in Skerries, a bit of a distance out, but I still decided I'd pay him a visit.

He met me off the train.

'I brought a story I wrote years ago,' I told him, 'I'll be looking forward to your comments. It's from the past but I kind of like it. I have some new stuff with me as well.' I brought everything but the proverbial 'I can hardly wait to read it,' he said as we walked to his house, 'By the by, mother is also looking forward to meeting you. She doesn't get out much anymore but she's very interested in people.'

The house was down a side-street and opened out onto the road. It was old fashioned and had a thick covering of ivy. Walking in the door was like journey into the past. A fire burned in the grate. The chimney mustn't have been cleaned for years because the living-room reeked of smoke. His mother sat before the open fire, her legs spread out. I could see abc marks all the way up to her fat thighs. She was a big woman and obviously had no shame. I wondered how she'd produced such a slight little bird of a man as Harry. He introduced me as one of his pupils from the writing class and she muttered

'You'll have a bit of salad?' Harry suggested.

I hadn't eaten so I said that'd be grand.

'I'll just drop down to the local shop for some lettuce and tomato. You and Mother can get acquainted.'

I stood clutching my bag with my manuscript. Not a word from the old dame. Eventually I drew up a chair and made an effort to talk to her.

'Not a bad day for the time of the year.'

No reply.

'Harry is a wonderful teacher. He's doing wonders with my work.'

She glared at me with a 'Cut the cackle' look.

'Harry has no intention of getting married,' she said, straight off the bat. That fairly flummoxed me. Not if he was the last man on a desert island would I ever have thought of him that way.

'He's spoiled rotten here with me,' she went on, 'and wouldn't even consider taking on a wife.'

'Right. Good for him.'

She looked a bit taken aback at this but continued unperturbed.

'So you needn't think you can be making sheep's eyes at him. I've seen wans like you before. Ye're all the same. I ran them before and by God I'll run you.'

I couldn't believe what I was hearing.

'I've never thought of Harry that way,' I said.

'I saw the way you looked at him.'

I was on the point of backing out the door quietly and leaving her to her darling boy when he came back with the salad. He looked a bit rattled. Maybe he'd witnessed this sort of scene playing itself out before. He put out a few wilted pieces of lettuce, cut up a tomato in four quarters and put some stale-looking white bread on a plate.

'Tea or coffee?' he asked me.

'Tea if you wouldn't mind,' I said.

The meal was taken in total silence, each morsel savoured by Harry and his doting mama. Afterwards I helped him clean up and he gingerly suggested a walk on the beach. That would be nice but the time is getting on. Maybe we could go over my writing.'

'A walk will blow away the cobwebs, make me fresher in myself to give you a better commentary. The trains run until eleven, you know.'

It seemed selfish not to agree so the pair of us put on our coats.

'Bye, mother,' he called on the way out. That drew a grunt from the old crone.

There was quite a strong gale blowing and the sand got into my eyes. At one stage he linked me and I felt uncomfortable. I bent down, pretending to tie my shoelace. When I stood up again I stuck my two hands into my pockets. It was only a small gesture on his part but I felt he'd crossed a line. Maybe I was still thinking about Box 101 and his mother's ramblings. For the rest of the walk he was quiet, as if I'd hurt his feelings.

When we got back to the house there was no sign of Mommie Dearest.

'She's gone for a lie-down,' he announced. 'She's so considerate. Doesn't want to interfere with our work.'

I produced my pages and we both sat on the sofa. He rummaged through them with a look of great intensity as if I was the new Sylvia Plath.

'I'll read you out the bit from the past,' I said, 'my handwriting is terrible.'

'Off you go, my dear. I'm all ears.'

'It's a piece I did years upon years ago. I just happened to keep it.'

'I'm waiting.'

I cleared and my throat and stated to read:

166

In the final mad dash for the train Rosie ran straight into the ticket collector.

'Watch it, watch it there. Jesus, you're a fine lump of a woman.'

She threw herself into a seat leaving her bags every way and any way. Time enough, girl. Have a ciggie and relax.

'There's no smoking on trains nowadays,' said Harry.

'Yes, but like I said, it was done a long time ago.'

'Fair enough. Continue.'

When the train was well out of Dublin she paid a visit to the toilet. In the mirror she saw herself not with kind Rosie's brown eyes but with cold measuring female ones. Men's eyes? No. Men's eyes didn't measure. They just skimmed over her and passed on to the girl with the little waist and the small pert bum. Rosie's eyes would not have seen fat thighs nor straggly fair hair nor indeed a pimple on the top of the nose. Years of lining up at discos where she'd wilted like a stodgy piece of sliced pan while sleek little chocolate éclairs glided onto the floor in the arms of civil servants from Clare or secondary school teachers from Athboy had made Rosie's eyes not Rosie's eyes.

'Nice bit of imagery there,' Harry put in. Getting slowly more confident, I continued.

Hedges and fields. Hedges and fields. Rosie watched them and thought of men that might or might not come to her. They wouldn't have to be on white horses. They could be on little brown donkeys or walking on narrow country roads or crawling along behind hedgerows. Or. Or, Or they could be Mr Rochester.

The train sped on and she closed her eyes and thought of Rochester leaning down from his horse and grabbing her. Off they would ride until they reached a deserted white strand. He wrapped his greatcoat round her and they lay close and little bits of green seaweed trailed round their limbs. Mr Rochester would stroke her plump thighs and afterwards they would light a fire and drink port and make love.

'If I might interrupt,' said Harry. 'Surely Mr Rochester is from one of the Bronte works. Emily's, I'm inclined to think, but don't quote me on that.'

'Charlotte actually. Yes, he's from *Jane Eyre*. It's just in Rosie's mind. He's her knight in shining armour.'

'I see. Don't know if that's a good idea, my dear. You must draw on your own creativity. Surely you can create a knight in your own imagination.'

'Well Rosie liked him. I'm just trying to convey that. If you think it doesn't work I won't go on.'

'Don't be so touchy. I'm just giving you a few suggestions.'

'Maybe I'll leave it. It's probably useless.'

'You must learn to take constructive criticism. I love it. Please let me hear some more.' Not feeling so perky now I went on reading.

Rosie rooted in her handbag for another cigarette. Her hand touched something hard and smooth and she pulled out a grey stone with speckles of blue running through it.

'Where did this come from?' she asked herself.

'Howya keeping, Rosie?' said the stone, 'Long time no see.'

'What's going on here? Am I losing my marbles or what?'

'Divil a marble. Don't you remember me? I met you years ago. St Mary's Avenue, Galway city, circa 1965. Does that ring a bell? You picked me up and put me in a matchbox. In cotton wool I was wrapped because I was your stone. Afterwards you put me in a drawer with a paper flower you got off a boy in third class and a picture of Elvis.'

'Is this a child's story, might I ask?' said Harry, 'Stones can't speak.'

'Well I wasn't really thinking on those lines. Just sort of dreamy stuff in the woman's head.'

'The woman's head. Is it stream of consciousness you're after?'

'I suppose. I'm not really clear, it just came out that way.'

'Well you might as well go on. Maybe I'll see what you're trying to get at after a while.'

I felt a total fool at this stage but kept on reading:

I've lain in a bottom drawer with the flower and Elvis,' continued the stone, 'for years. I'm sick of the loneliness and nobody to throw a word at me. This morning I crept into your bag and here I am.'

'I faintly remember you,' said Rosie, 'but I'm surprised you recognise me. Look at the cut of me. I'm ugly and horrible and so awfully fat. I hate myself. But you haven't changed. Your still have your grey greyness and your blue blueness and your darling smooth smoothness.'

'Give over,' said the stone. I think you're just dandy. I like cuddly women myself. Something to hold onto. Give us a kiss there, Rosie. Just a small one.'

'Not in front of all the people I won't. Such behaviour would be considered most odd. Kissing stones on public transport is not acceptable.'

almost stopped. I thought it was Harry snuggled up under the covers. I was too frightened to move.

'Harry,' I called, 'what are you doing down there?'

No response, but the breathing continued.

'Harry, this isn't funny. You're frightening me.'

Nothing.

I started to scream. Lights went on everywhere and Harry and his mother came rushing into the bedroom.

'What's going on here?' she roared 'don't tell me you let the hussy stay the night.'

'Easy, mother, she missed the train.' He fixed his gimlet eye on me. 'What's wrong with you? Had you a bad dream?'

'There's something in my bed. For God's sake get a light.'

He pulled the covers off me and I saw a white furry ball with pink eyes.

It's only Tony Rabbit,' the mother harumphed. 'What sort of a baby are you? I won't sleep a wink for the rest of the night.'

'Get back into bed, mother, you'll freeze. I'll be into you with a cup of cocoa in a few minutes.' She stormed out of the room like a ship in full sail.

'Jesus, Harry, I nearly died of fright. What's a rabbit doing in the bed?'

'He sleeps here mostly. The bed is always empty. I forgot to move him out. You're very nervy in yourself, aren't you?'

'Not really. You just don't expect to feel something alive in the bed with you.'

Make yourself comfortable there. I'll attend to mother and be back with a cup of tea. I'll take Tory downstairs. He won't bother you again.'

I heard him foostering round downstairs and there were also a few shouts from the old bag. After a while everything was quiet and he arrived with the cup of tea. He had removed his dressing gown and was in a striped pair of pyjamas. I noticed he'd left the jacket buttons open. The bottoms were clinging to his little belly for dear life.

'Here, my little duckling, drink this up and you'll be fine.'

I grabbed the tea from him and sat up straight in the bed. To hell with Tony Rabbit, this fellow was much more frightening now. Where was the mild-mannered English teacher who was so interested in my literary works?

'Thanks, but I really must get some sleep now.'

'All I'm doing is offering you a drink. Is that such a big deal?'

'You better get back to bed I'll have to be leaving here in two hours.'

'Ah for God's sake don't be so practical. I want to talk to you about what you showed me. It might be better now while it's still fresh in my mind. I loved the bit about the woman who liked her boiled egg soft and runny. Very descriptive.'

He moved towards the bed, sitting on the end of it. I saw his hairy chest through the opened buttons.

'Hope you don't' think I'm being very forward.' he said. 'Did anyone ever tell you you're a very beautiful woman?'

'Harry, stop it. It's the drink talking. We're friends Harry, just friends.'

'We can be more. Mother liked you. I'm not asking for anything now but maybe in time you'd get to like me. I know I'm a bit older than you. Not by much mind you. I think we could make a go of it.'

The penny was finally dropping. My writing was probably crap. I was a fly in his web. I should have vamoosed as soon as I saw the bloody feckin rabbit.

'Harry, I've never thought of you that way. It's just a platonic friendship. I value your advice with my writing. No more than that.'

His face fell and I suddenly found myself feeling sorry for him.

'I thought you liked me in other ways too. Did I mis-read the signals?'

'What signals? There weren't any. What are you talking about?'

His mask slipped suddenly.

'We're talking about the fact that I'm giving you illusions about your substandard writing.'

'Is that what you really feel about it? Are you telling me this was all a set-up?'

'How can I put this? You're one of hundreds of hopefuls I see every year. No better, no worse. I didn't tell you any lies, just, well, you know.....'

'Exaggerated?'

'Not even that. Do you know how good you have to be to make it today? It's a rat race out there.'

'You're trying to get out of the fact that you lied to me. Isn't it as simple as that?'

'No, no. You're misquoting me now. Let's start again. I'll go to my room now and in the morning...'

'Hold on a minute. You were willing to fill me up with pipedreams to get me into your claws.'

'I didn't say that. I think you could have potential but I didn't think the writing was what this evening was about.'

'Well *I* did. Now get me a taxi.'

I was about to explode with rage and misery. He tried to speak again but I stopped him.

'Get me a taxi,' I repeated. I wasn't taking no for an answer. If he didn't go for the phone I was either going to make a run for it or hit him. I felt that vicious. After a few seconds he went to the phone like a dutiful son and dialled. He looked at me pleadingly as he left the receiver down but I turned away.

I asked him to leave me alone until the taxi arrived and he did. I looked around at the spareness of the room and wondered how in God's name I'd allowed myself to be hoodwinked again. There was one born every minute.

When the taxi arrived I grabbed my stuff and went out without a word. He held the door open for me, hopping from one varicose-veined foot to the other. His mother called him from upstairs then.

As I walked out the door I heard the pitter-patter of his feet again on the bare wood. He was so dominant in the class and so subservient here. I doubted his mother cared too much about Virginia Woolf or Emily Dickinson. Maybe he'd made a pass at the famous writer he talked about too and that's why she hadn't mentioned him in the introduction to her books.

I cried all the way home in the taxi. Cried for my love life and for my lost friends and my stupid fears and my even more stupid dreams, cried even for Tony Rabbit and my mother-obsessed creative writing teacher. And I cried for myself, cried that I wouldn't be the toast of the thinking people of Ireland, cried and cried all night in the apartment I did so I did.

CHAPTER 31

I called into Jack the following day, returning to him as I always did when my life was upended for one reason or another. It only took him a second to realise something was wrong with me.

'Come on,' he said 'spit it out.'

'It's' nothing. Well not really.'

'You're a bad liar.'

'All right. Remember I told you I was doing some writing?'

'I do, to be sure. And I said, good idea.'

'Well it wasn't. I got so full up of my own importance at the class I was going to that I started to believe what a teacher was telling me about myself. He said I had talent and I swallowed the lie. I won't even bore you with the dreams I had about myself. A fool of a fellow fills me up with nonsense and next minute I think I'm Shakespeare.'

'Do you actually believe the things people say? I stopped doing that years ago.'

'You're right there.'

'Take it as a lesson learnt. It will make a woman out of you.'

'I'll never be a woman, just a senseless child. Do you know what a young girl said to me in the supermarket the other day?'

'No but I have a strange feeling you're going to tell me.'

'There's no need for the sarcasm. She asked me if I was someone's mammy.'

'What's wrong with that, sunshine?'

'I had to pretend I had children of my own. I felt so embarrassed. It was at the checkout. Her mother had four other children and was nearly nine months gone with the next. You're a man, you wouldn't understand.'

'I wouldn't be too sure about that. I'm human, in case you haven't noticed.'

'I told a big fat lie and said I had three girls and two boys and the woman gave me a warm smile as if to say, "We're in the same club, the mammies of the world." A mother's love is a blessing, nobody cares about you like your mammy.'

'You still could have a few babies,' he said, 'You can't be that old. What age are you anyway?'

'I'm well into my forties and not a sign of a man on the horizon. How can I have a baby at this late stage? No, I'm nobody's mammy and never will be.'

I found myself filling up and he drew me towards him. I snuggled into his worn old coat, not caring about the strong smell of cider. For a while I just sat there feeling strangely comforted.

Later when I got home I saw there was a postcard from Minnie. She had a wonderful time in Australia and had gone straight on to visit Clem in Florida. She seemed over the moon. There wasn't any mention of John. In the same post I had a letter from the solicitor. Anna's estate had been wound up so all that remained was the sale of the house. The letter said there was to be an auction in early December and that if I liked to attend he was enclosing details. That was just a few weeks away.

I continued to turn up at the shop. It wasn't the same without Anna but it kept me in a routine. Now and again I had another shot at a story, but without the belief I had in Harry Browne my efforts were lacklustre.

On the day of the auction Minnie phoned. She asked if she could spend the weekend with me because she had so much she wanted to tell me. I told her I'd probably be loaded after the auction and that we could have a good knees-up for ourselves.

Fred and myself met in town and went to the auction rooms together. There were quite a few people interested, the kind of people I used to see sometimes in the office at work, dripping jewellery. You could smell the money off them. A gavel was pounded and they raised their fingers almost unnoticeably to up the ante. It was strange thinking that these raised fingers could determine the way I'd be able to live my future.

In the end it went for €300,000. The auctioneer was delighted, rubbing his hands in glee after the buyer left the building.

'You're in clover,' he beamed, 'We did a big marketing spree on this and it's paid off'. But I thought he must have been interested in his own fat fee too. 'There are three reasons it did so well,' he added, 'location, location and location'. Then he gave a hearty laugh. He told us we'd have our cheques in early January. We'd have to pay some tax but we'd have about €130,000 each in the finish.

To celebrate we went for a meal. Fred ordered champagne and made a big fuss of everything but I could see his heart wasn't in it. We were both flush and yet something felt empty. I got dizzy with the champagne and suddenly felt like bawling. When I told Fred, he admitted he was the same. We were a delightful pair, sitting there in all the luxury and looking like something a cat dragged in from the rain.

He was terribly lonely, he told me, when our glasses were empty. He said the few short months he had with Anna had been the best time in his life since his wife died. .

'I know I'm lucky to have my children and my grandchildren but Anna was a partner to me. You have to let your family get on with their lives.'

There was nothing I could say to comfort him. I suggested we meet regularly and have a meal together. Cold comfort for Fred, but it was all I could think of.

'We'll definitely keep in touch,' I promised, giving him a kiss on the cheek.

'Definitely.'

He had tears in his eyes. We both probably knew we'd have little enough contact now that Anna was gone he pulled his coat collar up and we went in separation directions for our buses. .

Minnie arrived that weekend. She'd changed her hair colour to a sort of rich auburn and looked better than I'd ever seen her in years.

'What's your secret?' I asked.

'Separation,' she beamed. 'I had a brilliant time. The weather was fantastic and Clem must have spent a fortune on me.'

'I'll have to watch yourself and Clem.' I said. 'It sounds as if there's something going on there.'

'Ah, no, we're just good friends'. But she got quite pink.

'How did Australia go?'

'It was unbelievable. The twins treated me like royalty. The have a lovely flat in Melbourne and both of them have great jobs Gracie is dating a fellow from Cork. I can see it lasting. And Greta is involved with an Australian. I'm not too sure about him. A bit up himself, but it's early days.'

'Fair play to them, I'm glad they're doing so well.'

Then I told her how rich I was going to be and demanded she let me bring her for a meal. We wined and dined ourselves in an expensive restaurant in Howth. Every chance she got she brought up Clem's name. He had a son who was married with two children. The wife was a bit of a pain but the son was easy going like Clem.

'Any news of John?' I asked when she took a breath.

'Who? Oh him. He's still with your woman. Have you heard the latest? Teresa met him recently and he told her her ladyship was pregnant.'

'I don't believe it.'

'I'm dead serious. Teresa was looking at his beer belly and she said, 'If that was on a woman she'd be pregnant.' He said back to her, 'It was - and she is!' The man has no shame, making a joke of something like that. It just shows you how heartless he is.'

'Oh God. Does that make it worse for you?'

'Not really. I couldn't care less. It'll put manners on him when he has to change dirty nappies at his age. There's another side to that coin. He wants his women pregnant, barefoot and in the kitchen, but I doubt the new lassies are up to that. She'll probably make him cut the cord. Maybe she'll even want him to get the morning sickness with her.'

'You're a panic, Minnie.'

Clem had done wonders for her self-image. I almost felt a bit jealous. She had a husband and children and now she was getting another chance. Why were things not more evenly balanced out?

The rest of the weekend I heard nothing but Clem Clem Clem. She phoned him twice and spent so long on the line I eventually went to bed leaving her whispering into the phone. This was serious stuff. If there was a sock for every shoe, she was well on the way to getting her second one.

On the Monday before she went back to Galway I gave her a few bob and told her to treat herself in town. I left her to shop on her own as we both preferred that. I told her I'd meet her in Stephen's Green near the fountain.

After what seemed like an eternity she came back laden down with bags.

'Thanks to you,' she panted, 'I've got some lovely stuff. I can't wait to show it to you. You're a real pal so you are.' And she gave me a hug.

The rest of that day, and the day after, we spent living on old memories. Before she left she invited me to come to Galway again for Christmas.

'I promise it won't be anything like last year. We're both alone. Why not spend it together?'

I was delighted to get the invitation. She said to come down about five days before Christmas. 'That way you can help with the decorating while I'm out earning my living.'

After seeing her off on the train I wandered into a nearby hotel to have my tea. The place was packed and the waitress asked me if I wouldn't mind sharing with another woman.

'Hope you don't mind me joining you,' I said as I sat down.

'Well I prefer to dine alone actually, but okay.'

'I'm sorry, it's just the place is so packed.'

She had dyed blonde hair and was laden down with gaudy jewellery. I felt I knew her from somewhere but couldn't quite place her. I was a little awkward after her snooty comment so took out a magazine and began to read. I could feel her eyes burrowing into me. She finally banged her fork off the table.

'I know you,' she said.

'Really? Your face is familiar to me too.'

A few seconds later I realised who it was: Moira Ryan-Burke from The Holy Faith Convent in Clontarf. She hadn't changed a bit. I sat beside her in fourth year. I'd spent my final year there after we came up from Galway. She was unfriendly and full up of herself. Made me feel like a thick culchie. I'd heard her laughing at my accent one day in the refectory.

'God this is amazing!' she trilled. She was dressed in fake fur, her perfume stinking to high heaven.

179

'It's a small world. What have you been up to?'

'Not much really, just poddling along.' I answered.

'Poddling along! Is that all you can come up with after all these years. God I can't believe this.' You'd think we were bosom pals the way she was rattling on. As far as I was concerned she might have been the man, or the woman, on the moon. We made small talk for a few minutes and then she got to the inevitable question.

'Are you married?'

'Yes.' I decided not to give the old bitch the soot.

'Same here. Kids?'

'Yes, four. May as well do it in style.'

'We just have the three. Where are you living? Maybe you'd call out sometime. I could show you the house.'

'We're a good bit out of town. County Meath actually.'

At this stage the waitress had taken my order. I wanted to get out of the place fast. I couldn't keep up the lies much longer.

She rambled on about her three darling children. Stephanie was in her first year at College and Jason in the IT business. Little Hilary was still at Secondary.

'But I'm going on too much about my lot. What are your four up to?'

'The eldest, Juanita, is named after Juan Carlos. He has Mexican blood in him. She's at Cambridge reading English Lit. Next we have Percy. He's named after his y granddad, who owned a string of horses in Lincolnshire. He's majoring in Economics at TCD. Beverly is studying Marketing and Design and little Charles is taking silk.'

'What does that mean?'

'Don't you know? Of course English was never exactly your strong point in school, was it? I. He's going to be a barrister. Juan's grandmother was the first female lawyer in her town many moons ago. It's in the blood, I always say.'

'Really? Stephanie is very bright, you know. She got the highest marks in the school for her Leaving Cert. George says it's not off the ground she licked it. You probably remember how good I was at maths in school. I don't think you were particularly bright in that department.'

'No, couldn't add for toffee. Just as well Juan Carlos is so wealthy. I have a Gold Card and he never minds what I spend. Couldn't imagine myself having to count all the euros.'

I could see her taking in my appearance. Fortunately I was fairly well turned out that particular day. I also had the highlights in the week before.

I said I was in a dash but she wouldn't let me go that easily.

'Let's meet again,' she pressed, 'Give me your phone number and I'll give you a bell. It would be great if the kids could meet too. I never see any of the girls from school.'

I felt like saying I wasn't surprised. I made up a false number and she said she'd remember it.

'You've made my day,' she said trotting off.

The experience cheered me up. I almost felt I should rush home to get a meal for Juanita, who'd be in from College soon. Then I remembered that Percy was going to a ball this evening so I'd have to race off to hire out his dress suit.

I treated myself to a few drinks on the way home. A handsome fellow with gypsy looks was eying me up. He asked if he could join me and offered me a drink. I said no thanks and   went home and took up my efforts from the writing class. In spite of Harry Browne I still made notes in a jotter that I kept in my handbag. I could never see it as a novel but perhaps a long short story. At the very least it was keeping my mind occupied. To the Bridget Small part I'd added a character called John Finnerty. They were an odd couple, to be sure:

John Finnerty had full board in a house off Fairview Strand. One damp Saturday afternoon he arrived in early from a day in town. In the middle of the floor, with her feet plonked in a basin of water, sat Bridget Small. The blue little bulging veins stood out on her skinny white legs. ' Pass us the soap, would you John?' she said and as she spoke his mind went back to a day he'd seen his mother sitting with her feet in water and saying the exact same words. He'd ignored her, instead hurrying out to see a football match. He'd been wracked with guilt since but in that moment he fell hopelessly in love with Bridget Small, a woman who was thirty years his senior and who in one split second made all the guilt go away. He handed her the slippy soap and she smiled.

CHAPTER 32

Christmas was on top of me in no time. I got my money just ten days before and waltzed into Arnotts. I splurged out on presents for Minnie. I sent a cheque to Angie and bought myself various items in the clothes department, surprise surprise. Nothing too elaborate, just a few pairs of trousers, two party dresses, some cuddly Christmas jumpers, a pair of drop-dead gorgeous green boots and a pure wool coat with leather trimmings. (Using restraint as usual).

As promised to Minnie, I made my way down to her on the early train on December 23. It was jammers with people going home for the holidays. I had quite a few of the old nervous complaints and made a number of shaky trips to the toilet. Checked all my bodily parts carefully but amazingly enough everything seemed in working order. Maybe a slight white fur on the tongue and perhaps the knees looked a little puffy but I managed to keep myself reasonably cool.

Minnie met me at the station. She was off work until after Christmas and looked glowing. She grabbed my suitcase and hauled me down to a nearby pub for a sandwich and a cup of coffee.

'You've lost a bit of weight, Minnie. It suits you.'

'Not intentionally. To be honest, I'm finding it hard to eat.'

'John isn't back on the scene, is he?'

'It's not John anymore, it's Clem.'

'Oh Minnie, I'm glad for you.'

'I knew you would be. We're getting on famously. He's hoping to be here on Stephen's Day. I can't believe how excited I am. I feel like a teenager. I'm walking into doors. I'm going to throw a party for him on the 27th and I want you to help me with the preparations.'

'Okay, but would you not prefer to be alone with him?'

'I'll have plenty of time for that. He has an open ticket. He might stay for a month or longer, depending how we get on. I just can't stop smiling to myself. I never thought I could feel this way again.'

'How old is he, do you mind me asking?'

'Middle sixties, in his prime.'

'Twenty years older than you. God, it seems a lot, Minnie.'

'Have you not heard? 60 is the new 50. Age only matters if you're a cheese. Look at Joan Collins. In her prime and lovely as ever. Anyway, he acts like a child most of the time. I'm the sensible one.'

'Don't say anymore or you'll make me jealous.'

'What's been going on in your own life? Any man on the horizon?'

'I wouldn't know what they even look like anymore.'

'Stop that. You're still a young woman. You know my feelings on Nigel. He held you back. Anyway, I was going to make a suggestion to you. Clem has a brother in Chicago. He looks gorgeous and he's free.'

What is he: S, W or D?'

'Come again?'

'Single, widowed or divorced.'

'D. But a good D.'

'I'll take your word for it. The next time I get desperate I'll hop on a Boeing 747. In the meantime, why don't we attack the infinitely more important activity of shopping?'

I snuggled up in the small room in Minnie's house that night. The nerves were still a bit wobbly and the heart giving funny beats. If I was a horse, I thought, they'd have to shoot me. But something in there was still ticking. I sat up in the bed after an hour of trying to sleep and added a few lines to my masterpiece:

The landlady of the establishment was a fat little button of a woman. Precise in herself with beady eyes and little curls permed tightly round her red ears. When she found him in the bedroom with Bridget Small's cold blue legs wrapped round him she stamped her little slippered feet and shouted that this kind of dirt was not acceptable in a decent home such as hers.

Then I fell asleep dreaming of myself and Daire walking the strand at Dollymount.

CHAPTER 33

Christmas Eve saw Minnie in a flurry of preparation for Clem. She scrubbed the house from top to bottom, a new experience for her. She even went as far as washing down the doorstep. (I don't think it had seen clean water for twenty years or more). In the afternoon she went into town to have her hair done while I went out Salthill for a walk.

I sat on a seat on the prom with my jotter on my lap and began to write:

John Finnerty never had any real schooling but in his head he had the makings of a concerto or sonata or even a symphony. He could hear the pounding of it everywhere he went. He saw himself up on a stand conducting like billyo with violins and cellos and oboes and flutes coming in at his beckoning. Oh to be able to shout it out for the world to hear. If it wasn't for the fact that he didn't know a quaver from a lump of a sausage he could be another Beethoven. Why oh why had he been born into a poor Irish peasant background. At times the noise reached such a crescendo he had to put his fingers in his ears to stop the loud banging.

As I walked in towards town to meet Minnie I felt I could hear the music in my own head, felt that I was becoming Finnerty. Crowds were milling round doing the last of the shopping. A musician was lashing out a tune I used to dance to called The Blackbird. I was tempted to get up and dance but contented myself with beating my foot to the melody.

I arrived in the bar before Minnie and had an Irish coffee. The place was packed to the gills. 'The Fields of Athenry' was being murdered by a group at the bar. I was tempted to have another peak at my jotter, and another Irish coffee. After a few seconds I put the jotter back in my bag it was too noisy to concentrate of my masterpiece. .

Minnie came bouncing in, laden down with parcels.

'I'm exhausted from the shopping, I got a brilliant bargain for Clem. A lovely tweed jacket. It was in O'Maille's. Daddy always told me that's where John Wayne got his jacket for *The Quiet Man.* I know I'm no Maureen O Hara but there's no harm dreaming, It was the last one in the shop. I hope he'll like it and that it'll fit. He's a big man, you know.' She gave a knowing wink as she babbled on,

'I'm sure it'll be fine.'

'I hope you like what I picked for you too. No peeping at it now until Christmas morning. By the way you'll never guess who I saw on Mainguard Street.'

'Who?'

'John. And your woman with him.'

'Go away. Did he see you?'

'He tried to avoid me but I marched up to the pair of them. And before you ask - yes, she's preggers.'

'Oh, Minnie, I'm sorry.'

'Well I'm not. I told you how I feel about him. I can't say much for his taste, though. As my mother used to say, her legs aren't the best part of her.'

'Well it's great you see it like that. I think Clem has a lot to do with how you're feeling. Did you say anything to him?'

'I asked him to introduce me to his fancy woman.'

'You didn't. How did he take that?'

'He couldn't wait to get away from me.'

'Are you sure you're not building Clem up too much, Minnie? You hardly know him.'

'No way. I have a good feeling about us.'

'It's early days yet. Don't rush into anything.'

'I'll rush as fast as my feet can carry me. Anyway, what's up with you? You look very grumpy.'

'I'm just a bit tense. It'll pass.'

'No doubt it will. Come on, have another drink.'

We had a quiet Christmas Day. Minnie was a changed woman from the person I'd spent last Christmas with. She'd bought a huge tree and decked it out in style. I wasn't in much humour for food or talk but for her sake I put on a mask and pretended to enjoy her attempt at cooking. Burnt turkey, ham too dry, sprouts all soggy, stuffing too wet, potatoes very lumpy. She talked non-stop about Clem's arrival and what time did I think he would arrive in Galway. Apparently he was flying into Shannon and hiring a car at the airport.

By 10 p.m. I felt a bit like the poor boy at the wake, as they saying goes. I told Minnie I was tired and heading for the hills. I knew she thought I was jealous and maybe she was right. It was just the luck of the draw, being in the right place at the right time. I knew I still looked reasonably presentable but maybe it was my manner that put men off. Maybe I needed to be remodelled and have my esteem built up in some sort of a course. Or maybe I needed to write some more. My two friends Finnerty and Bridget were good therapy for me:

..

In the early spring Bridget invited Finnerty for a walk in Fairview Park. It was a cold blustery sort of day and Bridget was in chatty form. 'The way of it is, John,' she said, 'I'm the kind of person that speaks my mind, direct and honest to a fault. Now Anjelica, remember her, she's the one who was the supervisor in Accounts. Well anyway she asked me straight out what did I think of her hair and I told her it wasn't a suitable style for a woman of her age. Well John, if you were to hear the way she turned on me. John, are you listening to me?'

'Sorry,' said Finnerty, and he cried inside his head. Would the woman ever shut up rattling on? He was just at the point of the flute intermezzo, or whatever you call it. She was a harmless poor devil, though. Her eyes were the same sort of green-grey as Mam's. One minute she was Helen of Troy to him the next Old Mother Reilly. Oh to hell with it, be nice to the woman.

'I heard every word you said, Bridget, he said, 'honestly I did. Now would you like me to take you for a slap-up meal tomorrow after work?' Bridget's little pink cheeks puffed out and she cuddled up to him like a fat little kitten.

I slept late on Stephen's morning and woke to hear voices. Blast it, Clem must have arrived. Now I'd have to act as if I was delighted for the pair of them.

He was sitting at the kitchen table and Minnie was getting him something to eat. He was younger-looking than I remembered and twice as handsome. Like a lumberjack with big strong arms and a check shirt open at the neck. A small bit of the Clint Eastwood going on.

'Pleased to meet you again,' he said, 'Here, take a seat. Can I get you anything?'

'No thanks but you're good to ask.'

'Oh Clem knows how to treat a woman,' Minnie assured me. Smugly, I thought.

We made polite chit-chat but I knew they wanted to be alone. I stayed at the table as long as I felt was reasonable and then told them I was going for a good long walk out the Prom to clear my head.

'Don't you pair be staying around for me if you have plans. Fire ahead. I'll be fine on my own.'

'Are you sure?' said Minnie half-heartedly, 'We could all go out to Spiddal in the afternoon. I want to show Connemara to Clem.'

'You'd be very welcome,' said Clem. .

'No, honestly, I really feel like a good bracing walk. I'll see you when I see you.'

Out Salthill again. Nobody much around. Passed happy houses with Christmas lights in the window. Poor little match girl outside looking in. No home to go to. Keep on walking. Don't think too much.

But I did. I thought about granny and granddad and mammy and daddy and Angie and Brian and all the people who'd meant something to me once but were gone now.

My mind carried me back to the past as I strolled along.

Granny had a pub in Cork and every summer the whole lot of us travelled down to it and stayed two weeks. She allowed Angie and me to go behind the bar. Lemonade in big glasses and swatting flies with rolled-up newspapers. Littlle old women in shawls. Neat and tidy in the snugs, sipping their glasses of Guinness. Grandaddy stayed up in the sitting-room looking out at the bottles coming into the yard and keeping a count. Granny ran the pub. No one better to get out rowdies. Firm but always a lady. Then when grandaddy died she came and lived with us in miserable Artane.

The houses on the road were new at that time. Every single one the same. Granny had to share the bedroom with me and Angie. We were absolutely horrible to her and used to stay awake whispering and sniggering. We hated having to share our room with the poor woman.

Of course we knew it all. Both of us dickied-up in our mini-skirts and beehive hairdos.. The Cricket Club on a Saturday night. Carnival in Donnycarney. A gorgeous fellow with slicked back hair working on the bumpers. Just like one of those teddy boys from the fifties. 'Spit on me Herbie, you're only gorgeous.' And then home to sharing a room with boring old Granny.

Granny was a very jolly sort of a woman. It must have been lonely away from all her friends. I could just imagine what her life must have been like:

'Can we have another Foxes mint, granny Give us a spray of your 4711. Go on, granny. Tell us about Tim West.' 'Well Tim West was up on the stool inside the door one night and a fight broke out with himself and Jim Barrett. Jim spilt a drink on Tim and Tim shouted out 'You're after destroying me father's drawers.'

Angie and myself would laugh and laugh and think ourselves as smart as new paint imagining Tim and his old dad with just one pair of drawers between them.

'Give us another Foxes mint, granny. Tell us about the woman waiting for the train in Cork station.' 'Well myself and Bridie Casey were in the ladies toilet in Cork station waiting for the train to go to Mallow. This woman came along with her friend, holding herself as if she was about to wet the floor any minute. 'Look Maisie,' said her friend, 'it only costs a penny to go.' 'A pinny! A pinny!' said your woman, 'I'll hould it till I get to Castleisland.'

Angie and myself would nearly choke thinking of it, chortling at poor people with one pair of drawers between father and son, or people who couldn't afford to go to the toilet, not realizing that they were infinitely more interesting than we'd ever be.

I passed by the Estoria cinema. Happy happy days. One time myself, Angie and Mammy had gone to the pictures every day for a whole week. It was summertime and they showed a different film every afternoon. We stuffed ourselves with Smarties and Crunchies and oh the treat of it. I'd never forget that. That and the sneaky joy of being let off school one day before Christmas,because I pretended to be sick. Mammy bought me a comic, *The School Friend*, and it was the Christmas edition so it had snow at the top. Every Thursday we got that comic. It had stories of English girls with lovely names - Pamela and Joyce and Princess Anita. The heroines would have little tip tilted noses and I'd often push my nose up and stare into the mirror wishing my nose wasn't so broad and boring.

I walked towards Salthill and turned up O'Leary's Lane. St Mary's Avenue was the new name. Our house looked good. Still the same low little gate at the front. The same green bush with its dark green leaves growing wild over the wall.

Across the road was the Monks field. It was a little housing estate now. Memories of grey-faced boys dressed in grey clothes. Young fellows from the Iindustrial School facing O'Leary's shop.

'Daddy, why do those boys have to dig potatoes?' 'They've no mammys and daddys, pet.' 'But Daddy, they're only little fellows.' 'I know, love, don't worry about it. Will I tell you another story and then promise to go to sleep?' 'Yes, Daddy, just one more story and I promise.'

So many sad grey boys. None of us snug in our little houses knew of the horrors of abuse they'd suffered. Where did they all end up? It was too awful to think of.

I passed Muddy Starr's house and thought of Muddy and her daughter Phil. Even as children Angie and I knew there was something different about Phil. No husband. Just her mother and son Ted. Not a widow. How come? Years later Mammy told us Phil was 'a deserted wife,'. A strange thing at the time. Separated sounded all right but deserted was such a cold word. We'd sit with Muddy, me and Angie, when Phil went out for a while. 'Can the girls come down to mind Muddy while I run into town?'

She was a bit like a moon, Muddy, far too round to be a star. A big woman with spectacles and white hair. Every Christmas she'd knit mittens for us.

'Sing us a song, Muddy, you know - the one about the person dreaming.'

'I dreamt I dwelt in marble halls with vassals and serfs by my side.'

I walked back and looked in at O'Leary's shop. All different now, turned into a supermarket. Open plan just like any other shop. There used to be a long counter and you could get broken biscuits for a few pennies. Mr O'Leary, small and bald, whistling as he sliced the bacon. One time daddy played a joke on him and sold him his own bike. 'God, Tom, it's better than my own one. How much are you looking for?' Poor man, he didn't even realise it looked familiar.

The year we left Galway, granny in Glenamaddy died. I remembered being in the shop having to take the message. Auntie Kathleen on the phone. I was so young I hardly knew how to hold it. 'Tell your mammy granny is dead. Tell her to get a black coat for me in town. Tell her we'll be at the phone in Collins at 7 p.m.on Christmas Eve. No Santy that year. No birthday cake. Me and Angie spent Christmas with the Mulcahys. The beginning of a terrible time. In the January we moved to cold bleak Dublin where the streets were so wide and you could hardly see the neighbours' houses across the road. I cried myself to sleep the first night, begging to be let home to O'Leary's Lane, the Monk's field and Muddy Starr.

Other memories came flooding back. Daddy and Mammy started in the Civil Service on the same day.

'Tell us about when you saw Daddy for the first time. Please, Mammy, tell us, will you?'

'Your father and myself started work the same day. The minute I saw him I knew immediately he was the man for me. The very exact thing happened with your granny and granddaddy. Granny looked out her window, saw granddaddy walking by and said, 'That's the man I'll marry.' I think women know before men when the right one comes along. I was the only woman that would go up to Dublin on the train to watch the hurling and football. Six or seven men and me. I think that was what took your Daddy's fancy first. Anyway we went out for a while. We'd go out Salthill for walks and one time a fellow met your Daddy and said, 'Where's your sister?' because I wasn't with him. I suppose we did look alike. Both of us tall. Your dad was lighting mad that anybody would think he'd be such a sissy out walking with his sister.'

'What happened when ye broke up, Mammy?'

'We weren't too serious in the first few weeks. Next thing he was taking out the Murray one from Fairhill. She was a teacher. I was heartbroken but never let on. One day I was bending down picking up files and he leaned over and straightened the parting in my hair. You know how particular your Daddy is. It was hard for me but I never pretended to care a bit. That's what ye should do, girleens, keep your feelings to yourself until you're sure of your man. Anyway he asked me out a few weeks after and I made him tell the Murray one it was finished. I wouldn't agree to go anywhere with him until he promised to do that. And so he did.'

'What happened the Murray one, Mammy'?

'She never married.'

'Imagine, Angie, you and me could be two little small butty ones. She was butty, wasn't she Mammy?

'Very butty, and aren't ye lucky you got me for a mammy?'

'Yes, Mammy, very lucky.'

I went into the Jesuit's church to say a prayer. Me and Angie sang in the choir here for three years. Hail Queen of Heaven, O Salutaris Hostia. Could still see the pair of us, all dressed up in our Sunday best. 'Your mother keeps you lovely on a Sunday' Angie was in firsts because she had a higher voice and me in seconds.

Going down the steps I thought of my Communion picture. Pretty faded now, like myself. It was picked out to be put in the window of the photographer's showrooms. Mammy and myself passing by, mammy as proud as punch. The little white dress and my hair all tangled and curly. Mammy put in ringlets the night before, but it rained and they fell out. It made me look as if I had natural curls. My dream then.

We'd played skipping after school at the bottom of the school steps.

'All in together girls, this fine weather girls, when I call your birthday please jump out.'

January, February, March, April. I had to skip all the way to December. Mammy called me a Christmas Present because I was born on Christmas Day.

'Raspberry, apple, my jam tart, tell me the name of your sweetheart.'

A, B, C, D, trying to get to P for Pom. Pom Barrett, my first big crush. When we were walking out the avenue of Canon Roche's grounds he said to me, 'Can I tie your ribbon, love?' I went pucey pink and thought about his words for months. Wellington boots and short corduroy pants and me in a blue dress with smocking and little ducks round the hem. I loved that dress. 'Can I tie your ribbon, love?' Minnie told me he was as bald as an egg now, with a big belly on him.

I passed the Regional Hospital and thought of the time Brian was so sick. Every day Mammy and Daddy went in to see him with presents of books He was just twelve at the time and he was kept in for months. They couldn't say what was wrong with him, just something in the blood. We went to Mass every morning for him, said novenas to Blessed Martin de Porridge, and mammy sent intentions to Lourdes.

Then I got sick myself and they thought I had the same problem. I was put into the fever wing. There were iron bars on the windows and Mammy and Daddy could just look in at me. No such thing as a children's ward then. I was seven and the person closest to me in age was twenty-five. Once Daddy had been visiting Brian and he thought he'd look in on me even though it was late. I heard a tap on the window and saw his Claddagh ring but he left because he thought I was alsleep. I roared crying for hours. Not much sympathy either from the battleaxe of a matron.

Different time now, different hospital. Children not shoved in behind bars with adults.

Another time I stuck a bead up my nose at school. Sister Aquinas asked me to blow into her big white hankie but I was terrified I'd cover it with snot. Instead of blowing, what did I do but suck it further up my nose. It was a yellow bead from a necklace out of Woolworths. A big girl from sixth class told me if it went into my brain I'd die but Dr O'Connor said he'd have it down in two shakes of a lamb's tail. It was the first time I'd ever heard that expression. It took my mind off the bead, thinking about the lamb and his little tail waggling.

'Mammy, tell us about Ned Fahy, please Mammy tell it again.'

'Well, poor old Ned wasn't the full shilling but he had his own wisdom. Your granddaddy would tease him that a man lived up the chimney and he'd get Ned to close his eyes. Your granddaddy would say, 'Tom Chimney come down and leave a cigarette for Ned.' Ned would close his eyes and there in his lap would land a cigarette.

'And what used he say about getting married?'

'There's more married than can churn milk.'

'True for him, girls. Remember that.'

'What does it mean Mammy? Tell us again?'

'It means, girleens, that anyone can get married. But it takes a special kind of person to churn milk.'

All these people were dead now. There was snow on the ground the day of granny's funeral. We all drove down to Mallow behind the hearse. It killed a sheep on the way. The graveyard was freezing. Bernie and Paddy travelled from Glenamaddy. Two tall men standing by the grave. They had cigarettes and kept them lighting all through the burial, their hands curled round them in their pockets. Some trick that. Every so often they took a sneaky puff. I watched them in fascination. It was good to see Mammy's brothers there.

My two worlds together: the Glenamaddy and the Cork.

CHAPTER 34

Minnie's cheeks were pink and her hair was tousled from her love-making the following morning. She looked embarrassed but beautiful. Clem was bright-eyed full of chat. He obviously worshipped the ground Minnie walked on. As she served him his cornflakes he devoured her with his eyes.

'Listen, you two,' I blurted out, 'I think I should head back today.'

'No way,' said Minnie, 'I need your help with the party tonight.'

'I'm sure Clem will give you a hand. I really should get back.'

'I'll be out all day, ladies,' Clem announced, 'I'm heading towards County Clare. My ancestors come from there.'

'Don't be a spoilsport,' said Minnie, 'I've invited loads of people. You've nothing to go back to.'

'Okay,' I said, though I really wanted to be inside my own door and have the space to be as miserable and old-maidish as I liked.

I had to listen to Minnie all of that day. She had a permanent grin on her face which really got on my goat. I didn't resent her happiness but wished she was more low-key about it. I felt she was almost gloating. Between the pair of us we made a huge spread for the party. The house looked lovely and Clem arrived back from Clare with a large supply of drinks. The minute he walked in the pair of them went upstairs together and the spinster sat in the corner sipping a drink to calm herself down before the guests arrived. In no time the place was hopping. Lots of couples, people I recognised from schooldays, the Flaherty one and her baldy husband, a girl called Mona Egan who hadn't changed a bit. I couldn't believe my eyes when Teresa arrived in with a small weedy-looking fellow in a tweed suit and a stripy yellow shirt.

'Hi,' she chirped, 'This is Tony, a friend from work.'

'Pleased to meet you.'

'Great news about Minnie. I couldn't be happier for her. I was just telling Tony here about Clem.'

'Yes, great news.' I wanted to get away from the pair of them but was stuck in a corner wedged in behind a little table.

'Is himself with you?' asked Teresa with a sly look on her mean little face.

'No, he's away on business. Canada actually. I'm expecting him back next week. Now, would anybody like another drink?' I was hoping Tony, who hadn't a word to throw to a dog, would have the manners to refill my glass. No such luck. He was staring into space. I pushed my way towards the drinks cabinet and banged straight into the Flaherty one. We looked through each other. Next thing Minnie, looking beautiful in a sea-green floaty concoction, comes up and says 'Girls, don't you recognise each other? Fourth class, remember Peig?'

'How are you, Peig? I said.

'Fine. Long time no see. You'll have to excuse me, I think my husband is calling me.'

The night dragged on. Most of it I spent drinking on my own. A few familiar faces approached me but I was too down in myself to make any effort. Minnie and Clem disappeared upstairs half way through the night. I wanted to go up myself but as I was staying there I felt it would be rude.

Somebody took up a guitar and songs were bellowed out. A small ratty-looking man asked me if I ever tried my hand at courting. I gave him a filthy look and had another drink. And then another one. After a while someone produced poteen, the lunatic's drink. I had enough to make me lose contact with the lower half of my anatomy. I can't remember the rest of the night.

It was bright before the last of them went home.

'Next time you're around, bring what's-his-name. Tony and I would be delighted to make a foursome, wouldn't we, Tony? That, of course, is if what's-his-name exists.'

'Teresa,' said Tony, 'you've had enough to drink.'

'I'm just curious. Surely if you're in a relationship he'd be with you at Christmas.'

'Sorry, she's had too much,' he said to me and gave me a wink. Not such a bad poor devil, I thought, far too good for that one. I made a small attempt to clean up the mess and went to bed. I was too tired to take my masterpiece out. I heard the squeaky bedsprings from next door before I dropped off to sleep. When I surfaced the next day Minnie was pottering round the kitchen.

'Sorry we deserted you last night. Clem's gone shopping.'

'I think I'll get the early train, Minnie. It's time to get back to Dublin.'

'What's your hurry? You're welcome to stay for a week if you like.'

'Maybe yourself and Clem would like some privacy.'

'No we wouldn't. Our life is an open book.' That certainly seemed the case from the way they'd been carrying on. Open at all the wrong pages, though, as Mae West used to say.

For some reason I felt very crabby towards her. She looked like the cat that got the cream, her cheeks rosy like a little girl's. That's why I got defensive. 'I know when I'm not wanted. I can see I'm in the way. Anyway, you're the hostess after all. I wish you didn't walk out last night. I had to entertain the delightful Teresa, not to mention that smug Flaherty one.'

'I said I was sorry. You know yourself when you meet somebody you care about. All you want is to be with them.'

'I know that wonderful husband of yours couldn't stick me. Clem probably hasn't much time for me either.'

Why was I being so cross? I just couldn't help myself.

'Don't be like that. Listen, I care about you, regardless of what John feels. And Clem thinks you're lovely, that's the truth.'

'I'm sure it is. I'd love to hear what he said behind my back.'

Minnie picked up on my aggressiveness and went one better, proceeding to lash into me. She told me I'd become a right jealous bit of goods. She went on about my values and the person I'd become. She even brought up the fact that my mother had ended her days in a nursing home.

'Surely to God you could have looked after the poor woman. You had the time for it. Angie was in the States. She had her own family but you weren't even married.'

'That's a bit below the belt, Minnie. You didn't live with a deeply depressed woman for ten years.'

'Agreed, but it didn't seem to affect you too much, swanning round the shops like a spendaholic.'

On and on she went. I ended up in tears. Nigel even got dragged into it.

'The way you stayed with that fellow Nigel when anyone with an eye in their head could see you barely tolerated each other.'

'Have you any more insults to throw at me before I go? Do you care nothing about me at all?'

'It's precisely because I care so much about you I'm saying it. If I didn't like you I wouldn't bother.'

I went back that evening. Clem and herself brought me to the train.

'Friends again?' Minnie asked as I got on.

'You don't need to say that.'

Her words were pounding in my head all the way back to Dublin. Had I changed that much? Were my values all skew ways? Should I have looked after my mother? She'd never have turned her back on me. Why had I stayed with Nigel for so long when I knew I never loved him? All the sweat I'd put into a pathetic kitchen. Did I worry too much about my figure and my clothes?

So what if I did. I didn't want the truth anymore, just enough pleasant lies to lull me into old age.

CHAPTER 35

Back in Dublin I turned up for duty three days a week at the shop. Once or twice a week I beavered away at my novel. The writing of it was like therapy for me - free psychiatry with me as both doctor and patient. I was really getting into it but didn't know if it was publishable. Not that that mattered. I kept the crumpled pages in a drawer like the old stone I used to have, taking them out the way you would a beloved toy. Maybe those ramblings were my substitute for having children. Creation instead of procreation. Whatever, they kept my nerves steady as I tried to live through them. Unlike solicitors' secretaries and undependable boyfriends, they couldn't hurt you, and they did exactly what you said.

One evening Bridget came home from work and shook the rain from her face and nobody saw her tender neck or her delicate white hands. John was gone down the country for a few days and as it was a long weekend the boarding house was empty. Even the landlady was gone away, to her sister in Manchester. She'd emigrated when she was 21 and was settled outside the city with her husband and four children.

Bridget stood by the electric fire and the steam and the smell of the rain reminded her of long ago when she'd once said to her mother, 'I'd love to go out and run in the rain with a bar of soap and to wash and have bubbles all over me'. Her mother had replied, 'Such talk is sinful'. Everything had been sinful to her mother, even talk itself, and now she was silenced forever and the spinster lady could stay out all night if she liked, and wouldn't it be a lovely thing to do with John Finnerty.

Poor Bridget Small, my heart went out to her. Maybe if I wrote some more and put herself and John together in wedded bliss, all would be well for both of them. He'd stop stravaging round in all weathers in that bit of a coat and let his mother lie easy in her grave and Bridget would let all her pent-up emotions run as they wished. She was older, of course, but Finnerty was so guilt-ridden because of not handing his poor mother a bar of soap to wash her feet with. Maybe the only way to give him peace would be for him to marry a mother figure.

I had a letter from Minnie a few days later. She wrote that she was sorry if she'd hurt me but some things needed to be said. Clem was staying until the end of February and then he might decide to go home, tie up his affairs and come back to live permanently with her.

'Sorry for being so happy,' she wrote, 'I know your day will come.'

I sent her back a big smarmy card about friendship and added a note telling her I was delighted for herself and Clem despite the way I might have sounded with my sour grapes on the day we traded insults.

In the middle of February I got a letter re-directed from Nigel. It was from a cousin of my father's, Jamesie Creane, who lived in Cork. He wrote that his wife Katie was now in a nursing home in Dublin and that he was old himself and rarely got to see her. He asked if I could possibly pay her a visit.

I was never very close to this couple. I vaguely remembered he had a drink problem.

I paid just one visit to Katie Creane. It brought back too many hurtful memories for me to go there again. She didn't recognise me and never spoke a word. I left a bag of oranges and *Woman's Own* magazine with the sour-looking nurse.

My own mother had been in a nursing home in Clontarf at the end of her life. She'd been suffering from depression for a long time. She fought her darkness at first but the more she struggled the more it seemed to take out of her. Then a useless doctor started to prescribe pills for her, too lazy to seek another cure. After a few months they gave her bigger problems than they ever looked close to solving and she became addicted to them. There were so many concoctions I lost count. She was forever visiting the doctor looking for a 'magic' pill that would take away her pain, but none was to be found.

She worried about the fact that she'd been a poor mother to Angie, Brian and myself, and a bad wife to daddy. Then the religious scruples began and she dragged up trivial incidents from her past to corroborate her case. She convinced herself she was unforgiveable to God, this woman who wouldn't kill a fly on a holy picture.

She spent months in St Pat's hospital and was prescribed other cocktails of pills there but the damage had been done by this time. When they let her home she took to the bed, her favourite haven, as ever.

She reminded me of Miss Havisham from *Great Expectations* as she lay in the darkness. I began to dread coming home from work because I knew what state she'd be in. She became so dependent on me that it was major work trying to persuade her to let me out for a night. Even when I went, she'd ask me to be home at a certain time. Sometimes I had to ring her to assure her I was all right. If I was late at all she had visions of me sitting in a car wrapped round a lamp-post. This was no good to me so I stopped going out after a while. Sitting with her was the lesser of two evils.

After much discussion she eventually agreed to go to the nursing home. It was a forbidding place where old women sat in chairs all day, some of them asleep, others with shrivelled hands gripping onto handbags. Sometimes you'd get a smell of urine in the room. The place was run by a man who seemed to be in it just for the money. Occasionally the Health Board came down on him for some hygiene infringement and he did the bare minimum to keep them off his back. Other than that he didn't lift a finger - except to collect the cheque I paid him dutifully on the eleventh of every month. She was a digit, nothing more. Patient No 27, Room 5E. No special needs. Slightly depressed. *Compos mentis.* Next of kin lived locally and called Mondays, Wednesdays, Fridays and Sundays.

When I visited her she'd be sitting in the parlour staring at a television. The game show Countdown was usually on but she seemed to be the only one who had the foggiest what it was about. Her quick brain would work out the longest words in seconds. There were times I felt she was a victim of that brain. It was too active for her state. Sometimes she'd come out with a huge insight into the political situation or current affairs and I'd think: What are you doing here? You should be out in the world But then she'd go back into her shell again. Maybe she'd have been better off to be as thick as two short planks. Maybe ignorance was bliss.

She'd been something of a nerve case all her life but things had got much worse in the nursing home. On every visit she'd tell me of another pain or another strange jump from her heart. When we lived together we used to exchange symptoms. If ever I got a strange sensation I'd ask her if she ever experienced it. She'd always reassure me by telling me she had the same thing loads of times. It became a family joke. 'That's nothing, I had it and it's harmless.' Between us we must have shared every ailment known to man and we were still alive and kicking.

The visits started to get me down after a few months. She stopped coming out with me for walks or meals, insisting on staying in her room instead. She lost interest in my life and eventually in her own too. I couldn't drag words from her no matter how I tried.

She also seemed to resent it when I chatted to the other patients, as if they mattered more to me than she did. As we sat in the silence on those endless hours I found myself looking at them half in pity and half in fear: a retired ESB official, widows with nerve problems, an ex-nun who kept staring at me, a poor unfortunate thin woman who traipsed up and down non-stop in a demented state.

'When is Saturday?' she'd ask me.

'Six more days,' I'd reply.

'Will my daughter be in then?'

'Yes.'

I asked one of the nurses if her daughter had been in one Sunday afternoon.

'She rarely comes in,' she told me, 'she just phones now and again.'

Mammy's scruples got worse and I started bringing her to priests for confession. She told the same trivial sins over and over again. Once or twice she asked me to take her home but just when it looked like she was fit to come back she'd slip back into inertia again, not bothering where she was. When the inertia got worse she was moved to Beaumont Hospital.

She died one day in September, her favourite month of the year. Angie came home from the States and Brian came up from Limerick. She was buried in St Fintan's graveyard beside my father. Her mental health problems had really only started to deteriorate after his death. He was a crutch to her all her life, a crutch she hardly even knew was there. Then one day he was gone and she seemed to lose the will to live.

He was only in his mid-fifties when it happened. He'd gone into hospital for an operation on his varicose veins. It was in early December and we were all relieved he was going to be sorted for Christmas. Myself and mammy brought him in. On the way we stopped for a drink in The Botanic House pub in Glasnevin. It wasn't a serious operation but I knew he was worried. He didn't say anything but you could tell. Thinking back afterwards I convinced myself he knew he wouldn't be coming home.

The operation went wrong and he never came out of the anaesthetic. Nobody knew for sure what went wrong but we didn't feel like blaming anybody.

I visited him the night before he died. He was his usual perfectionist self. My last memories are of him telling me to post the 'Spot the Ball' competition from *The Sunday Press* and to straighten the hospital chair. The last thing he said to me was to keep on never minding.

We got a phone call early the next morning telling us he was critical. We got a taxi in, praying all the way. Never was the rosary said with more fervour than that morning, both of us filled with some kind of crazy hope that he'd pull through. I wasn't aware of the streets we passed on the way in, seeing nothing but his sad face in my mind as he stood in the pub with that last pint in his hand.

A young doctor met us at the door and we knew by his face that he was already gone. The song 'Do They Know It's Christmas?' was playing in the background as he told us the news.

Poor Daddy. He'd wanted nothing but good for all of us. I thought of the hours he'd spend with me trying to teach me if one apple cost a penny, what ten of them would cost. I was so anxious to get it right my thoughts would be all over the place, picturing rosy red apples with pink insides when you bit on them. Just like the ones in

Muddy Starr's back garden. I'd give a totally outlandish answer and the poor man would go purple and start again. He had a little bit of hair that stuck up at the back and Angie and me used to comb it for him. He loved us doing that.

He spent all his life trying to help others but getting short-changed himself. Then he had a heart attack and took early retirement, I remember him telling mammy he got a very poor send-off from the job. He'd organised so many farewell parties all through his working career and this was his thanks. It hurt him so much but he'd never show it. He bottled it all up, which can't have been good for him. Maybe better to scream out your pain and let them know you have feelings.

Too late now.

CHAPTER 36

For weeks of that early spring I had little contact with anybody. I rarely phoned any of my old connections. I ate, slept, walked alone.

I cried a lot, a rare thing for me. I cried for Mammy and Daddy and for Bridget Small and John Finnerty and his poor mother reaching out for a bar of soap. My tears for Bridget were caused by a passage I'd just finished in my story:

She made herself tea and boiled an egg in the quiet of the long sad weekend house. She looked out into the evening. The street was empty and bare trees stood nakedly leaning out to her and she loved them as she always had. She hated cluttered up dressings on trees and on people. Deep down I'm a streaker, she told herself. She was in a strange mood that night. If John were here they might have gone to the pictures. Was she putting too many hopes and dreams into John? So much younger. Such a kind man. The strange mood intensified. The smell of the rain and the stark trees brought back sensations she had forgotten existed. She was eighteen years old again and she wanted not to go to bed, wanted not to put in curlers, not to put out the light and say her prayers, and not to get a good night's sleep. She wanted excitement but spinster ladies of 51 didn't get much excitement.

There are barriers preventing spinster ladies from entering places of entertainment. The young can congregate in warm lounge bars and comfortable couples of 82 can be smiled on in such places. Brash bachelors of 108 can be one of the boys, but spinster ladies of 51 are unacceptable.

'To hell with it,' she said, 'I'm going out.'

I'd grown to love Bridget. I wrote about her going out to a pub the night she was alone and proceeding to get drunk. Somehow I couldn't sort out what would happen to her. I made a decision that I'd become her. Go to a pub and get drunk, all for research, and see where it led me.

I dolled myself up in a tweed suit I borrowed from the shop and then rolled it up at the waist until it almost showed my knickers. My hair had gone long but I was too involved in my private world to even think of hairdressers. I shook it out round my face and put on a tarty red lipstick.

The pub was crowded, just like it would have been for Bridget. I knew I stuck out like a sore thumb, surrounded as I was by noisy groups of happy paired-up people. I drank brandy which I knew Bridget would have done. I was pushed in a corner with a group of women of around my own age. They were a raucous bunch and every time I excused myself to go to the bar, one particularly obnoxious-looking one would pass some smart comment under her breath.

The night wore on and I was feeling decidedly wobbly.

'Excuse me,' the obnoxious one piped up, 'Do you mind if I say something?'

'Let her alone,' one of the others cut in.

'No, it needs to be said. My mother gave me sound advice and I'm passing it on to you. Never wear a short skirt or long hair when you've passed 35.'

'Mind your own business,' I snapped back.

'Mutton dressed as lamb, do you know that saying? It's for your own good. Have you no friends to go to the pub with?'

I left after that but tripped on the way out and crashed down the stairs, ending at the bottom with my legs in the air and my tweed skirt up over my waist.

Black and blue I swayed home. I walked the whole way in the lashings of rain. I cried for myself as I thought Bridget would have done, cried for my dreary spinsterhood and all the chances I threw away in life. I thought of girls in Bridget's class who had five or six children and who lived in comfortable homes in suburban houses with neat little front gardens. Poor Bridget, poor me. The rain poured down and the wind cut through me.

When I got back to the house I flung myself on the couch. Yesterday's newspaper lay on the floor and I picked it up, only half seeing it through my bloodshot eyes. There, squashed in a corner of the front page, was a tiny item about a hobo found dead in Fairview Park under a bench. The article said he'd died from hypothermia and his only possession was a battered copy of the book Dracula. The words swam before me.

Jack. It had to be him. I looked at it but didn't see it. I must have read it five times before I took it in.

Jack dead. How could that be? My friend. How could I I not have taken more care of him? The tears dripped down my face again as I scanned the lines. I blamed myself. I hadn't seen him for a long time but didn't bother to think why, wrapped up as I was in my own selfish problems.

Why hadn't I asked him more questions about his life? He tried once to interest me in his passion for Bram Stoker but I was been too taken up with my own mediocre existence.

I would never see him again now, would never be able to tell him that he meant more to me than all the hundreds of 'respectable' people I knew. He never complained, this man who had more to complain about than any of us. How had he kept going so long? That was the surprise, not that he'd died.

For the newspaper he was just another statistic, another grim reminder of the dirty underside of the Celtic Tiger. A drunk. A hobo. A drop-out. The newspaper didn't see his charm, his chances, his secret answers. Maybe it was the rest of us who were the real homeless. He had a home on his bench, in his heart. You couldn't get cold in there.

He'd advised me about my life when the so-called intelligent and intellectual people hadn't a clue in hell how I was really feeling or what to do about it. The solicitors, the Nigels, the smug doctors, none of them had half his brain. They'd tut-tut about this poor lonely old soul throwing his life away. But what life did they have? Or me?

It would have been easy to drown myself in a flood of self-pity but what good would that be to Jack? Absolutely no good whatsoever. Instead I would just remember him quietly - forever.

CHAPTER 37

I must have been two months in a state of guilt and depression. During that time I lost a lot of weight and looked wretched. Then one morning in June I took myself to Dollymount. The sun was scorching and there were loads of people on the beach. For no reason the weight in my chest seemed to be lifting so I walked to the sea and paddled. Looking at the poor specimens of feet I had in the water, a feeling of forgiveness came over me. My own poor sad feet with nobody to love them. No daughters or sons to hand me soap as I bathed them in a basin.

I went into a pub on the way home and had the first good meal I'd eaten in weeks. There was post in the hallway when I got home. Two letters. One was the phone bill and the other was from Minnie.

She was moving to Florida in July and invited me down before she went off.

'Can't wait to get there,' she wrote, 'I know I'm going to love it. Don't write back and tell me I should wait. At this stage of my life I know what I want.'

I phoned her later and told her how pleased I was for her.

'Clem and myself are on the phone every day,' she told me, 'I just can't wait to be out there with him. I'm not selling the Galway house, just going to let it. Maybe after a few years we'll move back.'

'That sounds great. I'm delighted for you.'

'I know you are. Sorry I was a bit blunt with you at Christmas. I just wanted you to get back to being my friend. I should have phoned you months ago but you know the way time goes by.'

'There's no need to apologise. I have a lot of work to do on myself.'

'Not at all. It was unfair of me. Anyway, can I take it you're coming down next month? I'm finishing work on Friday week and we can have the week together.'

So here I was on another Galway train. Not much in my suitcase. Make-up, a few bits of summery things, the Bridget book which I had hopes of getting back to, that was about it. I no longer had an urge to have to buy clothes just for the sake of doing so. I no longer had jealous feelings towards Minnie. There was a peace about me that I hadn't experienced for years.

I dozed off on the train and dreamed Mr Rochester was riding by the tracks on his black stallion. He leaned down and grabbed me and put me behind him while his dog Pilot raced ahead of us. He took me to a white silent strand and wrapped me up in his greatcoat and we lay close, little bits of green seaweed trailing round our limbs. Afterwards we warmed ourselves by a roaring fire and drank port and made love. When I woke up, the train was empty and we were in Galway.

Minnie looked a million dollars. Her skin was glowing and her crisp black curls were shiny and springy like they'd been in the old days. The twins had been home for the month of May and were now heading back to America.

'The pair of them are a panic', she said, 'Gracie said the Cork fellow was cute but very tight with his money. And as for Crocodile Dundee, as Grainne called him, he was a real ladies man and you couldn't depend on him for two minutes. Better off free as the breeze is what I say. Let them their fly their kites, there's plenty of time to settle down.'

'Fair play to the pair of them', I said, 'they have the world at their feet.'

'When I'm settled in Florida,' she told me later while we sipped coffee in a restaurant off Eyre Square, 'they're going to come and stay for a little while with Clem and myself and maybe see a bit of the States later on.'

'That's great news. Are they happy about Clem - happy for you, I mean?'

'They're fine about it. They spent a few days with their father while they were in Galway. They don't think much of the lady friend so I don't think there'll be too much contact there. Not that I care. He's their dad and it's up to them.'

'You're so forgiving, Minnie. I wish I could be a bit like you.'

'That's because I'm so happy. I'm sure if I didn't have Clem I'd be a different kettle of fish.'

I relaxed during those warm sunny days. I wandered down the Father Griffin Road through what used to be a little winding lane that led to a small beach a little distance from where all the holiday makers went. Now it was lined with large mansions but the little beach was still there. I had a photograph of Mammy in my mind with poor Brian building sand-castles and myself and Angie holding hands. A lovely day, a lovely innocent time.

'What will I do when you're in the States?' I asked Minnie one night as we sat in a pub.

'You'll be fine. You're welcome to come out and visit us. That goes without saying.'

'That's very nice of you but it won't be the same. I've always felt I had you to go to no matter how bad things were.'

'We'll have to find you a man of your own.'

'No thanks. I've had enough of men.'

'You're out of practice, that's all.'

The week was almost over and I felt a sadness at going back to Dublin. Back to what? A dull job in a backwater charity shop and memories of too many good things gone down the swanee.

On Saturday evening Minnie was going out to meet some friends. Alone in the house I forced myself to write a bit about Finnerty and

Bridget Small. I hadn't made contact with her since she'd gone alone into the night, consumed some solitary brandies and made her way home. My hand shook frantically as I wrote:

Down the stairs tumbled Bridget and three people - one a retired civil servant, one a Miss Marilyn McDonald from Blanchardstown and one fellow of the student type - saw her warm pink knickers and on Friday evening a very private lady rolled into the gutter and a crowd gathered and discussed her.

Bridget was vaguely aware of many voices. She didn't know that the young man, of the student type put her into a taxi and gave the taxi driver his last few euro. She didn't know that he'd discovered her Fairview address by looking into her spectacle case. She never knew a thing about the journey home but here she was inside her small rented room and she was still very drunk.

She made her way to the shared bathroom and pulled down neat towels from the rail and flung the red facecloth that had been with her since mother's time up to the ceiling and eventually her drunken fingers came into contact with a fat bar of soap. Pulling off her clothes she ran like a mad person out into the pelting rain.

The rain poured down and soap bubbles ran into gutters and Miss Bridget Small tightly wrapped her thin arms around a poor brown tree and sang to it. This is the song she sang:

'Are you lonely, my little baby? Mammy has come to mind you. I'm sorry I left you for a while. Your father was a vulgar man. He went away and left me all alone and I had to give you up, my dote. I know the orphanage was bleak and awful and I know you missed your mammy but I'm here now. I'll give you shelter and protection from all of them, so I will, so I will. From all of them with their families and their engagement rings and their cheap jokes. Mammy will comb your dear brown hair. Did you eat your porridge today, love? If you didn't it doesn't matter. Your own mammy will smile and will let her little girleen eat cornflakes even if it's winter time. I have a treat for you, my love. Mammy and you will go to the pictures after school this evening. We'll leave the dirty dishes and you and your Mammy will buy sweets and we'll sit at the pictures like two friends and we'll laugh in the dark at the lovers on the screen and the lovers in the audience because your Mammy doesn't think you should be protected from seeing love and your Mammy loves her little darling girl and will give her millions of other treats as well.'

The rain poured down and Bridget Small's private body was exposed to wind and cold but she felt nothing. She sang to the tree of how her baby could bring friends home in the evening and how when she was old enough she could mix with the boys and have parties and she never mentioned sin or never told her about the things all men were out for.

Bridget was thin and Bridget was greying. She was typical of the typical spinster lady but tonight she was a warm fat Mamma baking cakes for her daughter's twenty-first birthday and she was someone to run to and tonight she was more motherly than all of the mothers in all of the houses in all of Fairview.

Paddy Grogan, the night worker, saw her at 7.10 a.m. He was shocked and his first thought was to protect the innocent. He wrapped his coat round her and telephoned Dr James Ward.

'Of course when the doc saw her condition he knew she'd had it', he told the lads in the local on Sunday morning.

There were many who gave opinions on what caused such a thing to happen. Sexual frustration was the agreed common cause..

When John Finnerty returned to town he was told the story by a lady called Amanda O'Brien. She shared a flat a few doors down and had seen Finnerty a few times at the bus stop. She thought him quite handsome in a skinny interesting kind of way.

'Stark raving mad,' said Amanda, 'I always knew she was a bit strange.'

'She's the most sane person I've ever known,' replied Finnerty, 'It's 'a pity there wouldn't be more Bridgets in the world today.'

'Excuse me,' said Amanda, 'I didn't know you were a couple,' and she gave a snort of laughter.

'We're close friends,' said Finnerty, 'nothing more and nothing less.'

'That's right, just good friends as they say on the telly.'

Bridget developed pneumonia and it seemed she might not survive but after all she did. She was treated for her nerves and the doctors were indeed of one mind. Her problem, it was agreed, was sexual frustration. The fact of the soap pointed to religious scruples and the contact with the tree was inhibited sex. They sedated her for a time and eventually said she was well enough to go home.

Finnerty came one afternoon in August to pick her up. When he saw the small little lost figure of her and how helpless she looked, a wave of love came over him. So she was older, so she was no beauty, so her hair was greying and her poor skinny little legs were a mass of varicose veins. But so what, he loved her. That was it. He loved her.

'Bridget,' he said as they sat on the bus heading for Fairview.

'Yes, John dear.'

'Bridget, will you marry me?'

'Oh John, are you sure you want to be landed with an older woman, an older woman with nerve problems, are you sure, John dear, are you sure?'

They married in September, when the trees in Fairview Park were all dandied up with orange and gold leaves. Two of the other lodgers, a Mr O'Keeffe from Bandon and a Miss Cleary from Skibbereen, were bridesmaid and best man, and Bridget's elderly uncle gave the bride away. That night they made love and afterwards John washed Bridget's tired feet which had been cramped all day in cream sandals, and gently lathered her varicose veins with soap.

CHAPTER 38

I must have fallen asleep in the chair because I never heard Minnie come in.

'Wake up,' she barked.

'What time is it, Minnie?'

'Almost midnight. Come on, have a drink. This is a celebration.'

'Okay, just a small whiskey then.' I toasted her and wished her well with Clem.

'Before you go back to bed,' she said, 'I have a bit of news.'

'What's that?' I asked.

'You'll never guess who I saw down town tonight.'

Who?'

'Guess.'

'I haven't a clue. I'm tired If you want to tell me, tell me.'

'Daire.'

'Who?'

'Daire, your Daire. And he looks great.'

I poured myself a large whiskey.

'You're not serious? Was he with someone?'

'No, he was alone.'

'Did he see you? Did you talk to him?'

'I had a chat with him. He looks great, as I already told you.'

'And?'

'No, he never married.'

My mouth felt dry. Take another slug of the whiskey. Calm down, deep breaths.

'Did he mention me at all?'

'He couldn't stop talking about you and was delighted to hear you're here, footloose and fancy free. Or should that be fiancé-free?'

CHAPTER 39

I became the tenant of the Galway house the following month, getting myself a job in a small shop in Lower Salthil as well. I loved the way I could walk everywhere in Galway.

It was a particularly beautiful summer. I put on some weight and let my hair go back to its normal colour. I went to a refresher course in Irish and took up line-dancing. I joined a drama group. Learned to drive. Climbed a ladder and painted the outside of Minnie's house, overcoming my fear of heights in the process. I did a great job on her back garden. Grew lettuce and r adishes and managed to have a few roses in a corner under her front window. They were yellow and had a lovely smell.

Time passed. Minnie settled in America and married Clem. They spent six months of the year in Florida and six in County Clare, close to where his ancestors live. The twins got mad into Irish dancing and started auditioning for Riverdance.

I take trips to Dublin now and again to meet the girls from the office for coffee. Some things have stayed the same and some haven't. Sandra is now Fiona's secretary but doesn't appear to be overly busy. She sits in the front office filing her nails and reading Stephen King novels with great relish. Joanie's husband joined AA and hasn't had a drink for months. She found herself unable to live with him when he was on the wagon, however, so maybe Rita was right. She's now living with another heavy drinker and there are rumours he beats her.

Marjorie's boyfriend ran off with a cashier from the Trustee Savings Bank and she threw herself into her career to get him out of her mind. She started studying Law in the King's Inn and giving out stink about the fact that she had to swot up on Irish again. Fiona wound down and took on a new Senior Partner to lighten the workload. She does yoga in the evenings in an effort to get in touch with her inner self. Nadine is still doing the ballet and wants to go to Moscow to appear in 'Swan Lake'. Fiona is all for it.

Rita took a year's leave of absence to go off to London, where she's supposed to be tripping the light fantastic. Leslie Smith had a nervous breakdown and is now making baskets in John of Gods. Anyone who visits him says he sounds much happier in himself. Mr Roberts was mentioned in connection with the Anglo-Irish business. No wonder he was so quiet.

John left the one from Rockbarton, having decided she was a bimbo. He can be seen most evenings in a pub in Eglinton Street, boring the pants off everybody with stories about his heartless wife. His lady friend produced a baby boy and moved back home to her mother. Apparently she's aged a lot and become very bitter. The baby is hyperactive and suffers from colic. Fred went back to the tea dances after a long interval. He ran into Alice there and they now meet twice a week in Wynn's Hotel for coffee.

Nigel and Laura split up after she fell in love with her old scuba-diving teacher, who came over to Ireland to check out if the Celtic Tiger was all it was cracked up to be. Nigel was all cut up about it but looked on it as a learning curve. He didn't think he'd have much trouble finding another bird and took to surfing the net for fellow lonelyhearts. He bought himself a Maserati because, as they said in the Clairol ad, he was worth it.

CHAPTER 40

It was yesterday when I put a bead up my nose in a Galway school, yesterday when I didn't know the sums for my father, yesterday when I listened to stories from Muddy Starr, yesterday when I played in the Monk's field. Yesterday was also when I invented John, my husband, or played cowboys in Uncle Bernie's car, or looked through the windows of the house he owned but could never live in, or stood at his graveside mourning a life only half lived. And yesterday it was when I first came to Dublin and thought it was as cold as Poland with the wide arid streets and no fields at all to play in and no friends to play with even if there were.

Yesterday was when I missed my single line in the play with Minnie. It was when Mrs O'Leary made a Christmas cake for me and me alone on account of it being my birthday. It was when Brian came to the hospital to see me as a baby and said, 'Mammy, she's very small'. Yesterday was telling Big Knickers I forgot my copy and hiding the raincoat I hated in a ditch and stuffing horrible convent food into my pockets so I wouldn't have to eat it. And it was asking Daire to give me a flake of his life as we sat at the Spanish Arch one day watching the Naomh Eanna head out to Aran.

Yesterday when we moved from Galway. Yesterday when Brian was told he had a few months to live. Yesterday when we listened to Dolores Keane's sad voice singing 'My Own Dear Galway Bay; in the crematorium and yesterday when we dropped his ashes into the sea at Spiddal.

Other times seem farther away. The interview for Purcell, Fennelly & Co., the years of nothing when I didn't even realise I was dead inside, living to a clock because I felt it was the only way to go. Nigel seems far away too, probably because he meant as little to me as that job, or any other one I had. That must be the reason we create our own personal clocks, and why the passage of the years don't really affect them because we can always give pride of place to the good moments.

After Nigel left me and I left the job, other things filled the gaps but none of them are as clear to me as the sights and sounds and smells of those early years which I call up now like old friends when the dull sad present fails to equal them.

Photographs help too. I keep them in an old tin box in the attic and take them out when I want to cry, or laugh. They're unsorted, and spanning many different years. Some of the faces are unclear. Characters from a simpler time, in sepia, with starched collars and hollowed-out faces and plastered-down hair. They're all dead now, but more real to me than people I meet every day.

My favourite is the one of my mother's family in Glan, taken by Lafayette more years ago than I want to remember. Grandaddy is in the foreground sitting on a *chaise longue*, looking out at the world as if he owned it. Granny is standing beside him with a more austere expression on her face and Mammy is between them, her eyes full of longing at the possibilities her future had to offer. Many of her dreams came true but most of them ended too soon and when they were gone she didn't know how to fill the gaps.

Another photograph has Brian in it, Brian who was so full of bravery no matter how sick he became, placid even in his frailty. Brian who chased different kinds of butterflies, some of them in monasteries and some outside, Brian who was so happy with so little, which was just as well because that was all he was given.

And then there was the one of me outside the school, my hands behind my back and my hair in plaits the way Mammy liked to do it. My forehead looks high in it, nearly taking over the photograph and I remember Daddy telling me that was a sign of intelligence. Dream on, young girl.

These pictures are like the furniture of my mind, changing like the spools of the celluloid they're composed of each time I look at them, regenerating themselves like rooms I go into to feel sad in an indulgent way, or maybe stave off more pressing fears. I find myself talking to them like I once talked to John, find myself even forming relationships with the people in them, people I had little time for when they were alive because I was so wrapped up in my own traumas, too busy to see the richness in their spartan expressions and their spartan rooms.

There were no fitted kitchens then and no integrated fridges either but they're the stock I sprang from and I take some little pride in that, no matter how many blind alleys my trivial little life lead me into when I was trying to convince myself another emotional crisis has been averted, or another relationship forged that was going to change the pattern of my future, and even my past.

CHAPTER 41

The following notice appeared in the *Connacht Tribune* on the 27th of June, 2003:

'The bride, a local woman, wore a cornflower blue dress, size 16. Her hair was greying at the sides and around her eyes wrinkles of experience criss-crossed. She may not have been in the first flush of youth but she looked radiant. Daire Naughton, newly-returned from the States, was paunchy around the middle and losing his hair. He sported a dress suit and set a new fashion by wearing brown boots.'

Reader, I married him.

Withdrawn from Stock